VINTAGE® AMERICAN & EUROPEAN

WRIST WATCH

PRICE GUIDE

BY
SHERRY EHRHARDT
and
PETER PLANES

ROY EHRHARDT — Editor

SHIRLEY K. SHELLEY — Copy Editor

JUDY A. EHRHARDT — Graphic Artist

FIRST EDITION
HEART OF AMERICA PRESS, KANSAS CITY, MISSOURI 64134

ACKNOWLEDGEMENTS

The illustrations shown in this book have been supplied by fellow collectors and dealers who have generously allowed us to use material from their libraries, or have helped us in other ways, such as price consultants and/or researchers. We would like to take this opportunity to say "thanks" for the help they have given us: Robert "Bob" Arnold, Atlas, Mich.; Don and Sharon Bass, Sandusky, Ohio; Steve and Marsha Berger, Buffalo Grove, Ill.; Bernie Edwards, Northbrook, Ill.; Alpha Ehrhardt, Kansas City, Mo.; Larry Ehrhardt, Kansas City, Mo.; Judy Ehrhardt, Kansas City, Mo.; Michael "Mike" Ehrhardt, Kansas City, Mo.; Luther and Vivian Grinder, Owensboro, Ky.; Spencer Hodgson, Arlington Heights, Ill.; David and Tamara Jenkins, Grandview, Mo.; William "Bill" Meggers, Jr., Ridgecrest, Calif.; Roland Thomas "Rod" Minter, Lombard, Ill.; Bob Nelsh, Modesto, Calif.; Roger Rees, Rockford, Ill.; Phil Sommers, Raytown, Mo.; Lisa Southards, Kansas City, Mo.; Ron Starnes, Tulsa, Okla.; Ralph Whitmer, Springfield, Va. A special thanks to the various auction houses for use of illustrations from their catalogs. A complete list is presented on page 328.

IMPORTANT NOTICE. All of the information, including valuations, in this book has been compiled from the most reliable sources, and every effort has been made to eliminate errors. The possibility of error, in a work of such immense scope, always exists. The authors and publisher will not be held responsible for losses which may occur, in the purchase, sale, or other transaction of items, because of information contained herein. Those seeking further information on watches or clocks, are advised to refer to the complete line of Price Guides published by Heart of America Press.

Published by

Heart of America Press
P.O. Box 9808
Kansas City, Missouri 64134
Phone (816) 761-0080

Printed in the United States of America

ISBN: 0-913902-51-9 / Paperback

INDEX

The wrist watches in this book are alphabetized by the name on the dial. Special features or unusual watches and special sections are listed below.

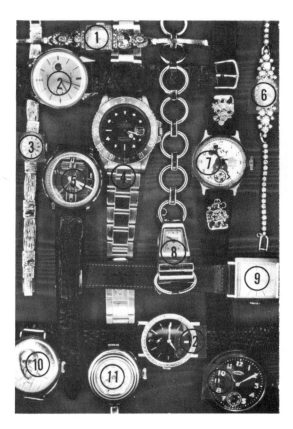

COVER PHOTO VALUES

6. **Hamilton "Diamond & Gold".** 14K white gold head and band set with 5 karats of brilliant cut diamonds. ca 1965 . . . . $2,500—3,000

7. **Mickey Mouse by Ingersoll.** "Antimated" Mickey's hands tell the time. Subsidiary seconds disc with tiny Mickey figures. Chrome tonneau case and original strap with chrome Mickeys. ca 1934. . . . . $50—75

8. **Art Deco Style.** 14K rose gold asymmetrical case set with 7 sapphires. Gold toned dial, Swiss movement. 14K rose gold link bracelet with each connecting link channel set with 4 baguette blue sapphires. ca 1945. . . $800—1,000

9. **Hamilton "Gold-Filled".** Silvered dial, subsidiary seconds. 17J, 8/0 size, 747 movement. 14K white gold-filled rectangular case. ca 1950. . . . . $30—50

10. **"R. Poincare, President"** with a large "R.F." and a lifelike bust embossed on the spring-loaded hunting style dial cover. White, glass enamel dial with Roman I to XII and inner chapter, red Arabic 13 to 24, with subsidiary seconds. Commercial grade, round, nickel, bridge, 10½''', 15 jewel, Swiss movement. Round, 800 fine silver, hinged back and front case with wire lugs. One of a series commerating the French Republic commanders during World War I. ca 1918. Estimate . . . . . $150—250

11. **Rockford.** Glass enamel, black numerals with red outside track, skylight dial. 15J, 0 size round movement. No. 884,093. Guaranteed permanent (marked Rockford), round 33mm. case with blue enamel on the bezel. ca 1914. Rare. Owner asking $450

12. **Hamilton "Tuxedo Masterpiece".** 14K gold, rhodium plated applied markers on a sterling silver dial. 22J movement, 14K white gold round case with 44-diamond bezel. ca 1958 . . . . $450—525

13. **Ingersoll Midget.** Radiolite black paper dial, subsidiary seconds. 6 size, round pin lever movement. Black gun metal finish round case with wire lugs and plain gun metal bezel . . . . $20—30

1. **Marcasite and silver** ladies watch with matching bracelet. 800 fine silver case and bracelet pave'd with marcasites. Swiss movement. ca 1925. . . . $135—170

2. **Le Coultre "Gold Futurematic".** Silvered dial with gold applied markers and hands. Window subsidiary seconds and power reserve indicator at 3 and 9. 12''', round nickel, 497, self-winding movement with back set and hacking device. Round, 35mm., 14K yellow gold case. ca 1960. New old stock with box and papers . . . . $300—350

3. **Heitel's "Gold Bracelet".** 14K yellow gold ladies watch. Oval dial and case with integral 14K, textured, tree bark finish bracelet. Swiss movement. ca 1970. . . . . $150—200

4. **Rolex "GMT-Master Oyster".** Brown dial with heavy gold luminous dots and markers, date window with Cyclop lens. Gold triangle 24 hour hand reads brown 24 hour rotating bezel setting in second time zone. Sweep second, 30J rotor chronometer movement in stainless steel and gold case, with stainless and gold band. ca 1978 . . . . $1,500—1,750

5. **Bulova "Accutron Spaceview".** Electric, sweep seconds. Round, gold-filled case. ca 1970. . $125—175

The author is a member of the National Association of Watch and Clock Collectors, Inc., and has attended many of their regional shows and chapter meetings. She has also attended hundreds of antique shows, flea markets, and jewelry stores in nearly all parts of the United States. She has been associated with and active in the Vintage jewelry wrist watch market for the past ten years.

SHERRY L. EHRHARDT

Peter has been in close touch with the wrist watch market for the past five years. He is a member of the AWI and the NAWCC, Inc., attending most of the regional and national shows and many of the chapter meetings that have a trading session or mart. During the last three years he has attended all of the major wrist watch auctions held in the United States, Switzerland, England and Germany as an active buyer and an observer of price trends.

PETER F. PLANES, II

HOW VALUES WERE DETERMINED

Peter has been in close touch with the wrist watch market for the past five years. He is a member of the AWI and the NAWCC, Inc., attending most of the regional and national shows and many of the chapter meetings that have a trading session or mart. During the last three years he has attended all of the major wrist watch auctions held in the United States, Switzerland, England and Germany as an active buyer and an observer of price trends.

Sherry has been associated with and active in the Vintage jewelry wrist watch market for the past ten years. She has attended many of the larger NAWCC marts, and hundreds of antique shows and flea markets in nearly all parts of the United States, with emphasis on the East and Midwest.

The prices in this book are based on what a wrist watch will sell for at the NAWCC marts and the top auctions, without the added buyer's premium. Recorded here are actual recent sales of rare or expensive watches, and averaged top values for the more common types which never make the auctions but which are usually bought and sold on a one-on-one basis.

Common commercial grade gold wrist watches that have nothing going for them other than the gold case were figured at gold spot of $400.00 per ounce.

No attempt has been made to predict the future prices but only to report the recent happenings in the market place among knowledgeablve collectors and dealers.

This book does not indicate the high prices asked and many times received by Madison Avenue, New York, or Main Street, U.S.A. jewelry stores, antique dealers at a major show, or, for that matter, any sale that would have to help support high overhead, travel, and marketing expense such as fancy showrooms, wages, and expensive advertising. Perhaps the value given in this book could be considered **high wholesale** or **low retail**.

This book is not a price list but an indication of value. It does not tell the buyer what he or she should pay but what they might expect to buy or sell for at the "top price" level outside of retail jewelry stores. Values in this book are based on the following concept of retail value: **THE PRICE A KNOWLEDGEABLE COLLECTOR OR INVESTOR WHO WANTS THE WRIST WATCH AND HAS THE MONEY, WILL PAY ANOTHER COLLECTOR OR DEALER WHO KNOWS THE VALUE.** Consequently, no watch sales have been used that occur among individuals and dealers who have no market information or the perception of actual supply and demand.

Use the values given in this book as a guide but, more importantly, use your own judgment based on your knowledge or desires of your particular collecting area and circumstances.

Remember, THE PRICE YOU PAY MUST ULTIMATELY BE YOUR OWN, and is the value of the wrist watch to you at that particular moment.

Despite the fact that the values shown are based on sales between knowledgeable persons, there are still many wrist watches for sale at bargain prices". In other words, many wrist watches have not yet been "discovered" by collectors, and, consequently, are available at prices far below those they will warrant when their real importance becomes generally known. It is our hope that this book will be of real value to you by helping you build your collection for the least possible cost and with a good chance for future value appreciation.

THINGS THAT DETERMINE THE VALUE OF A WRIST WATCH

TOP BRAND NAMES: The most popular and sought after wrist watch is one by Patek Philippe of Geneva, Switzerland, with all other things being equal; that is, case style, metal, features, type, etc. Other important top names, but not necessarily in the order of their importance, are Audemars Piguet, Baume & Mercier, Breguet, Cartier, Concord, Corum, Gubelin, Piaget, Rolex, Tiffany, Universal Geneve, Vacheron & Constantin.

These are followed by Agassiz, Buche-Girod, Chopard, Ditisheim, Girard-Perregaux, International, LeCoultre, Longines, Lucien Piccard, Matthey-Tissot, Mido, Movado, Ollendorff, Omega, Tissot, Touchon, Ulysse Nardin, Wittnauer, Zenith and Zodiac; again, not necessarily in that order. There are others but this is enough to give you a good idea of the better makes.

The most popular United States makers are Hamilton, Illinois, Hampden, Elgin and Waltham.

STYLE: Public popularity, fads, or fashion determines which style is preferred at any given time. Before a Vintage wrist watch is bought (to wear) at retail, the customer will always first put it on his arm to see how it looks or how someone else thinks it looks. Style is in the eye and mind of the buyer, and some styles are more popular than others.

UTILITY: A wrist watch has the advantage over most all other things to collect——**It is useful.** This single factor puts the wrist watch at the top of the list of Vintage items to collect, both for enjoyment to wear and for future long-term investment. An originally expensive wrist watch will always be in demand. Commercial grade "junk" will always be junk.

CASE METAL: The intrinsic value of the case metal is the only value some Vintage wrist watches have. Many metals and materials have been used for cases over the years. Some of them (in descending order of importance) are:

platinum, 22-18-14-10-9 karat gold, silver (both sterling and coin), gold-filled, gold plated, nickel, stainless steel, and plastic. Watches made by the top makers and cased in platinum and gold, are worth much more than the weight of the metal.

CASE MARKINGS: Many Vintage wrist watches by makers and jewelers such as Patek, Cartier, Rolex, LeCoultre, Tiffany, Hamilton, etc. were cased, boxed and timed at the factory. These watches in their original, marked cases are worth much more than watches in unmarked cases. All wrist watch companies making movements, at one time or another (and some for the entire life of the company), sold movements ONLY, with dials marked according to the specifications of the buyer, which were then cased in custom made or standard cases supplied by many American and European casemakers. These cases are sometimes described as "Contract Cases".

PRECIOUS AND SEMI-PRECIOUS STONES: Many different stones were used to decorate the dials, cases and bracelets of men's and ladies wrist watches. Several factors are involved in valuing watches with these stones. The size, color and quality of the stone are the most important factors in determining their value. The top name makers used only the finest stones available. Others used whatever the public would bear. It is very difficult to give a value for a watch containing stones without an actual examination of the watch and each stone. This was not possible for watches illustrated in this book, therefore, the actual value may be more or less than the value shown.

CONDITION: Here are some things to look for when buying a Vintage wrist watch. The condition of the dial, crown, case, movement, and bracelet (if permanently attached) must be considered.

Dial: Most wrist watches have metal dials. If it is a metal dial, has it been refinished or does it need to be? Refinishing costs from $15 to $75, and sometimes much time and effort on your part. On applied figure dials, are there any missing or damaged figures? Is the dial original? Are there scratches that cannot be removed, feet missing, dial bent or damaged? The more valuable the watch, the more valuable the dial.

Case: Notice the amount of wear. On a gold case, is it bent or dented from rough use; is the gold worn through; does it have bent or damaged or replaced lugs? Look at the spring bar holes. Are they worn, etc.? Initials or dedications hurt the desirability and therefore the value. On gold-filled cases, look closely at the corners and high edges of the case for wear (brass showing).

Bracelet: Be careful about buying a watch with a permanently attached bracelet that does not fit your wrist. Some types, such as mesh, costs a lot to shorten and even more to lengthen.

Movement: It should be original (this is more important in some watches than others). "Running" condition and complete without botched repairs is important. The finish should be good; the nickel or rhodium plating should not be worn off; no corrosion or rust; no scratches or non-original parts.

Crown: The original crown is important when they were marked, such as Patek or Rolex.

RECASING: There is an ever-growing problem in recasing the most expensive, top name wrist watches such as Patek, Cartier, LeCoultre, etc. The real value of these recased watches is the value of the movement, plus the value of the gold content of the case. There is some very good recasing being done that is difficult to tell from the original. If a recase is done well enough to be accepted by everyone, then it assumes the value of an original. When it is discovered that the watch is a recase, the apparent value will drop dramatically.

CASE STYLES PREFERRED ON PATEK PHILIPPE WRIST WATCHES: At this time, in the order of their importance, is the rectangular curved case, the rectangular; the square, and last, the round. Unusual lugs can increase the value tremendously.

CASE VARIATIONS THAT ADD VALUE: Hinged lugs, curved case, enamel case, tu-tone color, numerals on bezel, numerals on enamel bezel, large "Art Deco" style numerals on dial.

MOVEMENTS: Unlike pocket watches, movements play a small part in the value of the wrist watch, except for complicated watches. We look for some of the high grade Hamiltons and the more scarce Illinois, Hampden, and Rockford to get more attention in the near future, with a resulting rise in value.

WATCH BANDS OR BRACELETS: Most gold wrist watch bands and bracelets are not important and usually are worth a small premium (10% to 20%) over the precious metal content, if in mint condition. The exception is the marked ones made for or by the high-grade European watch companies such as Patek, Rolex, Cartier, etc. Exotic skin bands such as lizard, crocodile or alligator, enhance the look and value of the watch. Signed, original straps and buckles are sought after and have value, with a gold Patek bringing about $75.

ORIGINAL COST VERSUS VALUE TODAY: Expensive wrist watches are mostly hand-finished and the parts were hand-fitted. Very few of these expensive watches were made when compared to the millions of inexpensive commercial grade, machine-made watches. Therefore, these hand-finished watches are scarce to rare, and will still last a lifetime or more if properly cared for. They represent a status symbol that many people desire. Usually only the educated, moneyed, or people associated with the wrist watch trade are aware of top makers such as Patek, Cartier, Audemars or

Rolex. These companies only advertised to customers who could afford to buy expensive watches, therefore, the common folk would not be aware of these watches. Comparatively speaking, expensive high quality is still expensive high quality in a Vintage wrist watch, and junk is still junk.

COMIC CHARACTER: The comic character Vintage wrist watches are the exception to the above statement. Most of them are of low quality (pin pallet construction), but they have a wide appeal to collectors outside the watch market because of the collectibility associated with comic characters. They were offered for sale in beautiful and interesting boxes (sometimes worth as much as the watch), which appealed to the children then——and the child in us now.

JEWELRY WATCHES: Before World War I, wrist watches were considered to be ornamental jewelry and were not necessarily used as timepieces only. Until the soldiers started wearing them, it was considered "sissy" or "unmanly" to wear one. Expensive wrist watches that combined diamonds and other precious stones with platinum or gold (sometimes with enamel) in a decorative style have always been produced, even in the beginning.

Heavy markup, sometimes three, four or five times cost, was used as the sticker or retail price to cover fancy showrooms and expensive (usually national) advertising.

Collector value of a majority of these pieces is usually no more than the salvage value of the stones and the platinum or gold content of the case and bracelet.

Some designs that are considered popular now will bring a premium but it is usually limited to 10% to 20% above salvage value, except for the very special pieces or pieces by top name makers that command attention as status symbols.

COMPLICATIONS, ALARMS, CHRONOGRAPHS, CALENDARS, REPEATERS: Any feature added to the original time only wrist watch raises the value of a Vintage wrist watch. Complications increased the initial cost because of the added expense to the manufacturer, and the comparatively few people who wanted or needed one makes them scarce when compared to time only wrist watches. The value of each of these added features depend on many things; among them being the maker, the case metal and the case style.

MILESTONES OR FIRSTS: Many inventions either did not work well or, for one reason or another, did not find public acceptance and were not mass produced. Because of the enormous market for wrist watches, there has always been ample money available for research and development. Changes and improvements have been many and often, bringing us up to the electronic age. Of this work, the early varieties of "Self-winding" (being a good

example) are being collected by a few. In the past, information on wrist watches has been hard to find. Now with an occasional wrist watch book becoming available, I am sure that collectors for these will increase, and, because of short supply of collectible Vintage wrist watches, this will tend to push up the price.

ORIGINAL BOX — TIMING CERTIFICATES — GUARANTEES: All of these help the value of any wrist watch but the papers must have matching serial numbers. The more valuable the watch the more valuable the box and papers become.

COLOR OF THE CASE: At this time, solid gold watches are the most desirable (and worth more), in yellow gold, followed by green gold and then white gold. A rich yellow color is preferred in gold, gold-filled, or gold plated.

MULTI—COLOR OR TU—TONE CASES: Two or more colors in the case is popular now with Vintage wrist watch collectors. The separation between the value of a single color and a multi-color case increases as the value of the watch increases.

ALL PRICES IN THIS BOOK ARE FOR MINT CONDITION WATCHES.

OTHER USEFUL INFORMATION

AMERICAN & EUROPEAN WRIST WATCH MARKET: At this time, it appears that generally the European market is about twenty percent stronger than the American market.

AUCTIONS: There are four major auction houses in Europe, each holding about two auctions per year. Probably 800 to 1200 wrist watches are auctioned each year. There are two major and three minor auction houses in the U.S., which will probably auction about 400 to 500 wrist watches this year.

DEALERS: There are about six major Vintage wrist watch dealers that buy and sell full time in America. The other major buyers and sellers are mostly retail jewelry stores; for instance, stores on Madison Avenue in New York that cater to the public with Vintage watches. There are probably about ten major European wrist watch buyers. Most of them come to the auctions and the larger National Association of Watch & Clock Collector's regional marts. And, there are hundreds of "hip pocket" dealers everywhere that offer wrist watches to the public or collectors when supply permits.

COLLECTORS —— EUROPEAN VS AMERICAN: The Europeans began collecting wrist watches before the Americans. However, collectors are now springing up all over the U.S. They are beginning their collections with the companies who made railroad watches, such as Hamilton, Illinois, etc.

RARITIES: Wrist watch collecting is in its early stages now, and rare and valuable wrist watches will be found by collectors who are able to identify them. Many will be bought for very little money compared to their real value. We have tried to give you help in your search with this book.

PRIVATE LABEL OR JEWELER'S CONTRACT WRIST WATCHES: Watch manufacturers, importers and distributors make use of names that are found on either the dial, movement, or the case. There are various reasons for this: advertising, identification, etc. Some of these names were used for many years (example Tiffany and Cyma), others maybe only on one small batch of watches. A book issued in 1943 by The Jeweler's Circular Keystone called **Trade Marks of the Jewelry and Kindred Trades**, listed 148 company names and addresses of U.S. companies who were at that time using over 2500 names, many of which appear only on the dials. This book could not cover all of even this one year, much less 70 years of serious wrist watch production from around the world. We have instead selected from the material available to us the examples that we believe best represent the wirst watches that are available today.

The number of watches shown for each company in no way indicates its importance to collectors. We did, however, show as many as was practical for some companies that are important to collectors, such as Patek, Rolex, Cartier, Vacheron, Universal, Audemars, Hamilton and Illinois. Large numbers of other companies, such as Bulova, Gruen, Elgin and Waltham, were used because lots of these watches can be found. Others, such as Cyma, Tavannes, Longines and Marshall Field, were given because we had good pictures that represented many different styles or a large line for one year.

In future editions we will continue to give you the best information we have available.

CURRENT TOP NAME PRODUCT LINE CATALOGS: All companies issue periodic product line catalogs to regular customers and sometimes make them available to the public at a small charge. There are two ways to get these catalogs: (1) Go by your local jewelry store and get one if they have them available; (2) Order them directly from the company by paying the required fee. The companies with wrist watches for sale run advertising campaigns in selected over-the-counter magazines and how to order instructions are usually included in the advertisement. Also, Vogue Magazine does one or two special Holiday Preview issues about mid-Summer, in which they present their "Catalog Collection", with instruction on how to order them. The 1983 September issue included Cartier, Rolex, Baume & Mercier, Concord, Omega, Piaget and Corum. Prices for the individual catalogs run from $2 to $5. These catalogs sometimes include a retail price list which can give you an idea of what current styles are being offered, and, with your knowledge of

markups, will help you decide how much to pay for a used one.

1983 STYLES. For the past few years, top name companies such as Patek Philippe, Rolex, Cartier, Baume & Mercier, Concord, Piaget and Corum have been offering as their **top of the line**, wrist watches that are **identifiable from any angle**, which includes a bracelet just as distinctive as the watch. These companies are also the most heavily copied by the Far East companies who make fakes.

RAILROAD U.S. APPROVED WRIST WATCHES: The first wrist watch approved for railroad use was an Elgin B.W. Raymond on the Pittsburg and Lake Erie Railroad in early 1960. Here is a list of some of the railroad approved wrist watches, some of which are new and still available.

1. Ball, 13''' Size, 21 Jewel, Official RR Standard Model 1604B.
2. Ball 11½''' Size, 25 Jewel, Official RR Standard Trainmaster Model 2821.
3. Ball 11½''' Size, 25 Jewel, Official RR Standard Trainmaster Model 2620B.
4. Bulova Accutron Railroad Model 214.
5. Bulova Accutron Railroad Calendar Model 218.
6. Bulova Accutron Quartz Day-Day Model 92843 & 91818.
7. Bulova Accutron Quartz Ladies Model 92278.
8. Croton Railroad Timer.
9. Elgin 13''' Size, 23 Jewel, B.W. Raymond Chronometer.
10. Elgin 13''' Size, 21 Jewel, B.W. Raymond Chronometer.
11. Elgin 13''' Size, 21 Jewel, B.W. Raymond 1604-B.
12. Elgin 13''' Size, 21 Jewel, B.W. Raymond AS 10041.
13. Eterna-Sonic Model 133T—RA1550.
14. Hamilton Electric Model 505, 50, 51, and 52 Railroad Special.
15. Hamilton Electronic Product No. 910917.
16. Longines Ultronic Model 6312.
17. Pulsar Model JG041 and JG0385.
18. Rodania Quartz Model 09361, Ref. 3488.1.
19. Seiko Quartz Models FJ055M, FJ056M, HA163M, HA164M, and UX015M.
20. Universal Geneve Models 1205-0 and Unisonic RR52-0.
21. Wyler Models 1370RA, 4125RA, 3425RA, 1324, 1337-RA1550, 433T-RA1550 and 4176.

Collectors of Vintage railroad approved wrist watches prefer the Elgin, Ball and Hamilton Railroad Models but not much attention has been paid to the others.

GLOSSARY

Adjusted: Term applied to watch movements and some small clock movements to indicate that they have been corrected for various errors, such as isochronism, temperature, and positions.

Agate: A stone which is a variety of chalcedony, usually containing a pattern such as banding, eyes, etc.

Alarm: An attachment to a watch whereby, at a predetermined time, a bell is sounded.

Alloy: The mixing of more than one metal in order to produce one of greater hardness, malleability and/or durability.

Animated: Imitating or giving life-like movement to a watch dial. (Usually Comic Character)

Applied Figures: Figures which have been attached to the dial, usually with screws or small bolts with nuts.

Arabic Figures: Figures on a dial, such as 1, 2, 3, as opposed to Roman Numerals, such as I, II, V, IX.

Art Deco: A style of design between 1910—1935, most importantly influenced by cubist geometry.

Automatic Winding: See Self-winding.

Baugette: A step cut used for rectangular stones, of a small size.

Balance: The oscillating wheel of a watch, which in conjunction with the hairspring (balance spring) regulates the speed of a clock or watch. May be made bi-metallic to compensate for temperature changes and may be studded with screws for regulation.

Bearing: The support for a pivot or arbor. Jeweled bearings are used where there is danger of rapid wear on the pivots of fast moving parts such as the balance staff and also train wheel pivots.

Beat: The sound of the ticking of a watch, caused by the teeth of the escape wheel striking the pallets or arms of the escapement.

Beveled: Inclining from a right line to form a slant.

Bezel: The groove in which the glass (crystal) of a watch is set.

Breguet: A horological genius of the late 18th and early 19th century. The name applied to the type of hairspring which has its last outer coil raised above the body of the spring and curved inwards.

Bridge: Upper plates in a ¾ plate watch for the support of the wheels,. or pallet. Always has at least two feet or supports.

Brilliant Cut: The most beautiful form of cutting a diamond. It is also used for other clear stones. The standard brilliant has 58 facets, 33 in the crown and 25 in the base.

Bubbleback: Slang term for the early Rolex Oyster Perpetual (ca 1930 to 1950's).

Calendar, Moonphase: A disk, usually with a blue background, containing the moon phases and further decoration of stars which rotates one complete turn per month. Located at the 6th or 12th hour position. In reality, the moon rotates around the earth in 29 days, 12 hours, 44 minutes and 2-4/5 seconds.

Calendar, Perpetual: A perpetual calendar mechanism is self-adjusting, that is to stay it automatically indicates the months of varying length and is self-correcting for leap years.

Calendar, Perpetual Retrograde: The date hand moves through an arc on the dial and returns to 1 after reaching the proper date 28, 29, 30 or 31.

Calendar, Simple: Automatically registers one or all of the following: day, date, month and moonphase, and must be manually adjusted for months having total days other than 31.

Calibre: The size or factory number of a watch movement.

Cap Jewel: The flat solid jewel upon which rests the pivot end. Also called the "endstone".

Center-seconds hand: Sometimes called sweep-seconds hand. Mounted on the center post of watches.

Champferred: A beveled or sloped edge.

Champleve: Enameling done by cutting grooves in the metal into which the ground enamel is melted. The surface is then ground and polished.

Chapter Ring: The circle on the dial that contains the numbers for the hours and minutes. So called because in early clocks it was a separate ring attached to the dial.

Chromium: Very hard crystalline metallic chemical element with a high resistance to corrosion, used as plating on wrist watch cases.

Chronograph: A mechanical watch with hour and minute hand and a center sweep-second hand which can be controlled by one or more special buttons, in the side of the case or through the crown. The sweep-second hand may be started, stopped, and made to return to zero without interfering with the timekeeping of the watch.

Chronograph, Double Button: Stop and start on one button without returning to zero. One button to return to zero (flyback).

Chronograph, Simplified (One Button): Sweep-second hand runs continuously on this single button chronograph when at rest. Press completely down to return to zero, hold down until timing begins upon release, push down halfway to stop, release to start again, or all the way down to flyback. Usually of cheaper construction.

Chronograph, Split Seconds: Same as chronograph but is fitted with an additional center sweep-second hand (total of 2) with separate controls (buttons) to permit the timing of two events simultaneously. Example: The split-second chronograph with two chronograph hands permits ascertaining, in races of all kinds, the times of arrival of competitors following closely upon each others heels. The chronograph is set in motion by pressing a button whereupon both hands begin to move. At the arrival of the first competitor the one hand is stopped by pressing this button again and the time is read off. When the button is pressed a third time this hand catches up with the other in one jump, whereafter both move on together. At the arrival of the second competitor the first hand is again stopped and the time noted down. In this way, any desired number of time recordings can be made. A button fitted in the winder serves to return both hands to zero.

Click: A spring-tensioned pawl holding the ratchet wheel against the tension of the mainspring, enabling the spring to be wound, usually making the clicking noise as the watch is wound.

Cloisonne Enamel: A type of enamel work in which thin strips of metal are soldered to the base to form the outlines of the design. Colored enamel is then placed in each section.

Cock: An overhanging support for a bearing such as the balance cock; a cock has a support at one end only.

Compensating Balance: A balance with a bi-metallic rim made of brass and steel. The diameter increases or decreases with changes in temperature to compensate for these changes.

Conical Pivot: A pivot which curves back into the main body of its arbor, such as those used with cap jewels. (Balance staff pivots.)

Convertible Case: Watch case built into a sliding frame allowing the dial side to be turned over facing the wrist to protect it.

Convex: A domed surface.

Crown: A grooved circular piece fastened to the stem for winding the watch. (Slang term "Winding Knob or Button)

Curb Pins: The two regulator pins almost pinching the hairspring.

Curvex: Case with a slightly curved back to fit the wrist better. (Patented by Gruen)

Cushion: Square form with rounded edges.

Detent: The setting lever. A detainer or pawl.

Dial Train: The train of wheels under the dial which moves the hands. The cannon pinion hour wheel, minute wheel and pinion.

Diamond Dial: Dial set with diamonds for markers, numerals, etc.

Digital: See Jump Hour.

Doctor's Watch: See Duo-Dial.

Dollar Watch: A practical timepiece with a non-jeweled movement. The case and movement an integral unit with a dial of paper on brass or other inexpensive material. Ingersoll sold his first Dollar watch for $1.00 in 1892. (Taken from "The Watch That Made the Dollar Famous" by George E. Townsend.)

Double-Roller Escapement: A form of lever escapement in which a separate roller is used for the safety action.

Duo-Dial: Separate hour and seconds dials. (Slang term "Doctor's Watch")

Duplex Escapement: A watch escapement in which the escape wheel has two sets of teeth. One set locks the wheel by pressing on the balance staff. The other set gives impulse to the balance. The balance receives impulse at every other vibration.

Ebauche: A term used by Swiss watch manufacturers to denote the raw movement without jewels, escapement, plating, engraving. The manufacturers supply their ebauches to trade name importers in the U.S.A. and other countries who have them finished, jeweled, dialed, cased, etc., and engraved with their own (advertised) name brands.

Elinvar: A nonrusting, nonmagnetizing alloy containing iron, nickel, chromium, tungsten, silicon and carbon. Used for balance and balance spring. (Hamilton)

Elongated: The state of being stretched out or lengthened.

Embossed: To carve, raise or print so that it is raised above the surface.

Emerald Cut: A style of rectangular or square cut, featuring steps of elongated facets.

Enamel: (Soft) A soluble paint used in dials. (Hard) A porcelain-like paint used as an ornamental coating, acid-resisting and durable.

Engine-Turned: A form of machine engraving similar to etching.

Engraved: To cut into, to form a pattern or design either by hand or machine.

Filigree: Ornamental open work executed in fine gold or silver wire.

Flat Hairspring: A hairspring whose spirals develop on a flat surface. As opposed to the overcoil (Breguet) hairspring.

Fourth Wheel: Usually the wheel which carries the second hand and drives the escape wheel; it is the fourth wheel from the great wheel in the going train of a watch.

German Silver: A silver-white alloy composed mainly of copper, zinc, and nickel, called silver but containing none.

Gilded: To give a golden hue; gold plating.

Gilding: The process of coating the surface of metal with gold by painting on a mixture of mercury and gold and then heating to evaporate the mercury.

Gold: Pure 24K gold is yellow in color. It is very soft and not acceptable for use in articles subject to wear, unless alloyed with harder metal. The choice of alloy metals determines the color of the gold.

Gold-Filled: Another name for rolled gold.

Gold Plated: Electro-plated a few thousandths of an inch thick with pure or alloyed gold.

Grande Sonnierie: A quarter hour repeater; a type of striking in which the last hour struck is repeated at each quarter. Present day usage sometimes applies the term to a quarter hour which can be made to strike at will.

Green Gold: True green gold cannot be made of less fineness than 17 karat: usually made of 10 to 14 karat gold, alloyed with silver to make it as pale as possible and then the finished piece is electroplated with 18 karat green gold. True green gold is 17 parts pure gold and 7 parts pure silver.

Greenwich Civil Time: Also called Universal Time (UT). It is Local mean time as measured at Greenwich, England. (G.C.T.)

Hairspring: The spiraled spring attached to the balance to govern the speed of the balance oscillations.

Hexagonal: Six sided.

Hour Recorder: Small offset hour recorder dial has an indicator hand that advances one hour marker each time the minute recorder counts off 60 minutes. Usually placed over the 6th hour marker.

Hunting Case: Spring-loaded lid or cover over the face of the watch. (Example: See Hamilton Flintridge)

Independent Seconds-Beating: Fitted with a special center sweep seconds hand that advances by one jump every second. Sometimes called "Jump Second".

Index: The regulator scale. Used to help in adjusting the regulation. Most balance wheel clocks and watches had indexes.

Integral: A part that is permanently attached to another part, thus becoming one. As in a bracelet permanently attached to the head of a wrist watch.

Invar: A steel alloy containing about 36 percent nickel that remains the same length at different temperatures. Used in the making of balance wheels. Also used for pendulum rods in clocks for temperature compensation. Similar to Elinvar.

Isochronism: Quality of keeping equal time during the normal run of the mainspring, usually the qualities of a well-formed overcoil hairspring.

Jewel: Synthetic or semi-precious stones used for bearings in watches and precision clocks.

Jump Hour (or Digital): The hour indicator advances instantaneously at the beginning of the hour.

Jump Second: See Independent Seconds-Beating.

Lapis Lazuli: Synonym for lazurite, or ultra marine. An azure-blue stone with vitreous lustre, sometimes with gold specks used in jewelry and an occasional wrist watch dial.

Ligne (‴): A Swiss watch size, 2.2558mm. or 0.0888 in.

Luminous: Giving off light; glows in the dark. (See Radium)

Mainspring: The flat, ribbon-like tempered steel spring wound inside the barrel and used to drive the train wheels. Most American clocks eliminated the barrel.

Marquise Cut: A cut for diamonds in which the stone is brilliantly faceted and then shaped like an elongated almond or tear-drop with pointed ends.

Matte: A dull or flat finish.

Mean Time: When all days and hours are of equal length. This is oppsed to Solar Time where all days are not of equal length.

Meantime Screws: The adjustable screws in a better grade balance used to bring the watch to close time without the use of the regulator. Sometimes called "timing screws".

Middle-Temperature Error: The temperature error between the extremes of heat and cold characteristic of a compensating balance and steel balance spring.

Milled: Having the edge transversely grooved.

Minute Recording: Small offset minute recorder dial that advances 1 minute with each revolution made by the second hand. Usually one of three types: 1) Continuous; 2) semi-instantaneous; 3) Instantaneous. Usually placed by the 3rd hour marker.

Minute Repeater: A striking watch that will ring the time to the minute by a series of gongs activated by a plunger or push piece. A watch striking the hours, quarter hours, and additional minutes.

Nickel Silver: An alloy of nickel, copper, and zinc; usually 65 percent copper, 5-25 percent nickel, and 10-30 percent zinc, containing no silver.

Non-Magnetic: A balance and spring composed of alloys that will not retain magnetism after being put through a magnetic field.

Octagonal: Eight sided.

Open Face: A watch dial with the figure "12" at the winding stem.

Oval: Elongated circle.

Palladium: One of the platinum group of metals and much lighter. Will not tarnish and can be deposited on other metal by electroplating. Value is less than gold or platinum.

Pave: A style of setting stones where a number of small stones are set as close together as possible; to completely cover.

Pennyweight (DWT): A unit in troy weight equal to twenty-four grains or one-twentieth of an ounce.

Perpetual Winding: See Self-winding.

Phillips' Spring: A balance spring with terminal curves formed on lines laid down by M. Phillips. The term "Phillips' curve" is rarely used.

Pin Pallet: The lever escapement wherein the pallet has upright pins instead of horizontally set jewels. Used in alarm clocks and nonjeweled watches.

Poising: An operation to adjust the balance so that all weights are counterpoised. In other words, statically balancing a wheel or balance in a watch.

Position Timing: Adjusting a watch so that it keeps precise time when the watch is placed in a given position. Adjusted to three, four, five or six positions.

Power Reserve Indicator: See Up & Down Indicator.

Purse Watch: Folding, covered, or otherwise protected watch for carrying in the purse or pocket. (Example: Movado Ermeto)

Quick Train: A watch movement beating five times per second, or 18,000 per hour.

Radium: A radioactive metallic element that gives off light. Used on luminous dials.

Regulator: Part of the balance bridge which resembles a racquette (racket) and contains vertical pins which straddle the hairspring. When the regulator moves towards the stud, the effective length of the hairspring is made longer and the balance slows in speed; when the pins are moved farther from the stud, the hairspring is made shorter and the watch goes faster.

Repeating Watches: Usually one of six types: 1) Quarter repeaters—striking a deep note for the last hour (as shown on the dial) and two shrill notes, ting-tang for each quarter; 2) Half-Quarter Repeaters—striking the last hour, the quarters, and a single blow for the nearest half-quarter; 3) Five-Minute Repeaters—striking a deep note for the last hour (as shown on the dial) and one shrill note for each five minutes after the hour; 4) Minute Repeater—striking a deep note for the last hour (as shown on the dial), two shrill notes, ting-tang for each quarter, and one shrill note for each minute past the last quarter. The most complicated and popular today; 5) Clock Watches—the hours and quarters are struck automatically as the watch goes but the hours, quarters and minutes can be repeated at will by a slide in the case band; 6) Carillon—the quarters are struck on two, three, or four different notes. Sometimes known as "Cathedrals".

Repousse: Decorating metal by hammering out a design behind or on the reverse side in order to create a design in relief.

Reverso: See Convertible Case.

Rolled Gold: A metal plate formed by bonding a thin sheet of gold to one or both sides of a backing metal. Made by rolling the sandwich until the gold is at the desired thinness.

Rose Cut: Method of faceting stones with many small and usually not precision cuts.

Rose Gold: karat gold alloyed with copper.

Sapphire Crystal (Synthetic Sapphire Crystal): Extremely hard material used for watch crystals.

Self-winding: Wrist watch that will wind itself by use of a rotor or other mechanical means by swinging movement of the arm. If worn by a normally active person for four hours, it will remain running for 30 hours.

Setting Lever: The detent which fits into the slot of the stem and pushes down the clutch lever.

Silvered: Silver in color, not necessarily in metal content.

Sizes of Watches: The American sizes are based on 30ths of an inch. The Europeans use the ligne which is equal to .089 inches or 2.255 millimeters. In every case, the diameter is measured across the outside or largest part of the lower plate of the watch, right under the dial. In oval or other odd shaped movements, the size is measured across the smaller axis.

Staff: A pivoted arbor or axle usually referred to the axle of the balance; as the "balance staff".

Sterling: The minimum standard of purity of fineness of English silver; 925 parts pure silver to 1000 parts.

Stopwatch: A simple form of chronograph with controlled starting and stopping of the hands; sometimes also stopping the balance wheel. A timer in pocket watch form.

Stopwork: The mechanism on a barrel of a watch that permits only the central portion of the mainspring to be wound, thus utilizing that portion of the spring whose power is less erratic.

Subsidiary Seconds: Small dial, usually opposite the winding crown on a chronograph and at the 6th hour position on a time only watch, that indicates the seconds and makes one revolution per minute.

Sunk Seconds: The small second dial which is depressed to avoid the second hand from interfering with the progress of the hour and minute hand.

Sweep Seconds: See Center Seconds.

Tank Case: Flat, square, conservatively tailored case. (Introduced by Cartier, Patented by Gruen).

Tiger Eye: Silicified fibrous variety of "Riebeckite". A stone that when cut properly displays an eye-like effect.

Timepiece: Any watch that does not strike or chime.

Timing Screws: Screws used to bring a watch to time, sometimes called the mean-time screws.

Tonneau: Shape of case with its widest point across the center and tapering towards square ends.

Tourbillion: A watch in which the escapement, mounted on a cage attached to the fourth pinion, revolves around the mounted and stationary fourth wheel.

Train: A combination of two or more wheels and pinions, geared together and transmitting power from one part of a mechanism to another, usually from the power source (weight or spring) to the escapement.

Troy Weight: The system of weights commonly used in England and the United States for gold and silver. One pound equals 12 ounces, 1 ounce equals 20 pennyweights (dwt.) and 1 pennyweight equals 24 grains (gr.).

Tu-tone: Two colors of metal in the case or dial finish.

Up and Down Indicator: The semi-circular indicator hand or window indicator that tells how much the mainspring has been unwound and thus indicates when the spring should be wound. On wrist watches usually indicates how many hours are left. (Same as Power-Reserve Indicator).

Vermeil: Gilded silver.

Vibrating Tool: A master balance of certified accuracy as to vibrations per hour which is mounted in a box with glass top. The box may be swiveled to set the balance into its vibratory arcs. The balance to be compared or vibrated is suspended by its hairspring attached to a scaffold and when the box is twisted on its platform both balances will start vibrating. Thus the suspended balance may be compared (in speed) with the master balance and its hairspring lengthened or shortened until both balances swing in unison.

Waterproof: Airtight so that no water can enter.

White Gold: 24 karat yellow gold alloyed with nickel to make 14 or 18 karat white gold.

TABLE OF WATCH SIZES

1 ligne = 2.2559 mm.   1 inch = 25.40005mm.

American Sizes	Fractions of an Inch	Decimal Inches	Millimeters	Swiss Ligne
36/0	0	0.0	0.0	0
26/0	10/30	0.3333	8.46	3−3/4
20/0	16/30	0.533	12.73	6
18/0	18/30	0.600	14.41	6−3/4
16/0	20/30	0.666	16.10	7−1/2
14/0	22/30	0.733	17.78	8−1/4
12/0	24/30	0.800	19.47	9
10/0	26/30	0.8666	21.17	9−3/4
8/0	28/30	0.933	22.86	10−1/2
6/0	1−0	1.000	24.55	11−1/4
4/0	1−2/30	1.066	26.25	12
2/0	1−4/30	1.133	27.94	12−3/4
0	1−5/30	1.166	29.63	13−1/7
2	1−7/30	1.233	31.33	13−9/10
4	1−9/30	1.300	33.02	14−2/3
6	1−11/30	1.366	34.71	15−2/5
8	1−13/30	1.433	36.41	16−1/8
10	1−15/30	1.500	38.10	16−9/10
12	1−17/30	1.566	39.79	17−2/3
14	1−19/30	1.633	41.49	18−2/5
16	1−21/30	1.700	43.18	19−1/7
18	1−23/30	1.766	44.87	19−9/10
20	1−25/30	1.833	46.57	20−2/3

Sizes of Watches: The American sizes are based on 30ths of an inch. The Europeans use the ligne which is equal to .089 inches or 2.255 millimeters. In every case, the diameter is measured across the outside or largest part of the lower plate of the watch, right under the dial. In oval or other odd shaped movements, the size is measured across the smaller axis.

THE MAIN TYPES OF CHRONOGRAPHS EXPLAINED BY THEIR DIALS

NOTE: The following 17 pages were taken from a small booklet published by The Watchmakers of Switzerland in 1951.

Courtesy of F. H. (Bienne) and E. Bauches S.A. (Neuchatel)

From the library of Roland Thomas (Rod) Minter, Lombard, IL

THREE DIFFERENT TYPES OF MECHANISM

Each of the minute or hour-recording chronographs shown under No. 1 has a different type of mechanism.

I. Non-pillar-wheel chronograph mechanism, with adjustable hammer, adjustable minute-recording runner and adjustable minute-recording jumper (2 pushers).

II. Chronograph mechanism with pillar wheel and hour recorder (2 pushers).

III. Chronograph and split-second mechanisms with 2 pillar wheels for simultaneous observations (3 pushers).

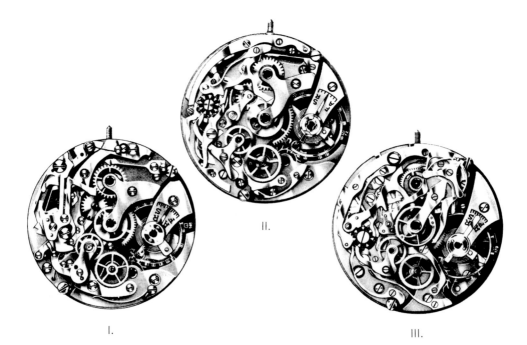

II.

I.

III.

OPERATING THE CHRONOGRAPH BY
MEANS OF THE PUSHERS

Some chronographs, those of the triple-action pusher type, have a single pusher on the side of the case or just inside the winding-crown O. This pusher is used successively for starting, stopping and returning the second hand to zero. Once it has been stopped, the chronograph cannot be restarted until the second hand has been brought back to zero. This triple-action system is no longer used for wrist chronographs.

Most chronographs to-day have two pushers, one of which has a single function and the other two. This double-action system has the advantage of enabling the chronograph to be restarted without the second hand being previously returned to zero.

The usual methods of operation are summarized below :

PUSHER FUNCTIONS			
Type	Pusher	Function	Operation
1	A	1 2 3	Starting Stopping Returning hand to zero
2	A B B	1 1 2	Starting Stopping Returning hand to zero
3	A A B	1 2 1	Sarting Stopping Returning hand to zero
4	A B O	1 1 1	Starting Stopping Returning hand to zero
5	A O A B	1 1 2 1	Starting Stopping split-second hand Stopping chronograph hand Returning hand to zero

A = Starting pusher
B = Return pusher
O = Stopping pusher

MINUTE-RECORDING CHRONOGRAPH

Timing to 1/5 second (C).
Timing up to 30 minutes (D).
Timing telephone conversations (E).

The dial of chronograph No. 3 is calibrated for timing to 1/5 second.

Timing up to 30 minutes, or in some cases 45 minutes, is possible with a minute-recording chronograph. For each rotation of the chronograph hand the minute-recording hand moves one division. Both hands return to zero simultaneously.

Charges for telephone calls are usually based on periods of 3 minutes; the special 3rd, 6th and 9th-minute divisions show at a glance the number of three-minute periods that have elapsed.

HOUR-RECORDING CHRONOGRAPH

Timing to 1/5 second.
Timing up to 30 minutes.
Timing telephone conversations.
Timing up to 12 hours (F).

For each complete rotation of the minute-recording hand (30 minutes), the hour-recording hand moves a single division representing one half-hour.

The three hands return to zero simultaneously.

CALENDAR CHRONOGRAPH

Timing to 1/5 second.
Timing up to 30 minutes.
Timing telephone conversations.
Timing up to 12 hours.
Indicating the date (G).
Indicating the day of the week (H).
Indicating the month (J).

The date is shown by the position of the blue pointer G which moves one division every 24 hours; it is set by pressing the pusher K. The day and the month are shown in the 2 dial openings. The date changes automatically every 24 hours. The month, however, is set by hand. The day of the week is altered by lightly pressing the double-action pusher L; the month is altered by full pressure on the same pusher.

The calendar mechanism is usually set by means of pushers on the side of the case. However, as there is no standard arrangement of their positions and corresponding functions, they are not necessarily the same as those shown above.

CALENDAR CHRONOGRAPH WITH MOON-PHASE INDICATOR

Timing to 1/5 second.
Timing up to 30 minutes.
Timing telephone conversations.
Timing up to 12 hours.
Indicating the date.
Indicating the day of the week.
Indicating the month.
Indicating the phases of the moon (M).

The moon-phase disc moves automatically. It is set by full pressure on the pusher K which in this case is a double-action pusher.

The calendar and moon-phase mechanism are usually set by means of pushers on the side of the case. However, as there is no standard arrangement of their positions and corresponding functions, they are not necessarily the same as those shown above.

K = Moon-phase pusher
M = Moon-phase disc

SPLIT-SECOND CHRONOGRAPH

Timing to 1/5 second.
Timing up to 30 minutes.
Timing telephone conversations.
Timing up to 12 hours.
Indicating the date.
Indicating the day of the week.
Indicating the month.
Indicating the phases of the moon.
Multiple timing by means of split-second hand. (N).

Chronographs with split-second mechanisms are particularly useful for timing simultaneous phenomena starting of the same time, but of different duration, such as sporting events in which several competitors are taking part.

In chronographs of this type, an additional hand is superimposed on the chronograph hand. Pressure on pusher A starts both the hands, which remain superimposed as long as the split-second mechanism is not blocked. This is done by pressing the split-second pusher O, fitted inside the winding-crown, which stops the split-second hand while the chronograph hand continues to move. After recording, the same pusher is pressed a second time, releasing the split-second hand, which instantly joins the still-moving chronograph hand, synchronizing with it, and is thus ready for another recording.

Pressure on pusher B brings the four hands back to zero simultaneously, provided the split-second hand is not blocked. Pressure on pusher O releases the split-second hand, which instantly joins the chronograph hand if the split-second hand happens to be blocked.

Pushers K and L, shown by arrows, on the side of the case of this chronograph, can be used to set the calendar and moon-phase mechanisms and are pressed down with the point of a pin.

As there is no standard arrangement of the positions and corresponding functions of the pushers, they are not necessarily the same as those shown above.

A = Starting pusher
B = Return pusher
K, L = Pushers for setting calendar and moon-phase mechanisms
N = Split-second hand
O = Split-second pusher

TACHOMETER CHRONOGRAPH

Timing to 1/5 second.
Timing up to 30 minutes.
Timing telephone conversations.
Tachometer scale (Q).

The tachometer scale is calibrated to show the speed of a moving object, such as a vehicle, over a known distance. The standard length on which the calibration is based is always shown on the dial, e. g. 1,000, 200 or 100 meters, or in some cases one mile. As the moving vehicle, for instance, passes the starting-point of the measured course whose length corresponds with that used as the basis of calibration, the observer releases the chronograph hand and stops it as the vehicle passes the finishing-point. The figure indicated by the hand on the tachometer scale represents the speed in kilometers or miles per hour. (See number 9).

On the tachometer scale of the chronograph illustrated opposite, the speed of a aircraft flying above a runway 1000 meters long is shown to be 700 kilometers per hour.

TELEMETER CHRONOGRAPH

Timing to 1/5 second.
Timing up to 30 minutes.
Timing telephone conversations.
Tachometer scale.
Telemeter scale (R).

By means of the telemeter scale it is possible to measure the distance of a phenomenon which is both visible and audible. The chronograph hand is released at the instant the phenomenon is seen ; it is stopped when the sound is heard, and its position on the scale shows at a glance the distance in kilometers or miles separating the phenomenon from the observer. (Calibration is based on the speed at which sound travels through the air, viz. approximately 340 meters or 1,115 feet per second).

During a thunderstorm the time that has elapsed between the flash of lightning and the sound of the thunder is registered on the chronograph scale as illustrated on the opposite side. The distance between the observation point and the thunderstorm, in this case, is 1600 meters.

On this dial there is also a tachometer scale, which is shown by blue circles (See number 8). This is used in the following way : if the minute-recording hand points to 0 the speed will be shown on the outer circle (speed between 1,000 and 60 kilometers) ; if the minute-recording hand points to 1 minute, the speed will be shown on the middle circle (speed between 60 and 30 kilometers) ; if the minute-recording hand points to 2 minutes the speed will be shown on the inside circle (speed between 30 and 20 kilometers).

PULSIMETER CHRONOGRAPH

Timing to 1/5 second.
Timing up to 30 minutes.
Timing telephone conversations.
Pulsimeter scale (S).

The pulsimeter scale shows at a glance the number of pulse beats per minute. The observer releases the chronograph hand when starting to count the beats and stops at the 30th, the 20th or the 15th beat according to the basis of calibration indicated on the dial. The hand shows at a glance the number of pulse beats per minute.

ASTHMOMETER CHRONOGRAPH

Timing to 1/5 second.
Timing up to 30 minutes.
Timing telephone conversations.
Pulsimeter scale.
Asthmometer scale (T).

The asthmometer scale shows at a glance the number of respirations per minute. The observer releases the chronograph hand as the patient begins a respiration and stops it on completion of the 15th, the 20th or the 25th respiration, according to the basis of calibration indicated on the dial. The hand shows at a glance the number of respirations per minute.

PRODUCTION-COUNTING CHRONOGRAPH

Timing to 1/5 second.
Timing up to 30 minutes.
Production-counting scale (U).

The production-counting scale is especially useful to large-scale manufacturers, as it enables them to determine the number of articles produced per hour.

The production-counting scale U on the dial of this model shows the production rate per hour ; no calculation is necessary if the basis of observation (the time taken to manufacture a single article, for instance) does not exceed 60 seconds. The observer releases the chronograph hand at the beginning of the observation and stops it when the observation is completed ; the figure shown by the hand on the scale represents the number of articles produced per hour.

If the time of manufacture is very short (up to 5 seconds, for instance), it is necessary to take as the basis of observation the time taken in manufacturing several pieces. The product of the number of pieces taken as the basis and the number shown on the scale represents the production rate per hour.

The chronograph dial on the opposite page shows the sweep hand pointing to 770 after the production of one piece. This would be the number of pieces produced per hour. If 5 pieces were produced during the same time, the production per hour would be 5 times 770, or 3,850 pieces.

It is of course possible to observe production times exceeding 60 seconds ; the quotient obtained by dividing 1 hour (3,600 seconds) by the time of manufacture taken as the basis represents the production rate per hour.

CHRONOGRAPH WITH MEMENTO DIAL

Timing to 1/5 second.
Timing up to 30 minutes.
Timing telephone conversations.
Timing up to 12 hours.
Tachymeter scale.
Memento dial (V).

The dial of this chronograph is fitted with a special reminder dial for noting the time of any given event. An independent setting mechanism for the hands is controlled by the crown (W).

V = Memento dial
W = Setting-crown for memento dial

MULTIPLE-PURPOSE CHRONOGRAPH

Timing to 1/5 second.
Timing up to 30 minutes.
Timing telephone conversations.
Tachometer scale.(Q).
Pulsimeter scale (S).
Telemeter scale (R).

The dial of this chronograph has several scales for various purposes.
The illustration shows one of the many combinations that can be supplied.

Q = Tachometer scale
R = Telemeter scale
S = Pulsimeter scale

TIDE CHRONOGRAPH

Timing to 1/5 second.
Timing up to 30 minutes.
Timing up to 12 hours.
Special calibration for yachting (X).
Dial showing " solunar periods " (Y).

The minute-recorder dial of this chronograph is divided into 6 sectors, each representing 5 minutes, and is specially designed for yachtsmen. In yacht racing a gun signal gives warning that in five minutes' time another gun signal will start the race. Thus the yachtsman is able to manœuvre his yacht so that he crosses the starting line on the second signal. This small dial thus shows at a glance how much time remains before the starting signal.

This chronograph shows the "solunar periods" as well as the official time. These periods, which are marked on the small dial Y, show the daily tidal times for a given port or latitude. This lunar dial is fitted with a rotating disc divided into 4 coloured sectors. The two opposite blue sectors represent high tide, while the two yellow ones represent low tide. As tidal times differ from place to place, a pusher Z is fitted for setting the coloured sectors accordingly.

Lunar time is also used by anglers, hunters and naturalists who are familiar with the " solunar theory ", for which tables have been published since 1930 by Mr. J. Alden Knight. These give a daily forecast of the feeding-times of fish and game, or in other words the most favourable times for fishing and hunting.

According to the scale of the chronograph shown   the tide will be its lowest around 6 a. m. and 6.30 p. m. that day.

X = Yachting dial
Y = " Solunar period " dial
Z = Pusher for setting lunar time

CHRONOGRAPH WITH CENTER MINUTE-RECORDING HAND

Timing to 1/5 second.
Timing up to 60 minutes. (C')
Timing telephone conversations.
Center minute-recording hand. (D')

In this model the minute-recorder calibrations are shown round the edge of the dial and the minute-recording hand works from the center D', which facilitates reading.

C' = Timing up to 60 minutes
D' = Minute recording hand

CHRONOGRAPH WITH DIRECTION HAND
(INDICATING NORTH)

Timing to 1/5 second.
Timing up to 45 minutes.
Timing telephone conversations.
Indicator hand showing North. (E')
Adjustable second hand. (F')

This chronograph is fitted with a small red indicator hand E' bearing
the letter "N"; this hand completes one turn of the dial in 24 hours
and is adjusted by means of crown O.   Bearings may be taken by
turning the watch, held horizontally, so that the hour hand points towards the sun, in which case the direction of North is shown by the
indicator hand E'.

This model is so constructed that the small second hand F' can be
set to the exact time. Crown G' is simply pushed in and turned ; this
moves the second hand F', which can thus be set, for example, to
correspond exactly to the time given by the time signal.

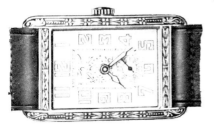

Abra "Rolled Gold Plate". Luminous numerals & hands, engraved center, subsidiary seconds dial. 10½''', 6J or 15J movement. Engraved rectangular, rolled gold plate or chrome case, detachable lugs. ca 1928 . . $3—5

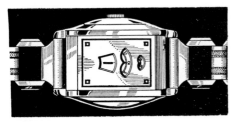

Abra "Jump Hour". Hour, minutes & seconds windows. 10½''', 7J movement. Chrome tonneau case. ca 1933 . . . . $40—50

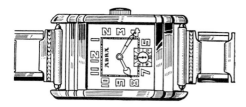

Abra "Chrome". Subsidiary seconds. 10½''', 7J movement. Rolled chromium plate, rectangular case. ca 1933. . . . . $4—8

Abra "Tu-tone Gold-Filled". Luminous numerals & hands with engraved center, subsidiary seconds. 14K gold-filled, engraved square case, detachable lugs. ca 1928 . . . . $35—55

Abra "Enamel". Plain dial. 10½''', 6J or 15J movement. Square, chromium plate case, calibrated black enamel bezel, detachable lugs. ca 1930 . . . . $20—30

Abercrombie & Fitch Co. Chronograph, subsidiary seconds, 30 minute & 12 hour registers. Highly jeweled, matte silver dial. 18K gold round case . . . . $275—325

ADMIRAL
Swiss Watch by Schwob

Admiral "Chrome Automatic". Waterproof. Luminous dial, center seconds. 17J movement. Round chrome and steel case. ca 1953 . .$7—15

Admiral "Moonphase Calendar". Raised figure dial, day, date windows, with outer date ring. 17J movement. Round yellow gold-filled case. ca 1953. . . . . $80—110

Admiral "Executive, Gold". Subsidiary seconds. 17J movement. 14K yellow gold, molded square case. ca 1953 . . . . $90—110

Aerotel "Chronograph". Subsidiary seconds, 30 minute recorder, with telemeter ring. 10½''', 17J movement. Round stainless steel case. ca 1939 . . . . $25—40

Agassiz "Platinum, Diamond & Sapphire". Ladies. 17J adjusted movement. Platinum rectangular case set with 14 diamonds & 6 Oriental sapphires. ca 1928 . . . . $300—400

Agassiz. Curvex, gold dial. 18J movement. 18K gold, elongated oval, 42mm. case. ca 1918. . . . . $400—600

Agassiz "Gold Curved". 18J movement. 38mm. 18K gold, curved tonneau case. ca 1920. . . . . $400—600

Agassiz. Diamond numeral dial. 18J movement. **Platinum** rectangular, 19x44mm. unmarked American contract case. ca 1928 . . $500—525

NOTE: All values are given for the head only unless the bracelet is included in the description.

Agassiz. Luminous numerals & hands. 14K gold or platinum rectangular curved case. ca 1931. Platinum . . . . $25C—325
14K gold . . . . 175—225

NOTE: Read Page 6 before using this book to value your wrist watch.

Agassiz. Luminous numerals & hands. 14K gold or platinum tonneau case. ca 1931. Platinum . . . . $150—185
14K gold . . . . 135—165

Agassiz, Universal Hours. 24 Hr. rotary dial, world time with 32 cities. 17J, 9¼''' movement. Round 14K gold case. 30 mm. ca 1935. . . . . $1,500—1,800

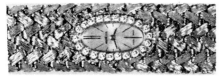

Angelus "Diamond and Gold Bracelet". Ladies. Oval dial. 14K gold, wide mesh bracelet. ca 1966 . .20% to 30% over gold & diamond value

Angelus Watch Co. Moonphase, calendar, tachometer chronograph, base 1000m., subsidiary seconds. 30 minute recorder, window day & date. GF 35mm. round case. ca 1945. 14K gold . . . . $850—1,000

Angelus "Chronograph". Tachometer base 1000m. with subsidiary seconds & 45 minute recorder. Round case with heavy lugs. ca 1947.
Stainless steel . . . . $ 25— 40
Gold filled . . . .   35— 50
14K gold . . . .   175—250

Angelus "Chronograph". Subsidiary seconds & 45 minute recorder. Round case. ca 1947.
Stainless steel . . . . $ 25— 40
Gold filled . . . .   35— 50
14K gold . . . .   175—225

Angelus. Calendar, chronograph. White dial, subsidiary seconds & 45 minute recorder, day & month windows with outer date ring. 18K gold, round case. . . . . $225—275

Angelus "Gold Bracelet". 14K gold, hammered round case and band. ca 1966.
. . . . 10% to 20% over gold value.

Americas 8-Days. Silvered dial, subsidiary seconds. 18K gold, tonneau case . . $350—450

Arbu, Split-Seconds Chronograph. Subsidiary seconds & 30 minute recorder. 17J, 13½'" movement. 18K polished & satin-like gold, 35mm. round case. ca 1950 . . . $1,200—1,400

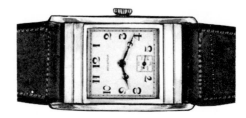

Ariston "Gold Curved Back Rectangle". Subsidiairy seconds. 17J movement. 14K white gold, curved, molded rectangular case. ca 1932 . . . . $120–150

Ardath "Duo-Movement" For the "Long Distance" traveler. Duo-Dial with local and home time and home date window. Two, 17J self-winding movements. Stainless steel round case with polished bezel. ca 1963 . . . . $50–75

Ariston "Gold Curved Back Rectangle". Silvered dial, black enameled figures, subsidiary seconds. 17J movement. 14K white gold, curved rectangular case. ca 1932 . . $100–130

ARISTON
Trademark of Marshall Field & Co.
Chicago, Ill.

Ariston "Gold Curved Tonneau". Subsidiary seconds. 17J movement. 14K white gold, curved tonneau case. ca 1932 . . . . $100–130

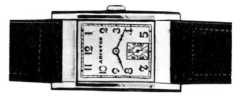

Ariston "Gold Curved Rectangle". Silvered dial, black enameled figures, subsidiary seconds. 17J movement. 14K white gold, curved, molded rectangular case. ca 1932 . . $110–140

Ariston "Gold Curved Back Rectangle". Silvered dial, black enameled figures, subsidiary seconds. 17J movement. 18K gold, curved, molded, rectangular case. ca 1932 . $140–175

Ariston "Gold Curved Back Rectangle". Silvered dial, black enameled numerals, subsidiary seconds. 17J movement. 14K white gold, curved, molded rectangular case with faceted corners. ca 1932. . . . . $90–120

Ariston "Gold Curved Back Rectangle". Silvered dial, raised etched figures, subsidiary seconds. 17J movement. 14K white gold, molded, curved rectangular case. ca 1932.
. . . . $100—130

Audemars Piguet "Diamond & Platinum Bracelet". Ladies. 6 baguette diamonds in the head and 34 brilliant diamonds in the platinum bracelet. Originality, condition, quality and size of the diamonds will affect the value. ca 1962.
. . . . $1,800—2,200

Audemars, Piguet & Co. "Platinum & Diamond". Ladies, 18J movement with 7 adjustments. Platinum rectangular case set with 10 diamonds. ca 1928 . . . $1,000—1,400

Audemars Piguet & Co. Astronomic, moonphase calendar. Silvered dial, subsidiary seconds, day, date & month recorders. 18J, 9¾''' movement. 18K gold, 26x36mm., rectangular case. ca 1931 . . . .$11,000—13,000

Audemars, Piguet & Co. "Platinum, Diamond & Sapphire". Ladies, 17J adjusted movement. Platinum rectangular case set with 46 diamonds & 42 Oriental sapphires. ca 1928.$1,200—1,600

Audemars Piguet. Moonphase calendar, subsidiary seconds, day & month windows with inner date ring. 8J, 9''' movement. Round, 18K, polished gold, 37mm. case. ca 1950.
. . . . $3,500—4,500

Audemars Piguet. Ladies, white matte dial. 18K gold rectangular 20mm. case with lug extensions. Backwind & set. ca 1930 . . . $500—700

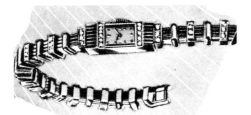

Audemars Piguet "Ladies Diamond & Platinum Bracelet". ca 1954 . . . . $1,200—1,600

Audemars Piguet, Geneva. Silvered dial, subsidiary seconds. 18J, 8¾''' movement. 18K, 30mm., round, polished gold bezel, with Roman numerals. ca 1950 . . . . . $750—850

Audemars Piguet "Gold Ultra-Thin". 18K yellow gold, square molded, tank-type case. ca 1954. . . . . $650—750

Audemars Piguet "Moonphase Calendar". Subsidiary seconds, day, date, month and moonphase dials. 18K yellow gold, round case, with polished bezel. ca 1954. . . . . . $7,000—8,000

Audemars Piguet. Slim 18K gold, 23x31mm. rectangular case. ca 1960. . . . . . . $600—800

Audemars Piguet "Gold Strap". 18K yellow gold, round case, with hour markers on polished bezel. ca 1961. . . . . $750—850

Audemars Piguet. Center seconds. 18K gold round case. ca 1961. . . . . $400—500

Audemars Piguet "Man's Gold Strap". Tu-tone champaigne dial with black markers. 18K yellow gold round case with hour markers and decoration on bezel. Hidden strap lugs. ca 1962 . . . . $750—800

Audemars Piguet, Geneve. Chronograph. Subsidiary seconds, 30 minute & 60 minute recorders. 21J movement. 18K gold, 39mm. round case . . . . $2,400—2,650

Audemars Piguet "Man's Gold Bracelet". White dial with white gold applied chapters. 18K white gold, textured case and matching band . . . . $2,000—2,400

Audemars Piguet, Geneve. Minute Repeater, round platinum case set with diamonds, platinum bracelet. . . . . $15,000—18,000

Audemars Piguet "Man's Gold Strap". Silvered dial with black markers. Sweep second movement. 18K yellow gold round case with heavy lugs and polished bezel. ca 1954 . . $650—750

Audemars, Piguet & Co., Geneva. 17J movement, 18K basket weave oval case, 31mm. . . . . $700—800

Audemars Piguet, Geneve. Gold finished dial, extra flat 1.7mm. movement. 18K gold square case . . . . $700—950

Audemars Piguet, Geneva. Silver matte dial, 17J movement. 18K gold ultra-thin, 33mm. rectangular case . . . . $600—800

Audemars Piguet. Silvered dial, molded round platinum, 35mm. case . . . . $800—950

Audemars Piguet, Geneve. Silvered dial, 17J movement, 18K gold round, 37mm. case with engine-turned bezel. 18K gold mesh bracelet. $800—1,000

Audemars Piguet. Modern, diamond dial. 18K gold oval case with rope twist border, 28mm., and matching 18K signed band . $2,200—2,800

Aureole "Alarm". Waterproof. Luminous hands & markers. Center seconds & red alarm hand. 17J movement. Round, case. ca 1957.
Gold plated yellow top. . . . . $20—35
Chrome. . . . . 15—25

Aureole "Chronograph". Gold-filled, raised figured dial, sweep seconds, 30 minute recorder with outer tachometer ring. 17J movement. Round chrome case. ca 1957 . . . . . $25—50

Axa. Radium silvered dial. 16J, 8¾''' movement. Rectangular case. ca 1924.
18K gold. . . . . $150—175
Silver . . . . 30— 45

Axa. Radium silvered dial. 16J, 10½''' movement. Tonneau case. ca 1924.
18K gold. . . . . $150—175
Silver . . . . 35— 45

Axa. Radium silvered dial. 16J, 10½''' movement. Sterling silver, molded rectangular case. ca 1924. . . . . $35—50

Axa. Elongated numeral, silvered dial. 16J movement. Plain rectangular case. ca 1924.
14K gold . . . . $250—275
Silver . . . . 35— 55

Axa. Radium silvered dial. 16J, 10½''' movement. Rectangular case. ca 1924.
14K gold . . . . $150—165
Silver . . . . 35— 50

Axa. Radium silvered dial. 16J, 8¾''' movement. Sterling silver, octagonal case. ca 1924.
. . . . $35—45

Axa. Radium silvered dial. 16J, 6¾''' movement. Faceted rectangular case. ca 1924.
14K gold . . . . $140—160
Silver . . . . 35— 50

Ball "Trainmaster Official RR Standard". White painted metal dial with the typical "Ball" hour markers and bold black numerals. Sweep second, 21J, adjusted 5 positions, Model No. 1604-B. 13''' stemwind movement made by A. Schild. Round stainless steel, railroad approved case, with heavy strap lugs. ca 1963 $100—150

Ball "Official RR Standard". White painted metal dial, sweep second, 21J, adjusted 5 positions, Model No. 1604-B. 13''', stemwind movement made by A. Schild. Round railroad approved, 10K YGF case, with heavy strap lugs. ca 1964. . . . . $150—200

NOTE: Read Page 6 before using this book to value your wrist watch.

NOTE: All values are given for the head only unless the bracelet is included in the description.

Ball "Indimatic". White painted metal dial with raised gold numerals & markers, with a power reserve indicator window. Sweep second, self-winding, 17J, unadjusted Model 1256. 11½''' movement made by ETA. Round case with heavy strap lugs. (Not Railroad Grade) ca 1963. 10K YGF. . . . . $150—200
Stainless steel . . . . 125—150

Ball "Official RR Standard Trainmaster Automatic". White painted metal "Ball" dial. Sweep second, 25J, adjusted 5 positions, Model No. 2821. 11½''' self-winding movement made by E.T.A. Round railroad approved case with heavy strap lugs. ca 1975. 10K YGF $175—225
Stainless steel . . . . 100—150

NOTE: Add $15 to $40 if complete with inner and outer Ball & Co. boxes on all of the watches illustrated. Also, 24-Hour Canadian dial would be about the same value.

Baume & Mercier. Moonphase calendar, center seconds, window day & month & outer date rings. 18K gold 37mm. round case. ca 1945. . . . . $700—800

Baume & Mercier "International". Ladies. 18K gold oval watch with sapphire stem. Flexible textured gold bracelet. ca 1969 . $700—800

NOTE: All values are given for the head only unless the bracelet is included in the description.

Baume & Mercier. Calendar chronograph, subsidiary seconds, 30 minute & 12 hour recorder, center seconds. 36mm. round 18K gold case. ca 1950. . . . . $350—400

Baume & Mercier. Rectangular case with moulded sides stamped Baume & Mercier, 23x31mm., ca 1970 . . . . $450—495

NOTE: Read Page 6 before using this book to value your wrist watch.

Baume & Mercier. Automatic skeleton, the dial with bar numerals & pierced plates to reveal the mechanism in an 18K gold circular, 34mm case. . . . . $800—1,000

Baume & Mercier. Champagne dial, 18K round case, 33mm. ca 1973 . . . . $375—450

Baume & Mercier "Curvex". Champagne dial. 18K gold, 26x37mm. rectangular case, with double border set with diamonds. ca 1975. . . . . $1,050–1,200

Baume & Mercier. Champagne dial, 18K gold round case, 25mm, with matching 18K gold band. ca 1977 . . . . $700–800

Baume & Mercier "International". Ladies 18K gold watch with diamond circled, white face, black Roman numerals on an intergal braid, textured, 18K gold bracelet. ca 1969. . . . . $1,200–1,600

Baume & Mercier. Ladies round, diamond and gold watch on a bracelet of textured, braided 14K gold. ca 1963 . . . . $550–625

Bedford "Venus". Ladies, 14K white gold filled tonneau case with numerals enameled on bezel. ca 1928. . . . . $25–40

Belforte "Gibraltar". Waterproof. Center seconds. Self-winding, 17J movement. Round gold-filled case. ca 1962 . . . . $10–15

Benrus "Embraceable". Ladies, 17J movement. Gold-filled tonneau case and molded bracelet. ca 1946. . . . . $10–15

Benrus "Sky Chief Chronograph". Subsidiary seconds, 30 minute & 12 hour recorders. 17J movement. Round 14K gold case. ca 1945. . . . . $200–250
Stainless steel 60– 85

Benrus "Prince Victor". Subsidiary seconds. 17J movement. Square gold-filled case. ca 1946 . . . .$25—35

Benrus "Dial-O-Rama". Waterproof. Hour & minute windows. 17J movement. Round yellow rolled gold plate case. ca 1957. . . . . .$30—45
Bracelet . . . . 2— 4

Benrus "Alarm". Waterproof. Luminous hands & dots, center seconds & alarm indicator. 17J movement. Round chrome case. ca 1957.
. . . .$25—35

Benrus "Diamond Galahad Automatic". Waterproof. White or charcoal diamond dial. 39J movement. Round stainless steel case. ca 1964.
. . . .$15—25

Benrus "Viking Automatic". Waterproof. White or black dial, center seconds. 25J movement. Round yellow case. ca 1963 . . . . . .$10—20

BLACK STARR & FROST

A New York 5th Avenue jeweler who offered a very exclusive line of jeweled wrist watches that are real objects of art. Value is in the eye of the buyer.

Black Starr & Frost. Platinum, diamond & sapphire. ca 1924. Size & quality of stones is important in valuing this type of watch.
. . . . $550—650

Blancpain "Diamond & Platinum Bracelet". Platinum rectangular case and geometric molded lugs, set with diamonds. ca 1947.
. .20% to 30% over diamond & platinum value

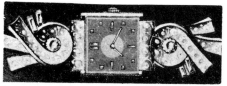

Blancpain "Diamond & Platinum Bracelet". Tu-tone gold dial with polished 18K gold markers. Square platinum case and heavy molded lugs set with 40 diamonds. Thin, snake, 18K gold attached bracelet. ca 1946.
. . . . $300—375

Borel Fils & Cie. Gold finished dial, subsidiary seconds. 14K gold, round case. ca 1920.
. . . . $210—235

Borel "Cocktail". Rotating dials create an interesting effect. Good 17J Swiss movement. Round, rolled gold plate top & stainless back. Black hour markers enameled on bezel. ca 1961 . . . .$7—20

Borel "Cocktail" (by Synchron). Black & white antimated dial. 17J movement. Yellow gold-filled oval case & matching bracelet. ca 1975. . . . .$15—25

Borel "Cocktail" (by Synchron). Date, self-winding. Black & white antimated dial. 17J movement. Round gold-filled case & lugs. ca 1975 . . . .$15—25

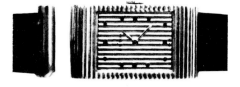

Boucheron Paris. Rectangular case, platinum with geometric pattern & chamfered ends. 17x30mm . . . . $450—500

NOTE: Read Page 6 before using this book to value your wrist watch.

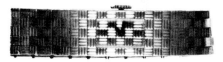

Boucheron, Paris. Horizontally lined, gold finished dial. Omega movement. Horizontally lined, 18K gold, rectangular case . . $400—500

Boucheron. Plain dial, with continuous geometric design on case & band, 18K gold, 11mm. wide. ca 1963 . . . . 20% over gold

NOTE: All values are given for the head only unless the bracelet is included in the description.

Boucheron. Quartz, dial with angled lines, in a 18K gold square 22x28mm case with similar lines. ca 1980 . . . . $500—700

Breguet "Self-winding Calendar". Engine-turned, silvered dial, black Roman numeral, subsidiary seconds & calendar dial, up/down indicator. 1-3/8''' long, platinum rectangular case with winder at 12. ca 1933. $3,000–3,500

Bovet "Catch-up Split Seconds Chronograph". Tachometer base 1 mile, with subsidiary seconds & 30 minute recorder. 17J, precision movement. Round waterproof case. ca 1946. 14K gold $350–450
Stainless steel 150–200

Breguet. Perpetual moonphase, calendar, silvered dial, center seconds, day & month windows with outer date ring. 18K gold, 34mm. round case $800–1,000

Bradley "Aquatrol and Seamate". Silvered or black dial, luminous numerals, center seconds. Non-jeweled Swiss movements. Round chrome plated case, stainless steel backs. ca 1961 $3–5

Breguet. Moonphase calendar, chronograph. Silvered dial, subsidiary seconds, 30 minute & 12 hour recorders, day & month windows, with outer date ring. 18K gold, 36mm. round case. $1,200–1,350

Bradley "Time Teacher". White hours & hour hand, blue minutes & minute hand. Non-jeweled Swiss movement. Round chrome case. ca 1962. . . . . $3–5

Breguet. Matching case & movement numbers. 18K gold 11mm. case & triple link bracelet. ca 1965. . . . . $700–800

Breitling "Datora Calendar Chronograph". Subsidiary seconds, 30 minute & 12 hour recorders, day & month windows, with outer date ring. Stainless steel round case. ca 1948 . . . . $40–65

Breitling "Superocean". Black dial, luminous hands & markers, center seconds. Automatic, 17J movement. Round stainless steel case, revolving bezel. ca 1965 . . . . $35–55

Breitling "Transocean Calendar". Raised gold numerals, date window, center seconds. Automatic, waterproof, 17J movement. Round case. ca 1965. 18K gold $125–150
18K gold top 75– 85
Stainless steel 20– 30

Breitling "Chronomat Chronograph". Subsidiary seconds, 45 minute recorder. 17J movement. Round case, revolving slide rule bezel. ca 1965. 18K gold $175–225
Gold-filled top. 40– 60
Stainless steel 35– 50

Breitling "Unitime". Black dial, luminous markers, center seconds, date window & GMT time. Automatic, 17J movement. Round stainless steel case, revolving calibrated bezel. ca 1965. . . . . $40–55

Breitling "Superocean Chronograph". Black & luminous dial, subsidiary seconds, 30 minute recorder. 17J movement. Round stainless steel case, revolving bezel. ca 1965 . . . . . . $50–75

Breitling Premier. Chronograph, Gold finished dial, subsidiary seconds & 45 minute recorder. 17J movement. 18K gold, round case$175—220

Breitling "Copilot Chronograph". Black & luminous dial, subsidiary seconds, 15 minute & 12 hour recorders. 17J movement. Round stainless steel case, revolving calibrated bezel. ca 1965 . . . .$50—75

Breitling "Astro-Timer Chronograph". Black & luminous dial & hands, subsidiary seconds, 30 minute & 12 hour recorders. Outer KM & mile tachometer rings. 17J movement. Round case, rotating bezel calibrates logarithmic scales of navigation computer. ca 1965.
Gold-filled top. . . . .$60—85
Stainless steel . . . . 50—75

Breitling "Navitimer Chronograph". Black dial, white subsidiary seconds, 30 minute & 12 hour recorder, with outer KM & mile tachometer rings. 17J movement. Round case, revolving calibrated bezel for logarithmic scales of navigation computer. ca 1965. 18K gold .$250—300
Gold-filled top. . . . . 60— 85
Stainless steel . . . . 50— 75

Breitling "Chronograph". Subsidiary seconds, 45 minute recorder. 17J movement. Round gold-filled case. ca 1965 . . . .$35—50

Breitling "World Time Calendar". Multi-color dial with 12 hour and 60 seconds chapter ring, date window at 3. 24-Hour ring and major cities of the world on a ring attached to a moveable bezel. 18K yellow gold, round case. ca 1954 . . . .$300—400

Britix. Automatic, moonphase calendar, day & month windows, with outer date ring. Round, GF case. ca 1950 . . . . $175—195

Bucherer. Silvered dial, subsidiary seconds. 15J movement. 26x28mm. tonneau case. ca 1928.
14K tu-tone gold . . . . $300—400
Tu-tone chrome . . . . 20— 35
Chrome. . . . . 4— 8

Britix. Tachometer chronograph, 1000m. base & telemeter. Silvered dial, subsidiary seconds, 30 minute recorder. 17J movement. 14K gold, round case. ca 1950. . . . . $175—200

Bucherer "Hinged Lugs". Silvered dial, subsidiary seconds. 15J movement. Engraved, 24x38mm., rectangular case with moveable lugs. ca 1928. 14K white gold . . . $125—150
14K tu-tone green & white gold . . . $250—275

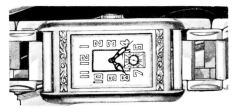

Brooks "Commander". Radium silvered dial & hands. 9''', 17J movement. 14K white gold-filled, engraved, curved rectangular case. ca 1933 . . . .$20—30
Bracelet . . . . 4— 8

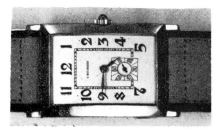

Bucherer. Silvered dial, subsidiary seconds. 15J movement. 25x34mm. rectangular tank case. ca 1928. 14K yellow gold . . . $110—130
14K white gold . . . . 100—120
Silver . . . . 30— 45

Brooks "Meridian Jump Hour". Hour, minute & seconds window. 10½''', 15J movement. 14K white gold-filled, engraved octagonal case. ca 1933 . . . .$30—45

Bucherer "Tank". Silvered dial, subsidiary seconds. 15J movement. 26x30mm. rectangular tank case. ca 1928. 14K tu-tone gold $250—350
Tu-tone chrome . . . . 20— 35
Chrome. . . . . 4— 8

Bucherer "Tank". Luminous dial, subsidiary seconds. 6J or 15J movement. 25x32mm. tank case. Made in square, rectangular, tonneau also. ca 1928. 14K yellow gold $120–150
14K white gold 100–125
Silver 30– 45
Chrome. 8– 16

Bucherer "Cushion". Luminous dial, subsidiary seconds. 15J movement. 25x25mm. cushion case. ca 1928. 14K yellow gold $90–150
Silver 25– 35

Bucherer. Luminous dial, subsidiary seconds. 15J movement. 32mm. round case. ca 1928. 14K gold $90–130
Silver 30– 45

Bucherer "Cushion". Luminous dial. subsidiary seconds. 15J movement. 28x28mm. cushion case. ca 1928. 14K yellow gold . . . $100–120
Silver 30– 45

Bueche-Girod. Ladies. Gold & lapis lazuli oval case. Matching gold ring bracelet . . $600–800

Bueche Girod. Ladies, malachite dial, 18K gold, 15x18mm. oval case with diamond & emeral set bezel. ca 1971. . . . . . . $700–800

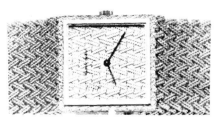

Bueche Girod. Gold mesh dial. 18K gold square case and continuing mesh band. ca 1966.
. . . . $600–800

Bulova. Ladies. Round dial, engraved center. 15J movement. 14K white gold, engraved octagonal case. ca 1922 . . . . $40–60

Bulova "Ladies". Round dial. 17J movement. 18K white gold, engraved tonneau case and fan-type lugs. ca 1922. . . . . $60–85

Bulova "Princess". Ladies. Hand-carved platinum, rectangular case and band set with 110 diamonds and 6 sapphires. ca 1927 . $750—900

Bulova "Czarina". Ladies, 17J movement. Hand-carved rectangular, platinum case and band set with 78 diamonds. ca 1927.
. . . . $500—600

Bulova "Sultana". Ladies, 17J movement. Hand-carved platinum, rectangular case set with 70 diamonds & 18 sapphires. ca 1927.
. . . . $300—375

Bulova "Marquise". Ladies, 17J movement. Hand-carved platinum, tonneau case set with 42 diamonds and 16 sapphires. ca 1927.
. . . . $250—300

Bulova "Ladies Sport". Silvered dial. 15J movement. 14K plain or engraved, white gold-filled rectangular case. ca 1927. . . . . $10—20

Bulova "Ladies Sport". Radium silvered dial. 15J movement. 14K white gold, engraved and faceted rectangular case. ca 1927 . . . . $35—55

Bulova "Debutante". Ladies, 15J movement. Engraved, yellow gold-filled rectangular case. ca 1927. . . . . $10—20

Bulova "Lady Bulova". Self-winding, 17J movement. Round, gold plated case. ca 1966.
Yellow plated . . . . $3—8
White plated . . . . 3—8

Bulova "Concerto". Ladies. 17J movement. Yellow or white gold plated, molded tonneau case. ca 1966 . . . . $3—5

Bulova "Goddess of Time". Ladies. Oval dial. 21J movement. 14K gold square case, faceted crystal and 14K gold matching bracelet. ca 1966 . . . . 10% to 20% over gold value

Bulova "La Petite, Diamond & Gold". Ladies. 14K gold oval case and leaf lugs, set with 8 diamonds, faceted crystal, matching band. ca 1966. . . . . $40—65

Bulova "First Lady". Oval dial. 17J movement. Oval, gold plated case with faceted crystal and twin twist bracelet. ca 1966 . . . . $3—5

Bulova. Radium silvered dial, luminous hands & numerals. 17J movement. 26x38mm., 14K yellow gold rectangular case. ca 1922 $175—250

Bulova "Gold Strap". Radium silvered dial, subsidiary seconds. 15J movement. 14K green gold rectangular case. ca 1927. . . . $110—140
14K white gold . . . . 100—130
14K green or white gold-filled. . . . 20— 30

Bulova. Radium silvered dial, subsidiary seconds. 17J movement. 14K gold rectangular case. ca 1924 . . . . $90—110
Sterling silver . . . . 20— 30
Yellow gold-filled. . . . . 20— 30

Bulova "President". Radium silvered dial, subsidiary seconds. 17J movement. Engraved, white gold-filled, curved rectangular case. ca 1929 . . . . $20—30
Gold-filled bracelet . . . . 3— 7

Bulova. Radium silvered dial, subsidiary seconds. 17J movement. 14K gold, engraved square case. ca 1924 . . . . $85—105
Green gold-filled . . . . 20— 30

Bulova "Ambassador". Radium silvered dial, subsidiary seconds. 15J movement. Engraved, white gold-filled, rectangular case. ca 1929.
. . . . $20—30
Gold-filled bracelet . . . . 3— 7

Bulova. Radium silvered dial, subsidiary seconds. 17J movement. 14K green gold, engraved rectangular case. ca 1927 . . $90—120
14K white gold . . . . 80—110
Bracelet . . . . . 10% to 20% over gold value

Bulova "Lone Eagle". Created in honor of Charles A. Lindbergh. Raised gold numerals & hands, subsidiary seconds. 15J movement. Embossed white gold-filled, rectangular case. ca 1932. . . . . $20—35

Bulova "Phantom". 17J movement. Curved and engraved, yellow gold plated, rectangular case and link bracelet. ca 1936 . . . .$7—18
White gold plated . . . . 7—18
Bracelet . . . . 2— 3

Bulova "Ambassador". Subsidiary seconds. 15J or 17J movement. Molded chrome tonneau case. ca 1936 . . . .$7—18
Yellow plated top. . . . . 8—20
Bracelet . . . . 2— 3

Bulova "Minuteman". Subsidiary seconds. 17J movement. 10K yellow rolled gold plate, curved tonneau case. ca 1940 . . . . .$35—55

Bulova "Brewster Plated". Subsidiary seconds. 17J movement. 10K yellow rolled gold plate, rectangular case & lugs. ca 1940. . . . .$20—30

Bulova "Corrigan Plated". Subsidiary seconds. 17J movement. 10K yellow rolled gold plate, molded rectangular case & lugs. ca 1940.
. . . .$20—30

Bulova "President". Subsidiary seconds. 14K gold rectangular case. ca 1940. . . . $125—150

Bulova "Montgomery". Subsidiary seconds. 17J movement. 10K yellow gold-filled, curved rectangular case. ca 1940. . . . .$35—55

Bulova "Banker". Subsidiary seconds. 15J movement. 10K yellow rolled gold plate, molded tonneau case. ca 1940. . . . . .$15—20

Bulova "American Eagle". Subsidiary seconds. 21J movement. 10K yellow gold-filled, rectangular case extending into curved lugs. ca 1940.
. . . .$15—20
Gold-filled bracelet . . . . 3— 5

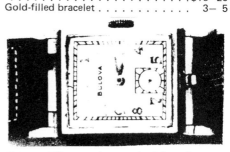

Bulova. Flips up to reveal picture frame on back. Silvered dial, 17J movement. Rectangular, RGP case . . . . $125—150

Bulova "Driver's watch". Subsidiary seconds, GF, 20x35mm., curved rectangular watch. ca 1950 . . . . $75—100

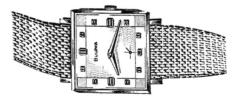

Bulova "Banker". Subsidiary seconds. 17J movement. Square, yellow gold plated case. ca 1966 . . . .$10—15
Mesh bracelet . . . . 2— 5

Bulova "Modern Sea King". Waterproof. Charcoal dial, raised markers, center seconds. 17J movement. Stainless steel round case with tapered expansion band. ca 1961 . . . .$10—20

Bulova "Accutron Astronaut". Black dial with sweep second and time zone triangle hand indicating 2nd time zone, on 24 hour rotating bezel. Stainless steel . . . . $ 75—100
14K gold . . . . 200—250
18K gold . . . . 250—350

Bulova "Commander". Waterproof, self-winding. Luminous dial, center seconds. Round, yellow gold plated case. ca 1966 . . . .$15—20

Bulova "Accutron Date". Oval, gold finished dial with hour markers on shadow ring and date window at 3. Sweep second. Gold plated top with stainless steel back & bracelet. ca 1975 . . . .$50—60

Bulova "Commander". Waterproof, self-winding. Luminous hands & dial, center seconds. 30J movement. 10K rolled gold plate, round case with etched bezel. ca 1966 . $30—40

Bulova Accutron. Skeletonized dial. Cushion case . . . . $75—100

BULOVA "ACCUTRON"

Bulova "Accutron" watches come in a large variety of case styles & metals. Among collectors at the present time, the most sought after is the "Spaceview" illustrated above, with the "Railroad Model" a close second. ca 1963.

Model	14K Solid Gold	Gold Filled Top	Stainless Steel
Spaceview	$225–300	$125–175	$100–135
Railroad Model	175–225	85–125	65–100
Other Styles	150–200	55– 80	50– 75

Other case styles are desirable and some more popular than others. This movement was U.S. Railroad Approved with the proper case and dial, and is marked with bold railroad numbers.

Buren. Gold plated dial, subsidiary seconds. 14K gold rectangular American case $100—125

BURLINGTON WATCH COMPANY
19th Street and California Avenue
Chicago, Illinois

Burlington Watch Company was a non-manufacturing mail order watch company who contracted with the Illinois Watch Company and Swiss companies to make watches for them. Early 20's and early 30's Burlington mail order catalogs (in the library of Raymond Rice, Aurora, Colorado) show about 20 styles of Illinois and Swiss-made wrist watches. "Burlington" on the dial and/or movement would add $5 to $10 premium over the same watch with "Illinois" or Swiss markings. A box and certificate would add $15 to $25 to the total value.

Butex. Tachometer chronograph, 1000 m. base, subsidiary seconds and 30 minute recorder. 18K gold round case. ca 1949 . . . . $175—225
Gold-filled . . . . 65— 80
Stainless steel . . . . 35— 55

Caldwell, J.E. Ladies. Rectangular, platinum, diamond & emerald bracelet watch. ca 1930.
. . . . $600—675

Henry Capt, Geneve, 5 Minute Repeater. Two gongs, white enamel dial. Plain round 14K gold case. 34mm . . . . $3,200—3,800

H. Capt, Quarter Repeater. Highly jeweled, silvered dial, subsidiary seconds. Plain round 18K gold case. 39mm . . . . $3,000—3,500

Carmen Bracelet Watch. (one of the first wrist watches introduced in the U.S. to the public nationwide from 1906 to 1914.) Glass enamel dial. Cylinder & 11J, pin set, Swiss lever movement. Case has enamel bezel & back in light & dark blue, green & red colors, or gold filled.
GF . . . . $15—30
Enamel . . . . 20—40

Cartier, France, European Watch & Clock Co., Inc. White matte dial. 19J, 8 adjustments, lever movement. 18K gold square case, white enamel bezel with gold Roman numerals, 22mm., gold string bracelet . . . . $2,750—3,250

Cartier, E.W.C. Co. 18K white gold, 34mm. rectangular lapel watch. Rose-diamond bezel & pendant fob set with 4 brilliants.
. . . . $1,500—2,000

Cartier, The European Watch & Clock Co.
Ladies 18K gold rectangular case, diamond
bezel & strap clasps. 33x13mm. ca 1925.
. . . . $2,200—2,600

Cartier, The European Watch & Clock Co. 18K
gold ladies 13x26mm. rectangular case. ca
1927 . . . . $1,100—1,350

Cartier, The European Watch & Clock Co.
18K gold ladies 20x28mm. rectangular case
with bowed sides. Original 18K band & clasp.
ca 1930. . . . . $1,400—1,600

Cartier, The European Watch Co. Ladies,
silvered dial, 18K gold 20x30mm. octagonal
case. ca 1935 . . . . $1,000—1,200

**Cartier, European Watch & Clock Co., Le
Coultre.** Ladies, silver dial. 16J movement.
18K gold, 25mm. round case with open work
ring of large & small beads, with braided 18K
gold Cartier band. ca 1940. . . . $1,000—1,200

Cartier. Ladies square case, inlaid borders with
diamonds. 20x27mm. Modern. . $1,600—2,000

Cartier. Ladies "Reversible", silver dial. 17J,
8''' movement. 18K polished gold rectangular
case. 32x21mm. ca 1965. . . . . $1,500—1,800

**Cartier (by Tavannes) "Diamond & Pearl
Bracelet".** White dial. Round case and links
paved with diamonds, and pearl bracelet.
. . . . $1,000—1,200

Cartier. Ladies. 1.80 carats diamond paved,
oval dial. 18K gold oval case, surrounded by
fluted coral and black onyx. Modern.
. . . . $2,000—2,200

Cartier. Ladies. Shaped lapis lazuli dial. 18K gold, shaped case. Modern . . . . . . $500—700

Cartier "Ladies Gold Tank". Textured gold finished dial. 18K gold, square tank case. Modern. . . . . $400—500

Cartier. Ladies. Lapis lazuli dial. 18K gold, lapis lazuli and diamond octagonal case. Modern . . . . $1,200—1,500

Cartier. Ladies. Lapis lazuli dial with diamond paved center. 18K gold hexagonal watch, braided bezel and band. Modern $1,600—2,000

Cartier. Ladies. Black onyx oval dial. 18K gold octagonal case set with alternating coral and black onyx sections, and 18K gold mesh band. Modern. . . . . $1,200—1,500

Cartier, E.W.C. "Elongated Curvex". 18K gold elongated curvex tank case. Length 45mm. ca 1925. . . . . $2,800—3,200

Cartier. Movement signed E.W.C., Paris. 18K gold back & gold diamond bezel. ca 1925. . . . . $2,200—2,800

Cartier, E.W.C. White dial, 18K gold, 27mm. round case, with diamond set inner bezel. ca 1925 . . . . $900—1,100

Cartier. 18J, 10''' European Watch & Clock Co. movement. Silver dial, 18K gold asymetric case. 32x25mm. ca 1928 . . . . . $2,000—2,250

Cartier, E.W.C. & Co. Silvered dial, 18K gold rectangular case . . . . $2,500—3,000

Cartier. The European Watch Co. Curved rectangular 18K gold case, 20x36mm. ca 1929.
. . . . $3,000–3,500

Cartier, The European Watch & Clock Co. Gold Hermitage watch, with spring levers opening two shutters revealing the dial. 33x48mm. 18K gold. ca 1930. . $2,500–3,000

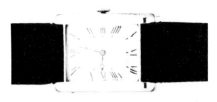

Cartier, European Watch Co. Tank, 18J movement, 18K gold rectangular case, 34mm. Back attached to front by 4 gold screws. ca 1930.
. . . . $1,500–1,800

Cartier, E.W. & Co. 18K gold case, bowed sides with a dotted border. 23x29mm. ca 1932.
. . . . $1,800–2,200

Cartier, France by E.W.C. & Co. White dial. 18K gold, square case. $1,500–1,800

Cartier, Le Coultre, France. Silvered dial, 18K gold, 37mm. rectangular case with back wind & set. ca 1932 . . . . $2,000–2,500

Cartier, Le Coultre. Desk watch, silver flat backed case with arched front & fluted panels at the side, one sliding to release hinged front panel. 80x52mm. ca 1935 . . . . . . $500–700

Cartier. Silver matte dial, 18K square case, blue enameled cover. 30mm. ca 1935 $3,600–4,000

Cartier, Paris, European Watch & Clock Co.
White enamel dial. 15J movement. 18K gold &
blue enamel square, 25mm. case. Maker's mark
JC. ca 1935 . . . . $3,500—4,000

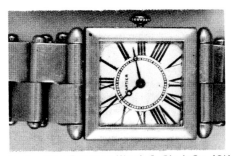

Cartier, The European Watch & Clock Co. 18K
gold square case with moulded strap lugs and
18K gold strap. ca 1936 . . . . . $3,400—4,000

Cartier France, Longines Watch Co., Santos.
White matte dial. 17J movement. 18K gold
square, 25mm. case. ca 1939 . . $4,500—5,000

Cartier, Touchon. White enamel face. 18K
gold, 27mm. square case, wide gold bezel with
blue enamel Roman numerals. ca 1940.
. . . . $3,500—4,000

Cartier, European Watch & Clock Co. Gilt
matte dial. 15J round movement. 18K gold
elongated hexagonal case. 23mm. $2,000—2,200

Cartier, France, Jaeger Le Coultre. Silvered dial,
18K gold rectangular, tank case, backwind &
set. 32mm . . . . $2,400—2,800

*NOTE: Read Page 6 before using this book to
value your wrist watch.*

Cartier. Santos Model, styled 18K gold square
case with heavy bold lugs. By E.W.C. ca 1952.
. . . . $4,000—6,000

Cartier. Sweep second in a stainless steel round
case, by E.W.C. ca 1952 . . . . . . $200—300

*NOTE: All values are given for the head only
unless the bracelet is included in the description.*

Cartier. 18K large round case with sweep
second hand, by E.W.C. ca 1952 . . $500—600

Cartier, Universal, Geneve. White dial, 18K gold round case, signed "Cartier"..... $450–500

Cartier, Jaeger Le Coultre. 18K gold, 35mm. octagonal case. ca 1969 .... $1,000–1,200

Cartier Movado. Modern, silvered dial signed Cartier. Slim, gold, round case. 32mm.
.... $450–500

Cartier, Jaeger Le Coultre. Automatic, 18K gold tank case. ca 1970..... $1,000–1,250

Cartier, Jaeger Le Coultre. White dial signed Cartier, 18K gold 20x24mm small oval case. ca 1965............... $1,400–1,600

Cartier. Modern. White lacquered dial, Swiss movement. 18K gold rectangular case.
.... $800–900

Cartier, Jaeger le Coultre. Dial signed Cartier. Lever movement with jeweled pallets. 18K slim square case with cone strap lugs. 25mm. ca 1969. With 18K deploiement clasp.
.... $1,300–1,400

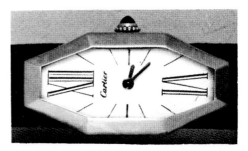

Cartier, Jaeger le Coultre. 18K gold case with chamfered sides. 19x38mm. Dial signed Cartier, hallmarked London 1972 .... $1,200–1,300

Cartier "Santos". Automatic, date aperture & center seconds. Steel case & octagonal gold bezel & gold screws on band. 30mm $650–750

Cartier. Gold oval, 20x28mm. case. ca 1976. . . . . $1,800–2,000

Cartier, Jaeger Le Coultre. Gold oval case with Roman & dot numerals on a blue enamel background. 23x30mm. Modern, ca 1976. . . . . $1,200–1,500

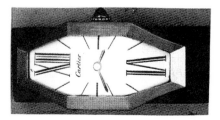

Cartier, Jaeger Le Coultre. 18K gold hexagonal case with chamferred sides, 20x38mm. $1,400–1,600

Cartier, Jaeger Le Coultre. White dial signed Cartier, London. 18K gold elongated oval case, 23x53mm $2,000–2,300

NOTE: Cartier watches are very desirable world wide and therefore have been faked and reproduced for many years. Currently, a few of the most popular models are being reproduced in the Far East and are being widely sold in the U.S. through flea markets, etc. Be careful that you are getting the real thing before paying top dollar.

Cartier, Jaeger Le Coultre. Grey dial signed Cartier, London. 18K gold moulded elongated oval case, 30x56mm. ca 1968 . . $2,200–2,600

Cartier, Jaeger Le Coultre. 18K gold, 23x31mm. tank case. ca 1975 . . . . $800—950

Cartier, Paris. Gold rectangular case with moulded sides, 28x14mm. Modern . $650—725

NOTE: Read Page 6 before using this book to value your wrist watch.

Cartier, Universal Geneve. Silver matte dial, 17J movement. 18K gold, 30mm. rectangular case with tortoise shell band & 18K gold clasp . . . . $1,100—1,250

Cartier, Paris. Modern, white enameled dial. 17J round movement. 18K gold elongated octagon case. 36mm . . . . $900—1,000

Cartier, Paris. Tank watch, white enameled dial. Square 18K gold case. 25mm. Modern.
. . . . $650—750

Cartier. Gold modern rectangular moulded case with bowed sides. 32x21mm. $900—1,000

NOTE: All values are given for the head only unless the bracelet is included in the description.

Cartier. Swiss, modern. 18K gold square case, 30x22mm . . . . $650—750

Cartier, LeCoultre, Reverse, white matte dial, subsidiary seconds, 18K, two tone square case, 22mm. . . . . $1,400—1,600

Cartier. Man's. Mother-of-pearl dial with black onyx frame. 18K white gold, square case with faceted corners, and 18K white gold mesh band. Modern . . . . $1,200—1,500

Cartier. 18K gold, 23x31mm. oval case, diamond set bezel. Modern, ca 1980 $1,200—1,500

Cartier. Man's. Honeycomb pattern, lapis lazuli dial. 18K gold hexagonal case. Modern. $900—1,000

Cartier. Modern, 18K gold 25mm. octagonal case. Double row diamond bezel, enclosing the winder . . . . $2,200—2,700

Cartier. Man's. Lapis lazuli dial. 18K white gold, square case with textured gold and square cut lapis lazuli bezel, and gold mesh band. Modern . . . . $1,200—1,500

Cartier. Automatic, gold octagonal case with double band enclosing winder, 31mm. . . . . $1,100—1,250

Cartier. Man's. Grossulaire dial. 18K gold and grossulaire case, gold mesh band. Modern. . . . . $1,200—1,500

Certina "Free Form". Mother-of-pearl dial, Gold-filled, octagonal case, set in rectangular frame for lugs. ca 1969 . . . . $30—60

Chopard, Geneve. Plain dial, 18K gold oval case, 40mm, wide peacock eye bracelet. ca 1972 . . . . 20% over gold

Chopard, Geneve. Plain champagne dial. 18K gold, 33mm. round case, with an inner black ring containing seven loose diamonds, stamped "Kutchinsky, .750". ca 1975 . . $1,200—1,500

CHRONEX
Trademark of Marshall Field & Co.
Chicago, Ill.

Chronex. Ladies. Silvered dial, black painted numerals. 7J movement. Hand engraved, white rolled gold plate rectangular case with graduated sides. ca 1932 . . . . $10—20

Chronex. Ladies. Matt finished dial, black painted numerals. 7J movement. Engraved white gold-filled, molded rectangular case. ca 1932. . . . . $15—25

Chronex. Ladies. Silvered dial, black painted numerals. 7J movement. White rolled gold plate, molded tonneau case. ca 1932 . . $10—20

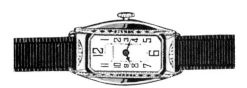

Chronex. Ladies. Silvered dial, black enameled numerals. 7J movement. Hand engraved, white rolled gold plate tonneau case. ca 1932 $10—20

Chronex. Ladies. Silvered dial, black painted numerals. 7J movement. White rolled gold plate, tonneau case, with oxidized design on front. ca 1932 . . . . $10—20

Chronex. Ladies. Silvered dial, black painted numerals. 7J movement. White rolled gold plate, tonneau case, with oxidized design on front. ca 1932 . . . . $10—20

Chronex. Ladies. Silvered dial, black enameled numerals. 7J baguette movement. White gold-filled, molded baguette case. ca 1932. . $10—20

Chronex. Silvered dial, luminous hands and figures, subsidiary seconds. 7J movement. Chrome finished, molded rectangular nickel case. ca 1932 . . . . $15—25

Chronex. Silvered dial, black figures, subsidiary seconds. 7J movement. Nickel, faceted rectangular case. ca 1932 . . . . $15—25

Chronex "20 Point Watch". Matt finished dial, luminous hands and figures, subsidiary seconds. 7J movement. Engraved, chromium finished, curved nickel cushion case. ca 1932 . . $30—45

CLEBAR

Made by the Swiss Company,
Zodiac

Clebar "Alarm". Waterproof. Radium silvered dial, alarm hand & center seconds. 17J movement. Round case. ca 1957. Steel . . . . $30—45
10K gold-filled . . . . $50—75

Clebar "Moonphase Calendar Chronograph". Radium silvered dial, subsidiary seconds, 30 minute recorder, day & month windows with outer date ring. 17J movement. Round stainless steel case. ca 1957 . . . . $175—225

NOTE: Read Page 6 before using this book to value your wrist watch.

Clebar "Chronograph". Waterproof. Radium silvered dial, subsidiary seconds, 30 minute recorder with outer tachometer ring. 17J movement. Round case. ca 1957.
Gold-filled top. . . . . $50—75
Stainless steel . . . . 25—50

NOTE: All values are given for the head only unless the bracelet is included in the description.

Clebar "Chronograph". Radium silvered dial, subsidiary seconds, 30 minute & 12 hour recorders, with outer tachometer ring. 17J movement. Round stainless steel case. ca 1957 . . . . $60—85

Clebar "Calendar Chronograph". Radium silvered dial, subsidiary seconds, 30 minute & 12 hour recorder, day & month windows with outer date ring. 17J movement. Round stainless steel case. ca 1957 . . . . $50—75

Clebar "Chronograph". Waterproof. Radium silvered dial, subsidiary seconds, 30 minute & 12 hour recorders. 17J movement. Round stainless steel case. ca 1957 . . . . . . $35—60

CLINTON

Advertised as "Cased and Timed in U.S.A.". ca 1957.

Clinton "Curved Rolled Gold Plate". Subsidiary seconds. 17J movement. Rectangular, 10K rolled gold plate top, stainless steel back case, large link lugs. ca 1957. . . . . . . $20—35

Clinton "Drivers'. Subsidiary seconds. 8¾''', 17J movement. 10K yellow rolled gold plate, round case, & large curved lugs. ca 1957. . . . . $20—35

Clinton "Curved Rolled Gold Plate". Subsidiary seconds. 17J movement. Curved rectangular, 10K rolled gold plate top, stainless steel back case. ca 1957 . . . . $12—20

COMIC CHARACTER

NOTE: Many comic character watches have been made and sold over the years, with the most famous being "Mickey Mouse". Only a selected few are illustrated here because of space limitations. MINT and IN THE ORIGINAL BOX are very important to the value of comic character watches.

Dick Tracy in red & blue on silvered dial. New Haven pin lever movement. Chromium plated, curved back case. ca 1933. . $ 40— 65
With box . . . . 100—125

Orphan Annie. In yellow, red, green & black on silvered dial. New Haven pin lever movement. Chromium plated, curved-back case. ca 1933. . . . . $ 40— 65
With box . . . . 100—125

Boy Scout by New Haven. Boy Scout activities in color on dial. Radium or plain figures, chromium plated tonneau case. ca 1934 $35—60
With box . . . . 75—100

Smitty. Silvered dial with Smitty in green. New Haven pin lever movement. Chromium plated case. ca 1935 . . . . $ 50— 75
With box . . . . 125—150

Popeye by New Haven, "Antimated". Disney characters in color on silvered dial. Popeye's hands tell time. White metal tonneau case. ca 1936. . . . . $ 50— 75
With box . . . . 125—150

Boy Scout by Elgin. Silvered dial, luminous dots. 7J round movement. "Official Boy Scout Watch" engraved on bezel. Chromium plated case with rolled gold plate back . . . . .$10—25
With box . . . . 30—35

Boy Scout by New Haven. Silvered radium dial. Pin lever movement. Chromium plated case. ca 1938. . . . .$ 5—15
With box . . . . 20—25

HI-YO, SILVER!

Lone Ranger "Hi-Yo, Silver" by New Haven. Colorful dial. Pin lever, tonneau movement. Chromium plated case. ca 1940 . . . . .$30—50
With box . . . . 65—95

Orphan Annie by New Haven. Silvered dial with Orphan Annie in color. 8/0 size movement Chromium plated, curved case, stainless back, red, blue or tan straps. ca 1942 . . . . $35— 60
With box . . . . 80—110

Babe Ruth. Colorful dial with picture of "Babe", his bat and autograph. Sweep second, luminous hands. Round stainless steel head & bracelet. ca 1949 . . . .$50—75
Complete watch in mint plastic, autographed baseball, with a sportsman's pledge card, "I have always tried to be a good sport, to play the game fairly and squarely. I believe in being a proud winner and a good loser at all times". Signed "Babe Ruth" . . . . $125—175

Hopalong Cassidy by U.S. Time. Grey dial with Hoppy's picture, red hands & small numerals. Chrome tonneau case, black cowboy band. ca 1951 . . . . $30— 50
With box . . . . 75—100

Fairy Story Wrist Watches for Girls: Alice In Wonderland, Little Red Riding Hood, See-Saw Marjory Daw. Animated characters swing back and forth on the dials. Colorful lithographed gift boxes. Round stainless steel cases. ca 1953. Head only . . . . $25— 50
Complete watch in mint box . . . . . 75—100

Hopalong Cassidy by U.S. Time. Grey dial with Hoppy's picture, red hands & numerals. Regular size, chrome tonneau case, black cowboy band. ca 1951. . . . . $35— 60
With box . . . . 85—110

Huckleberry Hound by Bradley Time. Full color dial. Round chrome plated case. ca 1962. . . . . $ 5—10
With box . . . . 10—25

Cinderella by U.S. Time. Pink dial, blue gown. Chrome plated case and blue band. ca 1951. . . . .$10—15
With box . . . . 35—80

Ballerina by Bradley Time. Colorful dial. Swiss pin lever movement. Chrome plated case. ca 1961 . . . . $ 5—10
With box . . . . 10—25

Comic Character Hero Wrist Watches for Boys: Dick Tracy, Gene Autry, Li'l Abner. Animated pistols, flags, etc. swing back and forth on the dials, all in special gift boxes with colorful lithographs. Round stainless steel case. Head only. ca 1953 . . . . $ 50— 75
Mint box & watch. . . . . 125—175

Yogi Bear by Bradley Time (Swiss). Full color dial. Round, chrome plated case. ca 1962. . . . . $ 5—10
With box . . . . 15—25

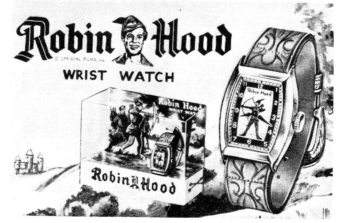

Robin Hood by Bradley Time. Colorful dial. Chrome plate, tonneau case. Stainless steel back. ca 1957 . . . . $25— 50
With box . . . . 75—100

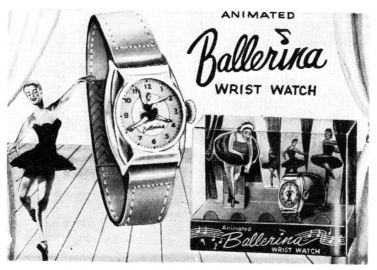

Ballerina "Antimated" by U.S. Time. Colorful dial with ballerina legs to tell the time. Chrome plated top, stainless steel back. ca 1957 $10—25
With box . . . . 30—40

Dale Evans & Buttermilk, Bradley Time. Autographed colorful dial, western tooled leather strap & fittings. Chrome plated top, stainless steel back. ca 1961 . . . . . . $30— 60
With box . . . . 80—110

Roy Rogers & Trigger by Bradley Time. Color autographed picture on dial. Chrome plated tonneau case, stainless back. ca 1961. $25— 50
With box . . . . 75—100

NOTE: Mickey Mouse by Ingersoll. Two strap models were offered on the same head and were made for 10 years or so. Over 2 million were sold in the first two years, 1934 to 1936.

Mickey Mouse by Ingersoll, "Antimated". Mickey's hands tell time. Subsidiary seconds with tiny Mickey figures. Chrome tonneau case & Mickey band. ca 1934.

With leather band	$ 50— 75
With metal band	75—100
With box	135—165

Mickey Mouse by U.S. Time, "Antimated". Mickey's hands tell time. Chrome rectangular tonneau case, red vinylite strap. ca 1949.

	$30— 50
With box	75—100

Mickey Mouse by Ingersoll, "Antimated". Mickey's hands tell time, subsidiary seconds. Small rectangular tonneau case. ca 1936.

Head	$ 50— 75
With charm bracelet & box	125—150

Mickey Mouse by U.S. Time. Red figured dial with Mickey's hands telling time. Pin lever movement. Small size, chrome case with red strap

	$25—40
With box	65—80

Mickey Mouse by Ingersoll, "Antimated". Mickey's hands tell time, subsidiary seconds. Gold plated or chromium-finished, rectangular tonneau case. ca 1940

	$ 40— 65
With box	100—125

Mickey Mouse by U.S. Time, "Antimated". Red figured dial. Mickey's hands tell time. Regular size, chrome tonneau case & red band. ca 1951.

	$25—40
With box	65—80

Concord. Ladies ribbon, 14K & enamel case. ca 1926. . . . .$40—75

Concord. Ladies. Elongated oval dial. Platinum & diamond tonneau case. ca 1926. Value varies according to size, quality and color of diamonds. . . . . $250—325

Concord "Diamond & Platinum". Silver dial. 17J adjusted movement. Platinum bezel with 8 diamonds, 18K white gold case back. ca 1927. . . . . $150—175

Concord "Diamond & Platinum". Silver dial. 17J adjusted movement. Platinum case set with 34 diamonds. ca 1927 . . . . $180—220

Concord "Diamond & Platinum". Silver dial. 17J adjusted movement. Rectangular platinum case set with 32 diamonds. ca 1927. $200—250

Concord "Diamond & Platinum". Silver dial, 17J adjusted movement. Platinum case with 72 diamonds. ca 1927 . . . . $500—650

Concord "Diamond & Platinum Bracelet". Silver dial. 17J adjusted movement. Platinum case and matching bracelet with 84 diamonds. ca 1927. . . . . $500—700

Concord. Silver dial. 17J adjusted movement. Platinum case with 24 diamonds and 10 sapphires. ca 1927 . . . . $180—220

Concord "Diamond & Platinum Bracelet". Silver dial. 17J adjusted movement. Platinum case with 72 diamonds and matching platinum mesh bracelet with 109 diamonds. ca 1927 . . . . $800—1,000

Concord Watch Co. Elongated rectangular case, extended lugs. Platinum, engraved & set with semi-precious stones. ca 1928 . . .10 to 25% over scrap value, more for exceptional beauty.

Concord Watch Co. Elongated rectangular case. Platinum with extended lugs set with diamonds. ca 1928. . . . . $1,000—1,200 More if diamonds are 10 points or more and good quality.

Concord Watch Co. Ladies, elongated rectangular case in 18K white gold & platinum, or 18K green gold, set with semi-precious stones. ca 1928. . . . . . .10% to 25% over scrap value. Buyers will pay more for exceptional beauty.

Concord. Ladies. 18K white gold with platinum top, or 18K green gold, rectangular case. "Art Deco" design set with semi-precious stones. ca 1928. Value varies according to the size, quality and color of the semi-precious stones.

Concord Watch Co. Ladies. 7½''', 17J movement. 18K yellow gold, faceted rectangular case, cord lugs. ca 1929 . . . .$70—90

Concord Watch Co., retailed by Tiffany & Co. Brushed gold dial, 17J movement. 14K gold, 40mm., plain curvex tonneau case. ca 1925. . . . . $150—200

Concord Watch Co. Square dial, 5½''', 17J movement. 18K 3-color gold (red & white links alternately with yellow gold border links), band & case. ca 1929 . . . .$450—600

Cornavin, Geneve. Tachometer calendar, black dial, 4 concentric chapter rings calibrated 0—25, 0—35, 0—60 & 0—70. Window date, round silver case, 35mm.. . . . . . . $150—175

Cortebert, Swiss. Moonphase, calendar, silvered dial, subsidiary seconds, window day & month, outer date chapter ring. 15J movement, 18K gold 35mm. round case. . . . . $650—750

Corum. Automatic, center seconds, 18K gold, 34mm. round case. ca 1961 . . . . . $250—275

Corum "Medicus". Center seconds and pulsometer. Round stainless steel case. ca 1962. $150—200

Corum "Medicus Calendar". Center seconds, pulsometer and date window. Round stainless steel case. ca 1962 . . . . $175—225

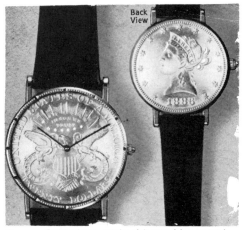

Corum. Gold piece watch with sapphire crystal. ca 1966. $20 piece . . . . $1,600—2,000
$10 piece. . . . . 1,000—1,200

Corum. Face embossed with symbols of the 12 tribes of Israel & "Long live the people of Israel" in Hebrew & English. Back embossed with Menorah flanked by two stars of David. 18K gold embossed with laurel wreaths, 35mm. round case . . . . $1,000—1,200

Corum, Swiss gold ingot, plain 18K gold rectangular case and gold buckle, 27mm.
. . . . $1,200—1,400

Corum. Silvered dial, 17J movement, 18K gold, 28mm. rectangular case, with original Corum signed band . . . . $1,000—1,200

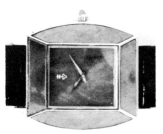

Corum. Rectangular dial. 18K white gold, bark finish bracelet watch. ca 1969. . . . . $750—850

Corum. Coral dial, 18K gold bowed rectangular shaped case. Movement by Corum . $700—800

Cosgrove & Pratt, Retail European jewelry store. Swiss 10½''' movement. 18K gold bowed square case. . . . . $200—250

Cyma. Ladies. Silvered dial, subsidiary seconds. 11''', 15J movement. 27mm., round silver Niello case. ca 1920. . . . . $40—60
Gold-filled enamel . . . . 25—35

Crown (by New York Standard, owned by Keystone Watch Case Co.) Most are 7J, 0 size. See "New York Standard" for description. ca 1912—20. 14K gold-filled. . . . . . . $10—20
Silver. . . . . 10—20
Silveroid . . . . 5—10

Cyma. Ladies. Round silvered, Roman numeral dial, subsidiary seconds. 11''', 15J movement. Octagonal case. ca 1920. Silver . . . . . $25—35
Gold-filled . . . . 20—30
Nickel . . . . 15—20

Cyma. Ladies. Luminous hands & numerals, subsidiary seconds. 11''', 15J movement. 27mm., Silver Niello case. ca 1920 . . . $40—60
Gold-filled engraved . . . . 25—35

Crown "Strap Watches". Glass enamel, plain or luminous dial, subsidiary seconds. 3/0 size, 15J, round movement. Round case with heavy strap lugs. ca 1920. Gold-filled case with Khaki strap, or Sterling silver case with Khaki strap, or gold-filled case with "Kitchener" leather strap . . . . $10—20

Cyma. White dial, luminous hands & numerals, subsidiary seconds. 13''', 15J movement. 33mm., engraved round case. ca 1920. Gold-filled . . . . $40—60
Nickel . . . . 25—40

Cyma (by Tavannes). White dial, Roman numerals, subsidiary seconds. 13''', 15J movement. 13''', 15J movement. 34mm. round, grooved bezel case. ca 1920. Silver . $100—125
Gold-filled . . . . 75—100
Nickel . . . . 35— 50

Cyma. White dial, subsidiary seconds. 15½''' 7J movement. 38mm. round case. ca 1920.
Silver . . . . $100—125
Nickel . . . . 25— 40

Cyma. Roman numeral dial, subsidiary seconds. 11''', 15J round movement. 29x45mm. oval case. ca 1920. 14K gold . . . . $350—400
Silver . . . . 100—150

Cyma. Luminous hands & numerals, subsidiary seconds. 11''', 15J round movement. 29x44mm. marquise case. ca 1920.
18K gold . . . . $360—410
Silver . . . . 100—150

Cyma. Roman numeral dial, subsidiary seconds. 11''', 15J round movement. 29x37mm. rectangular case. ca 1920. 18K gold . . . . $225—275
14K gold . . . . 200—250

Cyma. Black round dial, subsidiary seconds. 11''' round movement. 27x35mm. Silver Niello tonneau case. ca 1920 . . . . $35—50

Cyma. White round dial, subsidiary seconds. 11''' round movement. 27x35mm. Silver Niello tonneau case. ca 1920 . . . . $50—75

Cyma. Roman or Arabic dial, subsidiary seconds. 11''', 15J, round movement. 45x29mm. rectangular case. ca 1920. 18K gold $375—475
Silver . . . . 100—125
Gold-filled . . . . 100—125

THE REASON WHY
THE DEPOLLIER
Waterproof and Dust-proof Watch
MAINTAINED ACCURATE TIME
while worn by ROLAND ROHLFS on his three Worlds
Record Altitude Flights, finally to a height of 34,610 feet.

Patented in U. S. and Foreign Countries

Prestige Waltham Movement *Accuracy*

Had the atmospheric pressure within the case been permitted to equalize itself with the rarified atmosphere of the high altitudes, or the extreme cold of *44 degrees below zero* been permitted to reach the delicate movement, its compensation would have been seriously affected, rendering the watch undependable.

WORLD'S RECORD FOR ALTITUDE

THE CURTISS ENGINEERING CORPORATION
EXPERIMENTAL AND AERONAUTICAL RESEARCH LABORATORIES AT
GARDEN CITY, LONG ISLAND

Jacques Depollier & Son, 316 Herkimer St., Sept. 22, 1919.
Brooklyn, N. Y.
Gentlemen :

I wish to state that on my record breaking climbs to 27,000 feet, 34,200 feet, and 34,610 feet, of which two were official, I wore one of your Depollier Waterproof Wrist Watches.

The case number of this watch was 1935 and Waltham movement number 2114?830, and in all of these strenuous climbs the watch ran continuously and apparently without loss or gain, and it was this watch that I relied upon to give me the correct time on these flights.

I am very enthusiastic and thoroughly satisfied with the watch, and believe it to be the only one on the market that can undergo satisfactorily, a grueling test of this type.

Very truly yours,

Roland Rohlfs

Experimental Test Pilot

The WATERPROOF features of the Depollier Watch-case protected the movement from any change in the atmospheric pressure and from the sudden drop in temperature to 44 degrees below zero.

A watch keeping accurate time under such extreme conditions will certainly prove satisfactory for every day wear.

Each watch TESTED UNDER WATER. This Depollier Waterproof Watch-case is the same as adopted by the UNITED STATES ARMY since the war.

**Watch Complete, Waterproof Case and 15 jewel
Waltham Movement, $45.00**

Write for Booklet

JACQUES DEPOLLIER & SON
Manufacturers of High Class Specialties for Waltham Watches
Ateliers: 316 Herkimer Street, Brooklyn, N. Y.
Salesrooms: 15 Maiden Lane, New York
Dubois Watch Case Co. Established 1877

Roland Rohlf's
World's Altitude Record
34,610 Feet
Established Sept. 18, 1919.

Mount Everest
29.002 Feet

Pike's Peak
14,147 Feet

Woolworth Bldg.
750 Feet

TEMPERATURE TEST

WATER TESTED

Depollier "Waterproof". One of the first attempts at a waterproof case. ca 1919 . . . . $75—125

Depollier. Ladies. 14K gold, engraved rectangular case with faceted corners. ca 1926 . $40—75

Depollier. Ladies. Silver dial. 15J movement. 14K white gold, engraved case. ca 1927 $30—50

Depollier. Ladies. Silver dial. 15J movement. 18K white gold, engraved case. ca 1927 $30–50

Depollier. 14K gold-filled, faceted rectangular case. ca 1926 . . . . $15–25

Daving, Joseph "Rist Lid". Ladies. Enclosed round dial. Rectangular case. ca 1924. Value varies according to size, quality and color of diamond.
Platinum & diamond . . . $550–650
White gold & diamond 500–600
Plain platinum. 150–175
Plain white gold 125–150

Devon "Verndale". 14K white gold, highly engraved tonneau case & band set with 2 imitation emeralds or sapphires. ca 1928. . . . .$50–75

Devon "Marion". Ladies, 6¾''', 15J movement. 14K gold tonneau case. ca 1928. . . . . $40–60

Devon "Vanity". Ladies, 6½''', 15J or 6J oval movement. Nickel oval case with geometric blue, black, jade or red enameling. ca 1928. . . . .$10–20

Devon "Wichford". Radium silvered dial, subsidiary seconds. 10½''', 6J movement. Nickel tonneau case. ca 1928 . . . .$7–14

Devon "Duxbury". Radium silvered dial, subsidiary seconds. 10½''', 6J movement. Green rolled gold plate, molded square case with faceted corners. ca 1928 . . . .$7–14

DEVON
Trademark of Smith Patterson Co.
Boston, Mass. — ca 1928

Devon "Wall Street". Man's. Silvered dial, subsidiary seconds, 15J movement. White rolled gold plate "Art Deco" geometric case, black or blue enamel bezel calibrated with Roman numerals. Engraved & enameled molded lugs. ca 1928. . . . . $20–35

Diamond. Ladies, 17J movement. Rectangular platinum case, set with 4 marquise and 64 small round diamonds. ca 1932 . . . . . $475—575

Diamond. Ladies, 17J movement. Platinum rectangular case set with 2 large marquise and 46 small round diamonds. ca 1932. Value varies according to size, quality and color of diamonds. . . . . $350—425

Diamond. Ladies. 17J movement. Rectangular platinum case & lugs set with 8 baguettes and 80 round diamonds. ca 1932. Value varies according to size & quality of diamonds.

Diamond. Ladies, 17J movement. Rectangular platinum case set with 4 baguettes and 50 small round diamonds. ca 1932 . . . . . $375—475

Diamond. Ladies, 17J movement. Rectangular platinum case, set with 18 round diamonds. ca 1932. . . . . $150—180

Diamond. Ladies, 17J movement. Platinum rectangular case, set with 2 baguettes and 52 round diamonds. ca 1932 . . . . . $375—475

Diamond. Ladies, 17J movement. Platinum rectangular case, set with 4 marquise and 48 round diamonds. ca 1932 . . . . . . $450—550

Diamond. Ladies, 17J movement. Platinum rectangular case, set with 2 marquise and 68 small round diamonds. ca 1932 . . . $700—800

Diamond. Ladies, 17J movement. Rectangular platinum case set with 6 baguettes and 48 small round diamonds. ca 1932 . . . $475—575

Diamond. Ladies, 17J movement. Rectangular platinum case and lugs set with 10 baguettes and 68 round diamonds. ca 1932. Value varies according to size, quality and color of diamonds. . . . . $800—1,000

Diamond. Ladies, 17J movement. Platinum rectangular case, set with 10 baguettes and 38 round diamonds. ca 1932 . . . . . . $500—600

Diamond. Ladies. Enclosed dial. 14K gold, oval case, lid paved with diamonds, surrounded by petals, with matching gold mesh band. ca 1959. . . . . .10% to 20% over gold & diamond value

Diamond. Ladies. Enclosed dial. Round 14K gold case, diamond-set lid surrounded by petals, matching band. ca 1959.
. . . . .10% to 20% over gold & diamond value

Diana. Luminous hands & numerals, subsidiary seconds. 15''', 9J movement. 37mm. round case. ca 1920. Silver. . . . . . . $75—95
Nickel . . . . 20—30

Diamond. Ladies. Round white dial, raised gold markers. Gold case, diamond bezel, sunk into diamond-set V, and gold mesh band. ca 1959 . .15% to 25% over gold & diamond value

Diamond. Ladies. Raised gold markers on dial. 14K gold, engraved square case, matching gold band. ca 1959.
. . . . .10% to 20% over gold & diamond value

Diana (by Tavannes). White dial, subsidiary seconds. 15''', 9J movement. 37mm. round case. ca 1920. Silver . . . .$75—85
Nickel . . . . 20—30

Diamond (by designer "Marce"). Black dial, raised gold markers. Round, platinum & diamond case, extending out with swirls and scrolls of diamonds, and matching band. ca 1961. Value varies according to size, quality and color of diamonds . . . . . $5,000—6,000

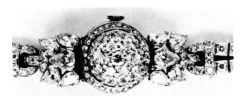

Diamond & Platinum Bracelet. Ladies round hunting case and band set with 7.50 carats of diamonds. . . . . $2,500—3,000

Diana (by Tavannes). Black dial, luminous hands & numerals, subsidiary seconds. 15''', 9J movement. 37mm. round case. ca 1920. Silver . . . .$60—75
Nickel . . . . 20—30

Digital Curvex. Windows for hours, minutes & seconds. 15J movement. 18K, two tone gold 40mm. case. ca 1925 . . . . $700—900

NOTE: Read Page 6 before using this book to value your wrist watch.

Ditisheim, Paul. Ladies. Octagonal dial. Diamonds and precious stone set in a platinum tonneau case. ca 1922. Value varies according to the size, quality and color of the diamonds and other precious stones . . . . . . $400—600

Ditisheim, Paul. Ladies. Diamonds and precious stones set in a platinum tonneau case, and diamond-set fancy lugs. ca 1922. Value varies according to the size, quality and color of the diamonds and other precious stones.
. . . . $1,000—1,250

NOTE: All values are given for the head only unless the bracelet is included in the description.

Ditisheim, Paul. Ladies, platinum and diamond tonneau case. ca 1922. Value varies according to size, quality and color of diamonds.
. . . . $1,200—1,600

Ditisheim, Paul. Silvered diamond dial, 17J movement. **Platinum,** 19x44mm. rectangular, unmarked American contract case, with extended lugs. ca 1928 . . . . $500—525

Ditisheim, Paul. Silvered diamond dial, 17J movement. **Platinum,** 20x42mm. square, unmarked American contract case with flexible lugs. ca 1928. . . . . $625—650

Ditisheim, Paul. Silver finish, diamond numeral & marker dial. 17J movement. **Platinum,** 26mm. round, unmarked American contract ladies case. ca 1928 . . . . $350—400

Ditisheim, Paul. Silvered ruby & diamond dial. 17J movement. **Platinum,** 20x45mm. square, unsigned American contract case with flexible lugs. ca 1928. . . . . $750—775

Ditisheim, Paul. Silvered diamond & sapphire dial, 17J movement. **Platinum**, 21x38mm. rectangular, unmarked American contract case. ca 1928. . . . . $700—750

Ditisheim, Paul. Silver finish diamond baguette dial. 17J movement. **Platinum** rectangular unmarked, 19x45mm., American contract, rounded corner, case. ca 1928. . . . . $475—525

Ditisheim, Paul. Silvered diamond dial, 17J movement. **Platinum & edged sapphire**, 18x45mm., curved rectangular, unmarked American contract case. ca 1928 . . $775—825

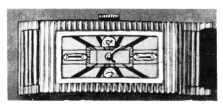

Ditisheim, Paul. Silvered diamond dial, 17J movement. **Platinum**, 19x51mm. moulded rectangular, unmarked American contract case, with moulded flexible lugs. ca 1928 $625—650

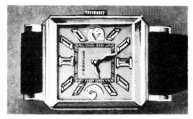

Ditisheim, Paul. Silvered diamond dial, 17J movement. **Platinum**, 24x40mm. rectangular, unmarked American contract case with extended lugs. ca 1928 . . . . $400—450

Ditisheim, Paul. Silvered diamond dial, subsidiary seconds, 17J movement. **Platinum**, 18x44mm., curved rectangular, unmarked American contract case. ca 1928 . . $450—500

Ditisheim, Paul. Silver finish, diamond numerals & baguette cut diamond marker dial. 17J movement. **Platinum**, curved rectangular, unmarked, 20x45mm., American contract case. ca 1928. . . . . $500—600

Ditisheim, Paul. Silver finish diamond numeral and baguette cut diamond dial, 17J movement. **Platinum**, curved rectangular, unmarked, 20x50mm, American contract case. ca 1928. $500—525

Ditisheim, Paul. Silvered diamond dial. 17J movement. **Platinum & Ruby edged,** 21x28mm. rectangular, unmarked American contract case. ca 1928. . . . . $775—825

Doric "Princess". Raised gold numerals on dial. 14K gold round case with large link band. ca 1945. . . . . . . 10% to 20% over gold value

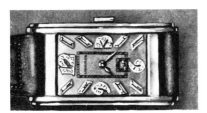

Ditisheim, Paul. Silvered diamond dial, subsidiary seconds, 17J movement. **Platinum,** 22x40mm., moulded rectangular, unmarked American contract case. ca 1928 . . $400—450

Doric "Diamond, Ruby & Gold Cord". Ladies. 14K gold square case. ca 1946. . . . $150—200

Ditisheim, Paul. Ruby & diamond dial, 17J movement. **Platinum,** 20x41mm. moulded rectangular, unmarked American contract case. ca 1928. . . . . $775—825

Doric "Diamond, Ruby & Gold Cord". Ladies. 14K gold square case. ca 1946. . . . . $90—120

Doric "Diamond, Ruby & Gold Cord". Ladies. 14K gold square case & lugs set with stones. ca 1946. . . . . $150—200

Ditisheim, Paul. Silvered diamond dial, 17J movement. **Platinum,** 19x45mm. elongated rectangular, unmarked American contract case with flexible lugs . . . . $550—575

Doric "Diamond, Ruby & Gold Cord". Ladies. 14K gold square case . . . . $90—120

Doric. Ladies Hunting. 14K gold "Art Deco" designed case set with diamonds and emeralds, with bracelet. ca 1946 . . . . . . $1,200–1,400

Doxa "Ladies Grafic". Assorted dial and strap colors. Manual wind movement. Plain square, intergal lug, case. ca 1959.
14K yellow gold. $75–100
Yellow gold-filled 25– 40
Stainless steel 20– 30

Doric "Ambassador". Raised gold markers on dial. 14K gold square case. ca 1945. $100–125
14K flexible link bracelet . 10% over gold value

Doxa "Chronograph". Tachometer dial with subsidiary seconds & 30 minute recorder. 17J movement. Stainless steel round case. ca 1945 . . . . $65–85

Doric "Diamond Dial". Diamond dial, subsidiary seconds. 14K yellow gold square case. ca 1946. . . . . $100–125

Doxa. Silvered dial with Breguet hands & numerals. 17J movement. Rectangular, ladies case. ca 1947. Stainless steel $10–15
Gold filled 10–15
14K gold . . . . 10% over gold

Doxa. Silvered dial with gold numerals & hands. 17J movement. Square case. ca 1947.
Stainless steel $10– 15
Gold filled 15– 25
14K gold 90–125

Doxa. Ladies. Silvered dial, raised gold markers on dial. 14K gold round case, flowered lugs set with diamonds, matching chain bracelet. ca 1949 . . . . $175–225

Doxa "Automatic". Silvered dial, self-winding center seconds movement. Round case. ca 1947.
Stainless steel $10– 15
Gold filled 15– 20
14K gold 85–110

Doxa. Silvered dial with black oxidized chapter ring. Subsidiary seconds, 17J movement. Tonneau case. ca 1947.

Stainless steel	$ 5— 10
Gold filled	10— 20
14K gold	75—100

NOTE: Read Page 6 before using this book to value your wrist watch.

Doxa. Black dial with subsidiary seconds. 17J movement. Round, tonneau case. ca 1947.

Stainless steel	$10— 15
Gold filled	15— 20
14K gold	75—100

NOTE: All values are given for the head only unless the bracelet is included in the description.

Doxa "Center Seconds". Tu-tone dial with Breguet-style hands & numerals. 17J movement. Round case. ca 1947.

Stainless steel	$15— 20
Gold filled	20— 25
14K gold	85—110

Doxa. Silvered dial with radium hands & numerals. Sweep second movement. Round, tonneau case. ca 1947.

Stainless steel	$ 5— 10
Gold filled	10— 20
14K gold	75—100

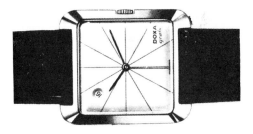

Doxa "Grafic Calendar". Assorted dial colors with date window at 10:30. Self-winding movement. Plain square, intergal lug, case. ca 1959.

14K yellow gold	$125—150
Yellow gold-filled	40— 60
Stainless steel	30— 50

Doxa. Moonphase, calendar, chronograph, contemporary, subsidiary seconds, 30 minute & 12 hour registers & outer date ring. 17J movement. Round stainless case. . . . . . $200—300

Driva. Quarter Repeater. Black dial, 14K plain rectangular case secured by screws, slide repeat between 1 & 2 o'clock . . . . . . $2,500—3,500

DUEBER HAMPDEN WATCH CO.
Canton, Ohio, U.S.A.

About 1913, Dueber Hampden started marketing ladies pocket watches that were converted to bracelet wrist watches. They continued to make a limited line until the company was sold to Russia in 1925. Before 1900, Hampden had marketed their 400 Series (3/0 size) stemwind, lever set movements (15J "Diadem", 17J, 16J & 11J "400", and 7J "Molly Stark"). These movements were both cased, timed & boxed at the factory as wrist or pocket watches in the case styles of the 1913 to 1925 period. Those common styles or shapes were round, cushion, tonneau, square, decagon and hexagon, which included some variations. Hampden, or Dueber-Hampden, continued to sell movements only to wholesale customers who cased them in whatever kind of case they could sell. During Hampdens short wrist watch production, they developed and sold round movements in 3/0, 5/0, 8/0, and a rectangular 11/0 size in 7 to 17 jewels.

NOTE: See Swiss-made Hampden on page 142.

Dueber Hampden "Mary Jane". Ladies. Engraved silvered dial. 15J or 7J, 8/0 size movement. Engraved cushion case. Cased, timed & boxed at the factory. ca 1923.
14K solid gold. . . . . $60—80
14K gold-filled . . . . 25—40

Dueber Hampden "Josephine". Ladies. Silvered dial. 7J or 15J movement. 8/0 size cushion case. Cased, timed & boxed at the factory. ca 1924. 14K gold . . . . . . $60—80
14K gold-filled . . . . 25—40

Dueber Hampden "Mary Jane". Sterling silver, raised figure, fancy dial. 15J, 8/0 size round movement. Tonneau ribbon case. Cased, timed & boxed at the factory. ca 1925. 14K white or green gold. . . . . $50—75
Gold filled . . . . 25—45

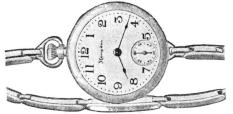

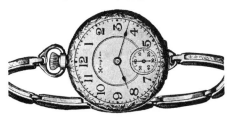

Dueber Hampden. Glass enamel or various color metal dial, subsidiary second. 7J Molly Stark or 15J Diadem, 5/0 size round movement. Round, engraved, or plain bezel, ladies bracelet case. ca 1920. 10K yellow gold $50—75
10K gold-filled . . . . 20—35

Dueber Hampden "Cushion". Plain or radiolite silvered dial, with & without seconds bit. 7J or 15J, 5/0 size round movement. Cushion case. Cased, timed & boxed at the factory. ca 1925. Gold-filled. . . . . $30—45
Rolled gold plate . . . . 25—40
Nickel . . . . 20—35

Dueber Hampden "Man-O-Fashion". Sterling silver, curved, plain or radium dial, subsidiary seconds. 15J, 8/0 size round movement. Made in green, yellow or white solid and filled, rectangular, engraved curved case. Cased, timed & boxed at the factory. Advertised as being the first **American Curved Case.** ca 1925

14K solid gold. . . . . $100—125
14K gold-filled . . . . 35— 55

Dunhill. Purse Watch with lighter. Silver. 43x47mm. case. ca 1927 . . . . . . $250—300

Dueber Hampden "Barrel". Plain or radiolite silvered dial, with & without subsidiary seconds. **Advertised as the first 5/0 size American Strap Watch Made.** 7J or 15J, 5/0 size round movement. Barrel shape men's strap case, made with removable lugs & buckles. ca 1925.

14K gold . . . . $75—100
14K gold-filled . . . . 30— 45

Dunhill. Purse Watch with lighter. 18K gold, 40x37mm. case. ca 1928 . . . . . . $900—1,100

Dunhill. Self-winding, alarm, window date. Round 18K gold case secured by screws.
. . . . $375—475

Dugena "Monza Automatic". Calendar. Diamond dial, date window. Stainless steel tonneau case. ca 1966 . . . . $10—15

Ebel Watch Co. for Van Cleef & Arpels. Ladies, oval, gold finished dial. 18K gold, long rectangular case, signed "UTI, Paris". Large moulded lugs . . . . $400—600

Eberhard. Chronometre, chronograph, white enamel dial, subsidiary seconds & 30 minute recorder with outer tachometer ring, 1000m. base. 18K gold, 39mm. round case. ca 1925.
. . . . $400–425

NOTE: Read Page 6 before using this book to value your wrist watch.

Edox. Moonphase, calendar. Contemporary, silver plated dial, center seconds, window day & month with outer date ring. 25J movement. Round GF case with steel back . . . $100–150

NOTE: All values are given for the head only unless the bracelet is included in the description.

Egona. Tachometer, Chronograph, base 1000m. Subsidiary seconds & 30 minute register. Gold brushed dial. 18K gold round case, 39mm.
. . . . $125–150

Elgin "Lady Elgin Bracelet". Open face and skylight. Dials made in various colors & finishes. 7J, 15J, 17J, 10/0 size, round movements were used. Early cases (1913–1916) were mostly round and in a variety of metals. ca 1912 to 1916. Cased, timed and boxed at the factory with matching bracelets.
14K yellow gold. $50–75
14K yellow gold-filled 20–30
Silver 15–25
Nickel 7–14

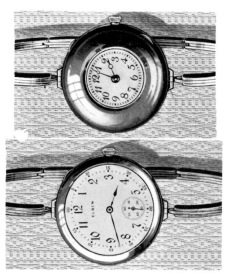

Elgin "Lady Raymond". Same as 10/0 size "Lady Elgin" except they are 5/0 size. ca 1913 to 1916. 14K yellow gold $55–80
14K yellow gold-filled 20–30
Silver 15–25
Nickel 7–14

ELGIN NATIONAL WATCH CO.
Elgin, Illinois 1867-1953

Wrist watches are like women. Everyone's idea and ideal varies. Realizing this, the case makers tried to make a watch to please everyone by letting their designer's imagination run wild. Therefore, we have literally thousands of case styles, dial colors, case and dial metals, and combinations thereof. In 1931, Elgin offered over 300 different wrist watches and each year some would be dropped from the line and new ones were added in the hope of finding a winner. What we have selected for this book is just a sampling of their more interesting watches. The U.S. manufacture of Elgins stopped in the mid-fifties, and thereafter many watches were sold that were Swiss made but marked with the Elgin name.

Elgin "Madame Susie 108". White oval dial, black numerals. 15J, Grade 484, 18/0 size movement. 14K WGF rectangular engraved case. ca 1928 . . . . $25—40

Elgin "Madame Jenny". White diamond-shaped dial, black numerals. Grade 484, 15J, 18/0 size movement. 14K WGF rectangular case with black, jade or ruby enamel & matching ribbons. ca 1928. . . . . $35—50

Elgin "Madame Lisa 211". White triangular dial, raised black numerals, luminous dots & hands. 10/0 size, 15J, Grade 484 movement. 14K green gold rectangular case with black & white hard enamel bezel. ca 1928. . $125—150

Elgin "Lady and Tiger". Raised gold figure dial. 15J, Grade 484, 18/0 size movement. 14K white gold case with design in gold and black enamel. ca 1928. . . . . $135—165

Elgin "Madame Premet 103". White geometric dial, black numerals. Grade 484, 15J, 18/0 size movement. 14K WGF rectangular case with black, jade or ruby enamel & matching ribbons. ca 1928. . . . . $35—50

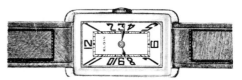

Elgin "Madame Patricia 110". Silvered black figured dial. 15J, Grade 484, 18/0 size movement. 14K, tu-tone, gold-filled case with white back & bezel & green extended center, including the lugs. ca 1928. . . . . $25—35

Elgin "Madame LouiseBoulanger 105". Square white dial, black numerals. Grade 484, 15J, 18/0 size movement. 14K WGF rectangular case in light blue or black & white hard enamel. ca 1928. . . . . $35—50

Elgin "Madame DeAnn 109". White dial, black figures. 15J, Grade 484, 18/0 size movement. 14K WGF, engraved rectangular case. ca 1928. . . . . $25—40

Elgin "Madame Amy 107". White oval dial, black numerals. 15J, Grade 484, 18/0 size movement. 14K WGF engraved, curved rectangular case. ca 1928 . . . . $25—40

Elgin "Madame Agnes". White diamond-shaped dial, black numerals. Grade 484, 15J, 18/0 size movement. 14K WGF rectangular case with black, jade or ruby enamel with matching ribbons. ca 1928 . . . . $35—50

Elgin "Lanvin 104". White elongated, hexagonal shaped dial, black numerals. Grade 484, 15J, 18/0 size movement. 14K WGF rectangular case with hard black enamel. ca 1928. . . . . $35—50

Elgin, designed by "Lucien Lelong 160". Ladies. Octagonal dial. Faceted 14K white gold-filled rectangular case. ca 1929 . . . . . $25—35

NOTE: The styles of Lucien Lelong, and others similar, are more popular with "Art Deco" fanciers than wrist watch collectors.

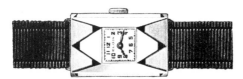

Elgin "Madame Shirley 118". Square white dial, black numerals. Grade 484, 15J, 18/0 size movement. 14K WGF rectangular case with moderinistic black enameled design. ca 1928 . . . . $35—50

Elgin "Lucien Lelong 181". Ladies. Tu-tone black & silvered dial. White gold-filled rectangular case with black enameling. ca 1929 . $40—60

Elgin "Madame Alpha III. Silvered oval dial, raised gold numerals with green enamel center. Grade 484, 15J, 18/0 size movement. 14K WGF engraved rectangular case with inlaid green enamel. ca 1928 . . . . $35—50

Elgin "Lucien Lelong 179". Ladies. 14K gold-filled rectangular case with red & blue or all black enameling. ca 1929 . . . . $35—50

Elgin "Madame Sherrie 112". Raised gold figure dial. 15J, Grade 484, 18/0 size movement. 14K WGF engraved case with green enamel. ca 1928. . . . . $30—45

Elgin "Lucien Lelong 108". Ladies. Round dial. Gold-filled rectangular case with red, blue, or black enameling. ca 1929 . . . . $40—60

Elgin "Lucien Lelong 178". Ladies. Diamond-shaped dial. 14K gold-filled rectangular case. ca 1929. . . . .$25—40

Elgin "Lucien Lelong 177". Ladies. Round dial. 14K white gold-filled, engraved & tapered rectangular case. ca 1929. . . . .$25—40

Elgin "Callot Soeurs Diamond 183". Ladies. Grade 514, 18/0 size, 15J or 17J movement. 14K white gold rectangular case with bars of blue & black enamel set with 2 diamonds. ca 1931. . . . . $75—100

Elgin "Style-Line 968". Ladies. Square dial. Grade 514, 18/0 size, 7J movement. 14K white gold, tapered rectangular case. ca 1931. . . . .$40—60

Elgin "Diamond 889". Ladies. Grade 488, 18/0 size, 17J movement. 18K white gold, engraved rectangular case set with 8 diamonds. 18K white gold mesh band. ca 1931 . . . $150—200

Elgin "Callot Soeurs Diamond 184". Ladies. Diamond-shaped dial. Grade 514, 18/0 size, 7J, 15J or 17J movement. 14K white gold, engraved rectangular case & lugs, set with 2 diamonds & 4 synthetic sapphires. ca 1931. . . . .$75—100

Elgin "Diamond 888". Ladies. Diamond-shaped inlaid enamel dial. Grade 488, 18/0 size, 17J movement. 18K white gold rectangular case, faceted corners, set with 14 diamonds & 18K gold mesh band. ca 1931 . . $175—225

Elgin "Diamond 801". Ladies. Diamond-shaped dial. Grade 488, 18/0 size, 17J movement. Platinum top & 18K gold rectangular case set with 42 diamonds. ca 1931. $350—450

Elgin "American Beauty 994". Ladies. Oval dial. Grade 514, 18/0 size, 7J movement. Nickel, chromium plated, engraved rectangular case. ca 1931 . . . .$5—10

Elgin "Style-Line 924". Ladies. Tu-tone dial. Grade 514, 18/0 size, 17J movement. 14K white gold embossed case. ca 1931. . . . . . .$40—60

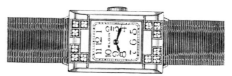

Elgin "Style-Line 958". Ladies. Grade 514, 18/0 size, 7J movement. 14K white gold-filled, embossed rectangular case. ca 1931. . . . .$20—35

Elgin "Style-Line 953". Ladies round dial. Grade 514, 18/0 size, 7J movement. Black enamel & 14K white gold-filled rectangular case with double lugs. ca 1931 . . . . .$20—35

Elgin "Professional 1635". Ladies. Subsidiary seconds. Grade 431, 6/0 size, 7J movement. Nickel, chromium plated, engraved tonneau case. ca 1931 . . . .$5—10

Elgin "American Beauty 964". Ladies. Oval dial. Grade 514, 18/0 size, 7J movement. Nickel chromium plated, engraved rectangular case. ca 1931 . . . .$5—10

Elgin "Ladies Gold-Filled 2955". 17J movement. Gold-filled, molded tonneau case and flexible loop lugs. ca 1939 . . . .$10—15

Elgin "Lady Elgin 3905". 19J movement. 14K gold, molded tonneau case and single lugs. ca 1939. . . . .$30—50

Elgin "Lady Elgin 3906". 19J movement. Gold-filled rectangular case and single molded lugs. ca 1939. . . . .$10—15

Elgin "Ladies Gold-Filled 3711". Semi-baguette movement. Yellow gold-filled, molded tonneau case and lugs. ca 1939 . . . .$10—15

Elgin "Lady Elgin 2959". 19J movement. Yellow gold-filled, molded rectangular case and flexible loop lugs. ca 1939 . . . .$10—15

Elgin "Nurse". Center seconds. Gold-filled square case & molded single lugs. ca 1940. . . . .$10—15

Elgin "Lady Elgin—Henslee". White dial, raised gold numerals. 19J movement. 14K gold square case, single molded lugs & faceted crystal. ca 1949 . . . .$50—75

Elgin "Lady Elgin—Henslee". White dial, raised gold dots & numerals. 19J movement. 14K gold square case set with 8 diamonds, single molded lugs. ca 1949. . . . . $90—120

Elgin "Lady Elgin—Henslee". White dial, raised gold dots & numerals. 19J movement. 14K gold square case & molded single lugs. ca 1949. . . . .$30—50

Elgin "Lady Elgin". Round white dial, 19J movement. 14K gold square engraved case & lugs. ca 1950. . . . .$40—60

Elgin. Luminous dial. 3/0 size round movement. Round, plain polish, heavy lug, nickel case. ca 1918. 7J . . . . $30—45

NOTE: Read Page 6 before using this book to value your wrist watch.

Elgin "Men's Strap". Same as 10/0 size "Lady Elgin" except for value and they are 0 size. ca 1913 to 1916. 14K yellow gold. . . $150—200
14K yellow gold-filled . . . . 40— 55
Silver . . . . 35— 50
Nickel . . . . 8— 18

NOTE: Elgin, like most other U.S. and foreign movement makers, at this time sold movements to the trade. These movements were placed in a variety of cases chosen by the jobber or jeweler. The typical case styles of the time (1913—1925) were round, cushion, tonneau, square, decagon and hexagon.

Elgin "Admiral Benson". Glass enamel or radium dial. 3/0 size, round movement. Round, plain polish silver case. ca 1918. 7J . . $30—45
15J . . . . 30—45

NOTE: All values are given for the head only unless the bracelet is included in the description.

Elgin "Military Style". Glass enamel or luminous dial. 0 size, round movement. Round snap back case. ca 1917 . .7 or 15J silver . $30—45
7 or 15J, GF . . . . 30—45

Elgin "Admiral Evans". Glass enamel dial. 3/0 size, round movement. Silver octagon, jointed silver case. ca 1918. 7J . . . . $30—45
15J . . . . 30—45

Elgin "General Pershing". Glass enamel or metal dial. 3/0 size round movement. Round, jointed back & snap-front silver case. ca 1918.
7J . . . . $15—20   15J . . . . $30—45

Elgin. Luminous dial. 15J, 6/0 size movement. 14K white or green gold filled, curved oval case, rope bezel & molded lugs. ca 1928 $25—55

Elgin "Presentation 212 & 215". Octagonal dial with gold Roman numerals inlaid in blue enamel bezel. Grade 444, 10/0 size, 15J movement. 14K white or green gold square case, large lugs. ca 1928.
212, white 14k gold . . . . $300—350
215, green 14K gold . . . .   350—400

Elgin "Presentation 140". Silvered dial with luminous figures & hands. 17J, 18/0 size, Grade 488 movement. Rectangular, 14K solid white gold rectangular case. ca 1928 .$100—125

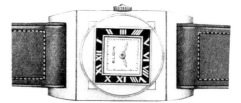

Elgin "Presentation 213 & 214". Square dial with gold Roman numerals inlaid in blue enamel bezel. Grade 444, 10/0 size, 15J movement. 14K white or green gold square case, large lugs. ca 1928.
213, white 14K gold . . . . $300—350
214, green 14K gold . . . .   350—400

Elgin "Senior 435". Silvered dial, subsidiary seconds, luminous dots & hands. 7J, 4/0 size, Grade 502 movement. Tu-tone tonneau case with 14K green gold-filled center. Nickel, chromium plated back & bezel. ca 1928. Chromium plated mesh band with green gold-filled edges not included in value . . . . $35—55
Bracelet . . . .   5— 7

Elgin "Presentation 227 & 228". Raised gold numerals on round dial. Grade 444, 10/0 size, 15J movement. 14K white or green gold square case,   large   lugs.   ca   1928.
227, white 14K gold . . . . $125—150
228, green 14K gold . . . .   150—175

Elgin "Thrift 449". Plain dial, subsidiary seconds. Roman numerals set in black enamel bezel. Grade 502, 4/0 size, 7J movement. 14K green gold-filled, tonneau case. ca 1931.
. . . . $75—100

Elgin "Avigo 461". Cushion dial, luminous hands & markers, subsidiary seconds. Grade 487, 4/0 size, 17J movement. Tonneau case. ca 1931. Silver. . . . . $30—40
14K white gold-filled . . . . 20—30

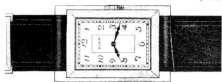

Elgin "Presentation 176 & 850". Raised gold numerals on dial. Grade 484, 18/0 size, 15J movement. 14K white or yellow gold, rectangular case with hammered bezel. ca 1931.
176, white 14K gold . . . . $110—135
850, yellow 14K gold. . . . . 120—150

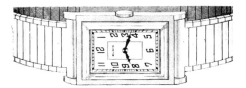

Elgin "Presentation 822". Raised gold numerals on dial. Grade 488, 18/0 size, 17J movement. 14K white and green gold-filled, beveled rectangular case. ca 1931. Tu-tone . . . . . . $50—75

Elgin "Avigo 426". Round dial, luminous hands & markers, subsidiary seconds. Grade 502, 4/0 size, 7J movement. Nickel chromium plate, cushion case. ca 1931. . . . . $20—30

Elgin "Presentation 841 & 1041". Grade 488, 18/0 size, 17J movement. Rectangular case with enclosed winder and Wadsworth gold-filled matching band. ca 1931.
841, 14K white gold . . . . $100—125
1041, 14K yellow gold-filled . . . . 35— 55

Elgin "Avigo 475". Black dial, luminous hands & numerals. Grade 502, 4/0 size, 7J movement. Nickel chromium plate tonneau case with wings on sides. ca 1931 . . . . $20—30

Elgin "Thrift 448". Plain dial, subsidiary seconds. Numerals set in black enamel bezel. Grade 502, 4/0 size, 7J movement. Nickel chromium plated, tonneau case. ca 1931.
. . . . $60—80

Elgin "Thrift 447". Silvered metal dial, subsidiary seconds. Figures set in black enamel on the bezel. 7J, 4/0 size, Grade 502 movement. Nickel chromium plated case. ca 1931 . $50—75

Elgin "Clubman Lord Elgin 218". Silvered raised gold figure dial. 15J, 10/0 size, Grade 444 movement. Tu-tone 14K white and green gold-filled, square tank case. ca 1931. . $45—65

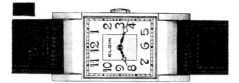

Elgin "Clubman 903". Silvered metal dial. 17J, 18/0 size, Grade 488 movement. Tu-tone 14K white gold-filled, rectangular case with yellow lugs. ca 1931 . . . . $45—65

Elgin "Clubman 902". Silvered metal dial. 17J, 18/0 size, Grade 488 movement. Tu-tone rectangular 14K white gold-filled, curved case with yellow gold-filled side bars & lugs. ca 1931 . . . . $45—65

Elgin "Clubman 163 & 844". Embossed Roman numeral dial on a black track. 15J, 18/0 size, Grade 484 movement. Rectangular case with swinging lugs to fit the wrist. ca 1931.
163, 14K white gold-filled . . . . $35—50
844, 14K yellow gold-filled . . . . . . 40—60

Elgin "Touchdown 925". Grade 447, 18/0 size, 17J movement. 14K white & green, tu-tone gold, rectangular case. ca 1931 . $50—75

Elgin "Clubman 1001". Round silvered dial. 17J, 18/0 size, Grade 488 movement. Tu-tone 14K white gold-filled, rectangular case with raised yellow bars. ca 1931 . . . . $65—85

Elgin "States 944". Raised gold numerals on dial. Grade 484, 18/0 size, 15J movement. 14K gold-filled, square case with faceted molded lugs. ca 1931. . . . . $45—65

Elgin "Home Run 1605". Raised gold numerals on dial, subsidiary seconds. Grade 429, 6/0 size, 15J movement. 14K yellow gold-filled, molded square case. ca 1931 . . . $25—35

Elgin "Clubman 911". Grade 488, 18/0 size, 17J movement. 14K white gold-filled, engraved tonneau case. ca 1931 . . . . $25—40

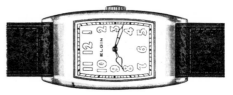

Elgin "Clubman 914". Luminous hands & numbers on dial. Grade 488, 18/0 size, 17J movement. 14K white gold-filled, curved rectangular case. ca 1931 . . . . $35—50

Elgin "Comrade 321". Raised gold numerals on dial, subsidiary seconds. Grade 462, 3/0 size, 7J movement. Engraved nickel, chromium plated, tonneau case & chromium plated mesh band. ca 1931 . . . .$10—15
Bracelet . . . . 3— 5

Elgin "Touchdown 202". Silvered metal dial with luminous numerals & hands, subsidiary seconds. 7J, 10/0 size, Grade 447 movement. Swell-center, rectangular 14K white gold-filled case with special "Mermaid" design engraved on bezel. ca 1931 . . . . . . $50—75

Elgin "Clubman 1602". Raised gold numbers on black track, subsidiary seconds. Grade 429, 6/0 size, 15J movement. 14K white gold, engraved tonneau case. ca 1931 . . . $125—150

Elgin "States 204". Silvered metal dial. 15J, 10/0 size, Grade 444 movement. Tu-tone 14K gold-filled tank case. White back & bezel with green bars running lengthwise of case. ca 1931.
. . . . $50—75

Elgin "Clubman 454". Silvered dial, subsidiary seconds with numerals on the bezel reflector under the crystal. 17J, 4/0 size, Grade 487 movement. 14K white gold-filled barrel case, with a specially designed 1/10 gold-filled flexible bracelet to match. ca 1931 . . .$35—55

Elgin "States 679". Embossed dial, subsidiary seconds. Grade 429, 6/0 size, 15J movement. 14K green gold-filled, molded tonneau case. ca 1931. . . . .$25—40

Elgin "States 682". Raised gold numerals on dial, subsidiary seconds. Grade 429, 6/0 size, 15J movement. 14K white & yellow tu-tone gold-filled, rectangular case. ca 1931 . $50—75

Elgin "Home Run 1630". Silvered dial, subsidiary seconds. Grade 429, 6/0 size, 15J movement. Cushion case. ca 1931. Chrome. . . . .$10—15
Bracelet . . . . 5— 7

Elgin "Legionnaire 404". Luminous hands & dots on dial, subsidiary seconds. Grade 487, 17J movement. 14K tu-tone gold-filled $35—55

Elgin "Home Run 1629". Silvered dial, subsidiary seconds. Grade 429, 6/0 size, 15J movement. Engraved tonneau case. ca 1931.
Chrome. . . . . $10—15
Bracelet . . . . 5— 7

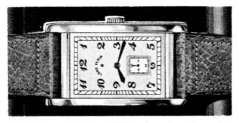

Elgin "Lord Elgin 2803". (Lord Elgin wrist watches introduced in 1937). Raised gold numerals, subsidiary seconds. Grade 531, 8/0 size, 21J movement. 14K yellow gold rectangular case. ca 1938 . . . . $115—145

Elgin "Lord Elgin 2845". Raised gold numerals, subsidiary seconds. Grade 531, 8/0 size, 21J movement. 14K yellow gold tonneau case. ca 1938 . . . . $125—150

Elgin "Lord Elgin 2843". Raised gold numerals, subsidiary seconds. Grade 531, 8/0 size, 21J movement. 18K yellow gold, lapped rectangular case. ca 1938. . . . . $110—140

Elgin "Lord Elgin 2805". Raised gold numerals, subsidiary seconds. Grade 531, 8/0 size, 21J movement. 14K yellow gold tonneau case. ca 1938 . . . . $100—125

Elgin "Platinum 2202". Silvered dial, raised gold numerals. Grade 483, 18/0 size, 17J movement. 10% Iridium platinum rectangular case. ca 1938. Platinum. . . . . $175—200
14K yellow gold. . . . . 100—135

Elgin "Lord Elgin 3505". Raised gold numerals, subsidiary seconds. Grade 531, 21J movement. 14K gold streamlined, curved, rectangular case. ca 1938. . . . . $90—120

Elgin "Curved Gold-Filled 2278". 15J movement. Yellow gold-filled, curved and engraved rectangular case. ca 1939. . . . . $25—35

Elgin "Curved Gold-Filled 2276". 17J movement. Yellow gold-filled, molded rectangular case. ca 1939 . . . . $25—35

Elgin "Curved Gold-Filled 3517". Subsidiary seconds. Yellow gold-filled, molded tonneau case. ca 1939 . . . . $30—40

Elgin "Lancer Gold-Filled 2280". 15J movement Yellow gold-filled, molded rectangular case. ca 1939 . . . . $25—35

Elgin "Flexon Gold-Filled 3816". Subsidiary seconds. 17J movement. Yellow gold-filled, molded tonneau case with hinged link lugs. ca 1939 . . . . $40—45

Elgin "Lord Elgin No. 3527". Subsidiary seconds. 21J movement. Yellow gold-filled, rectangular case with molded cylinder lugs. ca 1939. . . . . $35—55

Elgin "Lord Elgin 3831". Subsidiary seconds. 21J movement. Round, yellow gold-filled case with molded lugs. ca 1939 . . . . $30—45

Elgin "Lord Elgin 3503". Subsidiary seconds. 21J movement. 14K gold rectangular case. ca 1939 . . . . $100—125

Elgin "Tonneau 6703". White dial, subsidiary seconds. 15J movement. 10K yellow rolled gold plate, tonneau case with Veritas back. ca 1941 . . . . $20—35

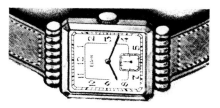

Elgin "Square 6704". White dial, subsidiary seconds. 15J movement. 10K yellow rolled gold plate, faceted square case with tubular lugs. ca 1941. . . . . $25—40

Elgin "Round 6705". White dial, subsidiary seconds or Boy Scout dial. 15J movement. 10K yellow rolled gold plate, round case with Veritas (stainless steel or oresilver) back. ca 1941 . . . . $20—35

Elgin "Wristfit 6612". Silvered or rose dial, subsidiary seconds. 15J movement. 10K YGF cushion case. ca 1941 . . . .$30—50

Elgin "Wristfit 3820". White dial, subsidiary seconds. 15J movement. 10K yellow rolled gold plate, molded square case with Veritas back. ca 1941 . . . .$25—40

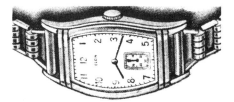

Elgin "Tonneau 6701". White dial, subsidiary seconds, 15J movement. 10K yellow rolled gold plate tonneau case. ca 1941 . . . .$20—35

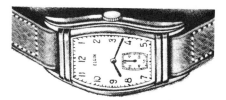

Elgin "Tonneau 6701". White dial, subsidiary seconds. 15J movement. 10K yellow rolled gold plate tonneau case with Veritas back. ca 1941.
. . . .$20—35

Elgin "Air Lord 6605". Avigo luminous dial, sweep seconds. 8/0 size, 15J movement. 10K YGF, 21mm. molded round case. ca 1941.
. . . .$25—45

Elgin "Sweep 6602". Waterproof. White dial, subsidiary seconds. 8/0 size, 15J movement. 10K YGF, 21mm. molded round case. ca 1941.
. . . .$25—40

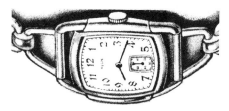

Elgin "Wristfit 6702". White dial, subsidiary seconds. 15J movement. 10K yellow rolled gold plate, rectangular case with large link lugs. ca 1941. . . . .$20—35

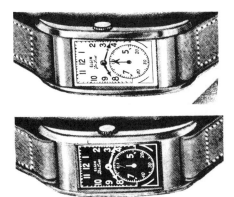

Elgin "Doctor's 5509". (Introduced in 1941). White or black duo-dial. 15/0 size, 17J movement. 10K YGF, 38x16mm. rectangular case. . . . . $75—125

Elgin "Diamond Presentation". Curved diamond dial. 17J deluxe movement. 14K yellow gold rectangular case. ca 1942. . . $250—300

Elgin "Lord Elgin". Raised gold numerals, subsidiary seconds. 21J movement. 14K gold rectangular case & large molded lugs. ca 1949.
. . . . $75—100

Elgin "Lord Elgin". Brushed dial, center seconds. 23J movement. 14K gold round case. ca 1957. . . . . $80—110

Elgin "Lord Elgin". White dial, raised gold numerals, subsidiary seconds. 21J movement. 14K gold square case, molded tapered lugs. ca 1949 . . . . $75—100

Elgin "Deluxe". White dial, subsidiary seconds. 17J movement. 14K gold-filled, molded square case. ca 1950 . . . . $35—55

Elgin "B.W. Raymond". Glass enamel dial, subsidiary seconds. 23J, round, railroad approved, stemwind movement. Round case with heavy lugs. ca 1961. 14K . . . $175—225
YGF . . . . 120—150
Stainless steel . . . . 90—120

Elgin "Lord Elgin". Raised gold dots & subsidiary seconds. 21J movement. 14K gold, curved & faceted rectangular case. ca 1950. $125—150

Elgin "Lord Elgin". Black dial, gold markers, subsidiary seconds. 21J movement. 14K yellow gold square case with large attached, moveable lugs. ca 1950. . . . . $150—175
Gold-filled . . . . 25— 40

Elgin. Subsidiary seconds & diamond set numerals. 14K gold, 32mm. round case. ca 1965 . . . . $200—250

Empire (American-made). 10½''', 7J movement. Chrome tonneau case. ca 1933. . .$7–16
Bracelet 2– 4

Empire "Jump Hour". 10½''', 7J movement. Chrome tonneau case, with hour, minute & seconds windows. Chrome $30–45
Bracelet 3– 7

Eska "Moonphase Calendar". Tu-tone gold or silvered dial with colorful moonphase at 6. Day and month window at 12, outer date ring. Self-winding, sweep second movement. Square case with polished, beveled bezel. ca 1956. 14K yellow gold $800–1,000
Yellow gold-filled 150– 200
Stainless steel 100– 125

Eterna. Ladies, 5¼''', 15J movement. 14K gold rectangular case, engraved and set with 6 sapphires. ca 1928 . . . .$50–75

ETERNA

Trademark for Schild Frerers & Co., Grenchen, Switzerland, and in 1928 was offering a full line made in platinum and gold and different metals with enameling.

Eterna. Ladies, 6''', 15J movement. 14K gold molded & engraved rectangular case. ca 1928. . . . .$35–55

Eterna "Ladies Gold Cord". 14K gold, molded oval case and lugs. ca 1940. . . . . . .$30–50

Eterna "Ladies Gold Cord". Black dial. 14K gold, round case and single lugs. ca 1940 . . . .$30–50

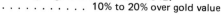

Eterna "Ladies Gold Bracelet". 17J movement. 14K yellow gold rectangular case & matching large link bracelet. ca 1942.
. . . . 10% to 20% over gold value

Eterna "Gold Strap". Center seconds. 14K gold, round case and molded lugs. ca 1940.
. . . .$120–140

Eterna "Gold Sweep Second". Luminous numerals & hands, center seconds. 17J movement. 14K gold case. ca 1946 . . . . $100—125

Eterna-Matic Centenaire. Center second, window date, 18K gold 33mm. round case. ca 1960 . . . . $150—200

EVKOB

Trade name for a large line of commercial grade Swiss watches in 6 or 15 jewels. ca 1928.

Eterna "Gold Strap". Subsidiary seconds. 14K gold, rectangular case. ca 1940 . . . $125—150

Evkob "Plated Strap". Radium numerals, subsidiary seconds. 10''', 15J movement. White or green rolled gold plate, chromium finish, three-piece case. ca 1928 . . . . $10—20

Eterna "Thin Gold". Subsidiary seconds. 14K gold, square case. ca 1940 . . . . . . $125—150

Evkob "Tu-tone Plated Strap". Radium numerals on silvered dial, subsidiary seconds. 10½''', 15J movement. White & green, engraved, rolled gold plate, three piece square case. ca 1928. . . . . $10—20

Eterna "Automatic". Center seconds. 18J, self-winding movement. Round case. ca 1947.
14K gold . . . . $110—135
Steel & 14K gold . . . . 75—100
Stainless steel . . . . 15— 25

Evkob "Plated Strap". Plain round dial, subsidiary seconds. 10''', 15J movement. Square case with engraved numerals on enamel bezel. White rolled gold plate, chromium finished case. ca 1928 . . . . $40—60

Excelsior Park. Tachometer chronograph, subsidiary seconds & 45 minute recorder, outer tachometer ring, base 1000m. Round, 14K gold, stainless steel or GF case. ca 1949.

14K gold	$175—225
GF	40— 60
Stainless steel	25— 50

FORTIS WATCH CO.

Factory at Grenchen, Switzerland, and distributed wholesale in the U.S. from New York.

Fortis "Sport". Radium silvered dial, 6¾''', 17J movement. 14K green or white gold rectangular case. ca 1923 . . . . $100—125

Gallet Duo—Dial. Ladies, top dial for 12 hours, bottom for subsidiary seconds. 7 or 15J, 4¾''' movement. 10K RGP or stainless steel rectangular case. ca 1934. RGP . . . . $50—75
Stainless steel . . . . 35—65

Gallet Duo-Dial, 1st dial for 12 hours & 2nd for subsidiary seconds. 7 or 15J, 8x12''' movement. Rectangular chrome case. ca 1934.
. . . . $125—150

Gallet Duo-Dial (Doctors). Top dial for 12 hours, bottom for subsidiary seconds. 7 or 15J, 8x12''' movement. 10K RGP, white or yellow, moulded rectangular case. ca 1934 . $100—125

Gallet. Chronograph, 30 minute recorder, 15J movement. Round stainless steel case. ca 1936.
. . . .$50—75

Gallet. Chronograph, double button, 30 minute recorder, 15J movement. Round stainless steel case. ca 1938 . . . .$50—75

Gallet. Decimal chronograph, 30 minute recorder, 15J movement, 30 minute recorder divides minutes into 100 parts. Round stainless steel case. ca 1938 . . . . $60—80

Gallet "Chronograph". Silvered dial with 5 scales and subsidiary seconds. Sweep hand times to 1/5 second with stop-start and flyback to zero. Tonneau stainless steel case with heavy lugs. ca 1940. . . . . $50—75

Gallet. Chronograph, radium finished or black dial, subsidiary seconds, 30 minute & 12 hour recorders. 17J, 14''' movement. Round, stainless steel or 14K gold case. ca 1960.
14K gold . . . . $175—225
Stainless steel . . . . 50— 75

Gallet. Calendar chronograph, subsidiary seconds, 30 minute & 12 hour recorder, day & month windows with outer date ring. 17J, 14''' movement. Waterproof, 14K gold or stainless steel round case. ca 1960.
14K gold . . . . $225—275
Stainless steel . . . . 85—110

Gallet "Flight Officer". Chronograph, subsidiary seconds, 30 minute recorder, outer ring calibrated for world time. 17J, 13''' movement. Round stainless steel case with revolving bezel. ca 1960 . . . . $75—100

Gallet "Decimal" Chronograph. Subsidiary seconds, 45 minute recorder & outer decimal ring. 17J, 14''' movement. Water & dust resistant, round, stainless steel case. ca 1960.
. . . . $25—50

Gallet. Chronograph. Plain or radium-finished dial, subsidiary seconds, 45 minute recorder with outer tachometer & telemeter rings. 17J, 14''' movement. Waterproof, round stainless steel case. ca 1960 . . . . $30—60

Gallet. Chronograph, subsidiary seconds, 30 minute recorder, with outer tachometer & telemeter rings. 17J, 14''' movement. Stainless steel round case. ca 1960. . . . . $25—50

Gallet. Chronograph. Radium finished dial, subsidiary seconds & 45 minute recorder. 17J, 14''' movement. 14K gold, stainless steel or 14K YGF round case. ca 1960. 14K . . . $150—175
14K GF . . . . 45— 65
Stainless steel . . . . 30— 50

Gallet. Chronograph, radium finished dial, subsidiary seconds, 30 minute, 12 hour recorders with outer tachometer & telemeter rings. 17J, 14''' movement. Round, stainless steel case. ca 1960. . . . . $40—60

Edmond Genet "213". (Casemaker). Ladies Hunting. 14K gold "Art Deco" designed case set with diamonds, rubies and sapphires. ca 1945 . . . . $800—1,000

Edmond Genet "214". (Casemaker). Ladies Hunting. 14K gold "Art Deco" designed case set with diamonds, rubies and sapphires, with bracelet. ca 1945 . . . . $1,000—1,400

NOTE: Read Page 6 before using this book to value your wrist watch.

Gerald Genta. Van Cleef & Arpels. Automatic skeleton. 18K gold octagonal case, onyx bezel. Case signed V. & A. Modern . . . $4,500—5,500

NOTE: All values are given for the head only unless the bracelet is included in the description.

Girard-Perregaux "Ladies Gold Strap". Black dial. 14K gold geometric case with scroll on one side. ca 1940. . . . . $60—80

Girard-Perregaux "Ladies Gold Bracelet". 18K white gold square case, molded flower lugs. ca 1940. . . . . . . 10% to 20% over gold value

Girard-Perregaux "Ladies Gold & Diamond Bracelet". Bangle style, 14K gold. ca 1940. . . . . 10% to 20% over gold value

Girard Perregaux "Ladies Gold Cord". 17J movement. 14K gold-filled square case and large molded single lugs. ca 1946 . . . . $30—50

Girard Perregaux "Ladies Watches". 17J movement. White or yellow gold cases. ca 1966.
D-3, 10K gold-filled. . . . .$5—10
D-4, 14K gold . . . . 10% over gold
D-5, 14K gold . . . . 10% over gold
D-6, 14K gold . . . . 10% over gold

FAMED FOR PRECISION

ca 1944. . . . . 20% over gold value

The beauty of a Girard-Perregaux Watch is more than skin deep. Inside the case there is the sheer beauty of mechanical perfection . . . to insure accuracy and long service. All vital parts, such as mainspring, hairspring, balance, escapement and gears are machined with rare precision and assembled by watchmakers whose skill is a tradition upheld from generation to generation. These distinguished watches are limited in number . . . yet unlimited in the pride and satisfaction they bestow. With 17 Jewels . . . at many leading jewelers . . . from $35. Write for interesting brochure G-4, "What's in a Fine Watch?"

GIRARD·PERREGAUX
Fine Watches since 1791

GIRARD-PERREGAUX, Rockefeller Center, New York 20, N.Y.
In Canada: Dominion Square Building, Montreal

Girard Perregaux "Chronograph". Silvered dial, subsidiary seconds, 30 minute recorder. 17J movement. Round case with rectangle push buttons. ca 1935. 14K YG...... $150—175
Stainless steel .... 50— 75

Girard-Perregaux "Gold Man's Strap". Subsidiary seconds. 14K yellow gold geometric case. ca 1940 .... $250—300

Girard-Perregaux "Gold Man's Strap". Tutone dial, subsidiary seconds. 14K yellow gold, molded rectangular case. ca 1940 .. $125—150

Girard-Perregaux "Chronograph". Subsidiary seconds, 30 minute & 12 hour recorder, with outer tachometer ring, 1 mile base. Round 14K yellow gold case. ca 1940 .. $175—225
Stainless steel .... 30— 45

Girard- Perregaux "Gold Strap". Subsidiary seconds. 14K yellow gold, round case. ca 1940.
.... $100—125

Girard-Perregaux "Calendar". Subsidiary seconds, date window. Stainless steel rectangular case. ca 1940 .... $90—110

Girard Perregaux "Gold Strap". Subsidiary seconds. 17J movement. 14K gold-filled rectangular case. ca 1946 .... $100—125

Girard Perregaux "Gyromatic". Self-winding, waterproof, shock resistant. Center seconds, 17J movement. Round case. ca 1953. 14K gold .... $100—135
Gold filled .... 20— 35
Stainless steel .... 15— 20

Girard Perregaux. Raised 14K gold numeral markers. 17J movement. 14K gold rectangular, satin-finished case. ca 1966 . . . . . $115—140

Girard Perregaux "Gold Strap". Chess-board dial. 14K gold square case. ca 1966. $125—150

Girard Perregaux "Gyromatic". Self-winding, Waterproof. Center seconds, with or without date window, 17J movement. 10K GF round case. ca 1966 . . . . $15—20
10K GF Date . . . . 20—25

Girard Perregaux "Gold & Diamond Strap". Oval dial. 14K gold rectangular case and oval bezel, set with 42 diamonds. ca 1966.
. . . . .20% to 30% over diamond & gold value

Girard Perregaux "Sea Hawk". Waterproof. Center seconds, date window, 17J movement. Round stainless steel case. ca 1966 . . .$15—20

Girard Perregaux "Chronograph". Waterproof. Black dial, luminous numerals, subsidiary seconds, 30 minute & 12 hour recorders. 17J movement. Stainless steel round case with revolving bezel. ca 1966 . . . .$50—75

Girard Perregaux "Alarm". Waterproof. Center seconds, Alarm indicator window, 17J movement. Round case. ca 1966.
14K gold . . . . $120—135
14K gold top . . . . 70— 90
Stainless steel . . . . 30— 45

Girard Perregaux "Sea Hawk". Waterproof. 17J movement. 10K Gold-filled round case. ca 1966 . . . . $15—20

Girard Perregaux "Gold & Diamond Bracelet".
14K gold round case, bezel set with 36 diamonds, matching mesh band. ca 1966.
. . . . .10% to 20% over gold & diamond value

Girard Perregaux. Waterproof. Black & silvered abstract dial. 17J movement. Round stainless steel case. ca 1969 . . . . $15—20

Girard Perregaux "Date Gyromatic". Waterproof & self-winding, date window, 17J movement. Beveled cushion case. ca 1966.
14K gold . . . . 20% over gold
10K gold-filled . . . . $25—30
Stainless steel . . . . 20—25

Girard Perregaux "Chronograph". Silvered dial, 30 minute & 12 hour registers, Tachometer. Stainless steel case. ca 1969 . . . . . . $25—40

Girard Perregaux "Date". Silvered dial, date window, 17J, Gyromatic, self-wind movement. High frequency. 10K GF, square case, round face. 10K GF bracelet. CA 1969 . . . . $20—30

Girard Perregaux "Gyromatic". Self-winding, white dial, center seconds, 17J movement. Round case, ca 1969. 10K GF. . . . . . $25—40
Stainless steel . . . . 15—20

Girard Perregaux "39J Observatory Chronometer". Self-winding & waterproof, date window. 39J, high frequency movement. 18K gold tonneau case. ca 1969 . . . . . $200—235

Girard Perregaux. Dress watch. Silvered dial, 17J movement. 14K gold, square case. ca 1969.
. . . . $100—125

Girard Perregaux "Day Date". Silvered dial, day/date window, 17J, self-wind, Gyromatic movement. Water resistant, stainless steel case. ca 1969. . . . . $15—25

Girard Perregaux "Diver". Black dial, revolving bezel shows elapsed time. 17J, Gyromatic movement. Water-resistant stainless steel case with bracelet. . . . . $25—30

Glashutte. Chronograph. Black dial. Subsidiary seconds & 30 minute register. Metal case secured by screws . . . . $350—400

Glycine "Diamond & Platinum". Ladies, 17J movement. Platinum oval case set with 10 baguette-cut and 52 round diamonds. ca 1930. . . . . $1,000—1,250

Glycine "Ladies Gold Bracelet". Raised gold markers on dial. 14K textured gold rectangular case with attached matching bracelet. ca 1966. . . . . .10% to 20% over gold

Glycine "Ladies Gold Bracelet". Raised gold markers on dial. 14K gold oval case with attached gold, flexible mesh bracelet. ca 1966. . . . . .10% to 20% over gold

Glycine "Ladies Gold Bracelet". Raised gold markers on dial. 14K gold marquise case with attached matching, textured gold mesh bracelet. ca 1966 . . . . .10% to 20% over gold

Glycine "Diamond Dial". Rose gold dial with 8 baguette & 8 round diamond numerals, subsidiary seconds. 17J movement. Rectangular, 14K gold curved case with stepped sides. ca 1940. 14K yellow gold . . . . . $275—325
14K white gold . . . . 250—300

Glycine. Tu-tone dial, subsidiary seconds. 17J movement. Rectangular, 14K gold case. ca 1940 . . . . $100—125

Glycine "Curved Gold". Tu-tone dial, subsidiary seconds. 17J movement. Rectangular, 14K gold curved case. ca 1940 . . . . . $115—135

Glycine "Rose Gold Curved". Rose gold, subsidiary seconds dial. 17J movement. Curved rectangular, 14K yellow gold case. ca 1940. . . . . $100—125

Glycine "Rose Gold". 14K raised gold numerals, subsidiary seconds dial. 17J movement. Rectangular, 14K rose gold case. ca 1940. $135—165

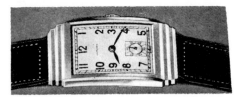

Glycine "Rose Gold". Dial with 14K raised gold numerals, subsidiary seconds. 17J movement. Rectangular, 14K rose gold, faceted case. ca 1940 . . . . $100—125

Glycine "Gold Strap". Yellow gold finish, tu-tone dial, subsidiary seconds. 17J movement. Round, 14K gold case, large curved cylinder style lugs. ca 1940 . . . . $135—165

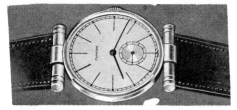

Glycine "Rose Gold". All rose gold dial, subsidiary seconds. 17J movement. Round, 14K rose gold case, large cylinder style lugs. ca 1940 . . . . $135—165

Glycine "Rose Gold". Tu-tone rose dial, subsidiary seconds. 17J movement. Square, 14K rose or yellow gold. ca 1940. . . . . $135—165

Goering, Elaine. Engraved dial. 6J movement. Engraved, rectangular chrome case with faceted corners. ca 1928. . . . . $15—25

Goering, Elaine. Luminous dial, subsidiary seconds. 14K white or green gold, curved rectangular case. ca 1928 . . . . $110—130

Grana "Gold Strap". Subsidiary seconds. 14K yellow gold square case. ca 1946 . . $100—125

Grandjean, Henry, Geneve, Minute Repeater. Silver matte dial, subsidiary seconds. 18K gold, 39mm. round, signed case, slide repeat. ca 1920 . . . . $6,000—8,000

Gruen "Wristlet N-8". Ladies. Engraved dial. Green, white or yellow gold, round case. ca 1912. 14K gold . . 10% to 20% over gold value Gold-filled . . . . $10—15

Gruen "Cartouche S-10". Ladies. Rectangular dial. Precision movement. 14K gold, engraved tonneau case. ca 1926.
. . . . 10% to 20% over gold value

Gruen "Cartouche 23". Ladies. Oval dial. Platinum, elongated cushion case, engraved and set with 4 diamonds. ca 1926 . . . . . . $75—95

Gruen "Cartouche 121". Platinum, engraved tonneau case, set with 4 diamonds & 2 sapphires. ca 1926 . . . . $60—80

Gruen "Cartouche 161". Ladies. Platinum, engraved tonneau case set with 6 diamonds & 2 sapphires, with matching solid gold mesh bracelet. ca 1926 . . . . $75—90

Gruen "Cartouche 189". Ladies. 17J "precision" movement. Engraved, rectangular, platinum case set with 12 diamonds & 8 sapphires. ca 1926 . . . . $90—110

Gruen "Wristlet 3P". Ladies. 17J "precision" movement. Diamond paved rectangular platinum case. ca 1926 . . . . $175—250

Gruen "Wristlet A-847". Ladies. 18J "precision" movement. Rectangular platinum case & lugs set with 79 diamonds & matching bracelet. ca 1926 . . . . $350—450

East View, The Gruen Watch Company . . . Time Hill, Cincinnati, U. S. A.

Gruen "Wristlet E-107". Ladies. Tu-tone dial, 17J "precision" movement. Platinum rectangular case, diamond pavèd bezel. ca 1926.
. . . . $125—165

Gruen. Ladies. 14K gold, engraved tonneau case. ca 1927 . . . 10% to 20% over gold value

Gruen. Ladies. Tu-tone oval case. 14K gold, engraved rectangular case. ca 1927.
. . . . 10% to 20% over gold value

Gruen "Cartouche". Ladies. 17J movement. Tonneau platinum case set with diamonds & 2 sapphires. ca 1927 . . . . $175—200

Gruen "Platinum & Diamond". Ladies. 17J movement. Platinum & diamond rectangular case. ca 1927 . . . . $375—475

Gruen. Tu-tone dial. 14K gold, engraved tonneau case set with 4 diamonds & 2 sapphires. ca 1927 . . . . $90—110

Gruen "Fifth Avenue". Ladies. 17J movement. Rectangular platinum & diamond case. ca 1928. Value varies according to the size, quality and color of the diamonds . . . . $600—800

Gruen "Park Avenue". Ladies. 17J movement. Rectangular platinum & diamond case. ca 1928. Value varies according to the size, quality and color of the diamonds . . . . $450—600

Gruen Precision. Ladies. Rectangular platinum case set with diamonds & semi-precious stone, matching band. ca 1928. Price varies according to size & quality of diamonds.

Gruen "Imperial Tank". Luminous hands & numerals. 37x25mm., 14K gold rectangular case. ca 1927 . . . . $125—160

Gruen "Rosemarie". Ladies. 17J movement. Rectangular platinum & diamond case & lugs. ca 1929. Value varies according to size, quality and color of the diamonds . . . . . . $275—400

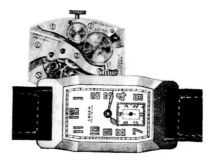

Gruen "Quadron". Luminous hands & numerals, subsidiary seconds. 17J square "precision" movement. 37x25mm., 14K gold tonneau case. ca 1927 . . . . $150—175

Gruen "Henrietta". Ladies. 17J "precision" movement. 14K gold, clover-shaped case & single lugs. ca 1951 .10% to 20% over gold value

Gruen. Luminous hands & numerals, subsidiary seconds. 17J movement. 14K gold square case, engraved bezel. ca 1928. . . . . $125—160

Gruen "Tank". Luminous hands & numerals, subsidiary seconds. 17J "precision" movement. 32x25mm. rectangular case. ca 1924. 14K gold . . . . $135—175
Gold-filled . . . . 30— 40

Gruen "Precision Cushion". 17J movement. 14K gold cushion case. ca 1926 . . . $100—120

Gruen "Quadron". Subsidiary seconds. 17J rectangular "precision" movement. 14K gold rectangular case. ca 1928. . . . . . . $120—145

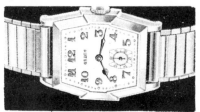

Gruen "EXSP-11". Subsidiary seconds. 15J movement. Molded tonneau case. ca 1930. 14K gold. . . . . $150—200
Gold-filled . . . . 15— 25

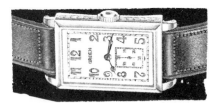

Gruen "Quadron". Subsidiary seconds. 15J movement. 14K gold rectangular case. ca 1930. . . . . $125—150

Gruen "Quadron". Luminous hands & numerals, subsidiary seconds. 15J rectangular movement. 14K gold rectangular case with faceted corners. ca 1930. . . . . $125—150

Gruen "Quadron". Luminous hands & numerals, subsidiary seconds. 17J "precision" movement. 14K gold, molded tonneau case & lugs. ca 1930. . . . . $150—175

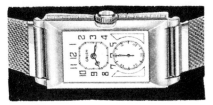

Gruen "Techni-Quadron" (Doctor's). Duo-dial, upper for hours, lower for seconds. 14K yellow gold, rectangular case. ca 1930 . . $750—1,000
Gold-filled . . . . 185— 200

Gruen "Varsity". Luminous hands & numerals, subsidiary seconds. 15J or 17J movement. 14K gold, molded tonneau case. ca 1930 . . . . $115—140

Gruen "Curvex Patroness". Silvered dial. 17J, curved precision movement. 14K YGF, long tonneau, curved case. ca 1937. . . . . . $25—40

Gruen "Curvex Majesty". Silvered black numerals, subsidiary second dial. 17J, curved precision, 14K gold-filled, long rectangular, curved case. ca 1937 . . . . $85—110

Gruen. Raised gold numerals, subsidiary seconds. 15J movement. 10K yellow or rose gold-filled tonneau case. ca 1940 . . . . $20—35

Gruen "Tonneau". Raised gold numerals, subsidiary seconds. 15J movement. 10K yellow gold-filled, molded tonneau case. ca 1940. . . . .$20—30

Gruen "Doctor's". Silvered duo-dial, raised gold numerals. Upper for hours, lower for seconds. 17J movement. 10K gold-filled, elongated tonneau case. ca 1940 . . $225—275

Gruen, "Curvex" Black dial signed Veri-Thin, diamond studded and bar numerals, subsidiary seconds. Gold 22x40mm. rectangular curved case, with arched faceted crystal, curved plates on movement. ca 1945 . . . . $350—400

Gruen "Precision Curvex". Raised gold numerals, subsidiary seconds. 17J movement. 14K yellow gold tonneau case. ca 1940 . . $80—110

Gruen "Precision Curvex". Raised gold numerals, subsidiary seconds. 17J movement. 14K yellow gold-filled, molded tonneau curvex case. ca 1940 . . . .$60—75

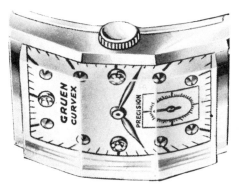

Gruen "Curvex". 3-diamond dial. 14K gold curved case with tri-facet crystal. ca 1946 . . . .$350—375

Gruen "Tonneau". Raised gold numerals, inner center seconds ring. 15J movement. 10K yellow or rose gold-filled tonneau case. ca 1940. . . . .$35—50

Gruen "Executive". 3-diamond dial, subsidiary seconds. 17J movement. 14K white, rose, or yellow gold, tri-facet case & crystal. ca 1947. . . . . $350—400

Gruen Watch Co. Curvex patent precision, silver matte dial, subsidiary seconds, 17J movement, 14K gold, 40mm. rectangular case. $250–300

NOTE: Read Page 6 before using this book to value your wrist watch.

Gruen, Curvex. 17J curved movement. Black signed dial, subsidiary seconds. 14K gold 38mm moulded rectangular tank case, also signed. $175–200

Gruen "Curvex". Tu-tone dial, subsidiary seconds. 14K gold-filled, curved rectangular case. ca 1940. . . . .$25–40

NOTE: All values are given for the head only unless the bracelet is included in the description.

Gruen "Curvex Executive." 5 diamond dial. 17J movement, 14K gold rectangular curvex case. ca 1951 . . . .$350–400

Gruen "Star Supreme". 21J veri-thin movement in square yellow GF case. $60–70

Gruen "Autowind Medallion". Self-winding, 23J precision movement in round 18K gold case . . . . 20% over gold

Gruen "Guns of Navarone". Silvered dial, center seconds. Automatic, 23J movement. Round stainless steel case. ca 1961 . . .$15–25

Gruen "Alarm-Cal". Silvered dial, date window at 3, center alarm setting indicator. 17J precision, sweep second movement. Round case with extra crown for alarm and matching band. ca 1965. Yellow gold plated . . .$50–70 Chrome top, steel back. 40–60

Gruen "Day–Nite". The hour markers jump automatically at 6 p.m., from conventional color to florescent nite-glo until 6 a.m. Self-winding, sweep second, 17J movement. Round case. ca 1965. Yellow gold plated. . . . $35–55
Stainless steel 30–50
Matching bracelet 2– 5

Gruen "Diver Autowind Steel". Black dial with rotating time elapse black bezel. 17J precision, self-winding, sweep second movement. Stainless steel, round, 600' waterproof case with expansion or rubber band. ca 1965.
. . . . $40–60

Gruen "Fleet Autowind". Luminous or black dial and hands. Sweep second, self-winding, 17J precision movement. Chrome top, steel back, round case. ca 1965. . . . . $10–20

Gruen "Airflight Jump Hours". Hour markers jump automatically at 1 a.m. to read 13-24. 17J precision, sweep second movement. Round waterproof case. ca 1965.
Yellow gold plated $85–110
Chrome top, steel back 75–100

Gruen "Chronograph". Telemeter and tacho-meter (base 1 mile) scales on silvered dial with 30 minute recorder and subsidiary seconds. 17J precision movement with stop, start and fly-back sweep second hand. Round, waterproof, stainless steel case. ca 1965 . . . . . . $25–40

Gubelin, E. "Ladies Diamond & Gold Bracelet". Square case and massive leaf-covered lugs, large link bracelet. ca 1940.
. . . . .20% to 30% over gold & diamond value

Gubelin, E. Black or silver dial, 17J. 18K gold Ladies. ca 1942 . . . . $150—185

Gubelin. Ladies, black dial, 18K gold & black enamel, 34mm. long tonneau case . $600—700

Gubelin. Ladies, stainless steel square case, or 18K gold round case, with moulded extended lugs. ca 1943. . . . .18K gold . . . . $125—150
Stainless steel . . . . 50— 60

Gubelin. Ladies, gold satin finished dial. 18J movement. 18K gold, 26mm. round case, diamond set bezel. 18K gold mesh strap.
. . . . $1,500—2,000

Gubelin. Ladies, 14K white gold square case. Lugs studded with two yellow sapphires & 10 diamonds on two sides. 17J movement. ca 1945 . . . . $375—450

Gubelin, E. Black or silver dial. 17J, sweep second. 18K gold case. ca 1942 . . . $250—275

Gubelin "Diamond, Ruby, Sapphire & Platinum". Ladies. Value varies with the size and quality of the diamonds and precious stones, and condition. ca 1954.

Gubelin. Black or gold plated dial, subsidiary seconds, 17J movement. 18K gold square case with moulded lugs. ca 1944 . . . . . $350—400

Gubelin. Moonphase calendar. Self-winding, silver dial, day & month windows, inner date ring. 25J, 12''' movement. Waterproof, 32x32mm., 18K gold square case. ca 1950. . . . . $2,500—3,000

Gubelin, E., Chronograph. Pink matte dial. Subsidiary seconds, 30 minute & 12 hour registers. 18K gold 40mm. round case . . $475—525

Gubelin "Gold Ipso-Day Timemaster". Silvered dial with applied gold square markers and hands, with date window at 3. 25J, self-winding, sweep second movement. Square, 18K yellow gold case. ca 1952 . . . . . . $500—600

Gubelin "Ipsomatic". Tu-tone dial with heavy applied gold markers and hands. 25J, self-winding, sweep second movement. Heavy round case. ca 1952. 18K yellow gold . . . $275—350
Stainless steel . . . . 100—125

Gubelin "Gold Ipsomatic Timemaster". Silvered dial with applied gold markers and hands. 25J, self-winding, sweep second movement. Square case. ca 1952.
18K yellow gold. . . . . $450—550
Steel and gold . . . . 250—350

Gubelin "Gold Ipso-Day". Silvered dial with applied gold markers and hands, date window at 3. 25J, self-winding, sweep second movement. Round, 18K yellow gold, tonneau case. ca 1952. . . . . $400—450

Gubelin "Man's Gold Bracelet". Brickwork pattern continued on dial. 18K yellow gold rectangular case with molded bezel and integral bracelet. ca 1954 . . . . $1,500—2,000

Gubelin, Minute Repeater. Matte gold dial signed Gubelin, movement signed E. Gubelin FAB. Swiss repeating on two gongs. 32mm. rectangular 18K gold case with repeat slide. $12,000–14,000

Haas, retailed by Van Cleef & Arpels. Solid gold dial, subsidiary seconds & minute ring, hour window. 18K gold, tonneau case. ca 1927 . . . . $1,800–2,200

Gubelin. White enamel dial, 18K gold, 39mm. moulded oval case. $500–700

Hallwatch. Ladies. Silver dial, 15J movement. 14K white gold, engraved case with 6 sapphires. ca 1927. . . . .$35–55

Gubelin. Gold dial, 18K gold, 39mm. faceted, elongated octagonal case $500–700

Hallwatch. Ladies. 17J movement. Platinum rectangular case and mesh bracelet set with 186 round and 6 baguette-cut diamonds. ca 1930. Value varies according to size, quality and color of diamonds $2,250–2,750

Hallwatch. Ladies. 17J movement. 18K white gold, engraved tonneau case, set with 6 diamonds and 12 emeralds. ca 1930 . . $100–135

Gubelin. Moonphase calendar. Silver dial with applied gold index, day & month windows, inner date ring, center seconds. 25J, 11½''', self-winding movement. 37mm., 18K gold, waterproof round case. ca 1960. $1,800–2,200

Hallwatch. Subsidiary seconds. 15J movement. White gold-filled, curved rectangular case. ca 1930 . . . .$15–25

HAMILTON WATCH COMPANY
Lancaster, Pa. U.S.A.
1893 to 1983

The Hamilton product catalog of 1911 does not show any wrist watches available at that time. The smallest pocket watch movement offered was 0 size, 17 jewel, and we have seen wrist watches made with round, converted pocket watch-style cases, with convertible or detachable bands. At this time, Hamilton was selling uncased 0 size movements, and in 1913, 6/0 size movements to the trade. The first Hamilton wrist watch to appear in their product catalog was a 6/0 size, 17 jewel, Grade 986, shown in the first illustration below. Hamilton went on to produce a long and varied line of case styles until they ceased U.S.A. production (in the 1960's) then used the Hamilton name on Swiss-made movements. Hamilton was a company of many firsts, including electric watches and the Computer Pulsar. They made fine watch movements and are considered by collectors to be the "Patek Philippe" of American wrist watch makers.

Hamilton "Round Detachable". Metal dial. Subsidiary seconds, 17J, 6/0 size 986-A movement. Plain or engraved 14K gold or GF ladies case. ca 1922. 14K Gold . . . . $60—80
14K GF . . . . 20—35

Hamilton "Ladies Decagon". Silvered dial, subsidiary seconds. Grade 987, 6/0 size, 17J round movement. Timed & cased at the factory in round, decagon, tonneau, and cushion cases. ca 1926. 14K white or green gold. . . . $60—80
14K white or green gold-filled. . . . . 25—40

Hamilton "Skylight". Silvered dial, subsidiary seconds. 17J, open face, Grade 986, round 6/0 size movement. Sold in both full open face with subsidiary seconds and skylight cases, cased & timed at the factory. ca 1914.
14K yellow gold case & bracelet . . . . $55—85
25 Yr. YGF case & bracelet . . . . . . 15—35

Hamilton "Cushion". Glass enamel or metal dial. 17J, 6/0 size, 986-A movement. 14K gold & GF ladies case. ca 1922.
14K Gold . $60—80   14K GF . . . .$25—40

Hamilton "Tonneau". Glass enamel or metal dial. 17J, 6/0 size 986-A movement. 14K gold & GF ladies case. ca 1922.
14K Gold . $60—80   14K GF . . . .$25—40

Hamilton "Round". Glass enamel or metal dial. 17J, 6/0 size 986-A movement. 14K gold or GF ladies round case. ca 1922 . 14K gold . $60—80
14K GF . . . . 20—35

Hamilton "Cedarcrest". Ladies 17J, 21/0 size 995 movement. 14K gold rectangular case with solid gold fittings. ca 1934. . . . . $60—80

Hamilton "Mayfield" Ladies 17J, 21/0 size 995 movement. 14K GF rectangular case. ca 1934 . . . . $30—50

Hamilton "Wellesley". 17J, 18/0 size 989 movement. 14K engraved GF rectangular case. ca 1934. . . . . $20—35

Hamilton "Bryn Mawr". Applied gold numeral dial. 17J, 18/0 size 989 movement. Ladies 14K gold rectangular case. ca 1934. . . . . $60—80

Hamilton "Aurora". Ladies 17J, 18/0 size 989 movement. 10K GF bowed rectangular case. ca 1934 . . . . $30—50

Hamilton "Chevy Chase". 17J, 18/0 size 989 movement. 14K gold engraved tonneau shaped case. ca 1934 . . . . $60—80

Hamilton "Gail". Ladies 17J, 18/0 size 989 movement. 10K GF rectangular case. ca 1934. . . . . $30—50

Hamilton "Diane". 17J, 18/0 size, 989 movement. Ladies 14K gold rectangular case. ca 1934 . . . . $70—90

Hamilton "Linden Hall." 17J, 18/0 size 989 movement. 14K GF rectangular case. ca 1934 . . . . $20—35

Hamilton "Fairmont". Ladies 17J, 21/0 size 995 movement. 14K GF bowed rectangular case. ca 1934 . . . . $40—60

Hamilton "Myrna". 17J, 21/0 size 995 movement, raised numeral dial. 14K GF round case. ca 1937. . . . .$30—50

Hamilton "Shirley". 18K gold or black numerals on silver dial. 17J, 21/0 size 721 movement. 10K GF round case. ca 1949. . .$15—25

Hamilton "Maxine". Ladies 17J, 20/0 size 997 movement, raised numeral dial. 10K GF round case. ca 1937 . . . .$30—50

Hamilton "Olivia". 18K gold numerals or black numerals and dots on silver dial. 17J, 21/0 size 721 movement. 10K GF bowed square case. ca 1949 . . . .$10—25

Hamilton "Nola". Ladies 17J, 21/0 size 995 movement. 10% iridium platinum rectangular case set with 22 diamonds, with solid gold fittings. ca 1937. . . . . $120—140

Lady Hamilton "K-6". 17J movement, 14K gold rectangular case with 6 diamonds. ca 1951 . . . .$75—100

Hamilton "Muriel". Ladies 17J, 20/0 size 997 movement. 10K GF rectangular case. ca 1937.
. . . .$30—50

Lady Hamilton "K-14". 17J movement, 14K gold rectangular case with 14 diamonds. ca 1951 . . . .$100—125

Hamilton "Celia". Ladies 17J, 20/0 size 997 movement, raised numeral dial. 10K GF rectangular case. ca 1937 . . . .$30—50

Lady Hamilton "PL-3". 17J movement. Platinum rectangular case with 20 diamonds. ca 1951 . . . .$100—125

Hamilton "Constance". Ladies 17J, 21/0 size 995 movement, raised numeral dial. 14K GF diamond-shaped case. ca 1937. . . . . .$30—50

Hamilton "Lynn". Black numerals on silver dial. 17J, 11/0 size 911 movement. 14K gold round case. ca 1949. . . . .$30—45

Hamilton "Diamond & Platinum Hunting Bracelet". 17J adjusted movement. 138 round brilliant, 62 baguette and 4 marquise-cut diamonds with 6.69 carat total, set in a platinum hunting case and bracelet. ca 1962. Value varies according to size, quality and color of diamonds. . . . . $6,000—8,000

Hamilton "Diamond & Platinum Hunting Bracelet". 17J adjusted movement. 137 round brilliant, 24 baguette and 1 marquise-cut diamonds with 4.60 carat total, set in a platinum hunting case and bracelet. ca 1962. Value varies according to size, quality and color of diamonds. . . . . $4,250—5,250

Hamilton "Diamond & Gold Hunting Bracelet". 17J adjusted movement. 121 round brilliant and 21 baguette-cut diamonds with 3.06 carat total, set in 14K white gold, hunting case and bracelet. ca 1962. Value varies according to size quality and color of diamonds. . $2,000—2,600

Hamilton "Diamond & Gold Hunting Bracelet". 17J adjusted movement. 101 round brilliant and 16 baguette-cut diamonds with 2.18 carat total, set in 14K white gold, hunting case and bracelet. ca 1962. Value varies according to size, quality and color of diamonds. . $1,850—2,250

Hamilton "Diamond & Gold Cord". 17J oval adjusted movement. 30 round brilliant and 6 baguette-cut diamonds with 1.00 carat total, set in 14K white gold case. ca 1962. . . $525—650

Hamilton "Diamond & Platinum Cord". 17J adjusted movement. 38 round brilliant and 8 baguette-cut diamonds with 1.38 carat total, set in a platinum case. ca 1962. Value varies according to size, quality and color of diamonds . . . . $1,200—1,500

Hamilton "Diamond & Gold Cord". 17J adjusted movement. 28 round brilliant and 20 baguette-cut diamonds with 1.32 carat total, set in a 14K white gold case. ca 1962. Value varies according to size, quality and color of diamonds. . . . . $950—1,200

Hamilton "Diamond & Platinum Cord". 17J adjusted movement. 46 round brilliant, 20 baguette, and 2 marquise-cut diamonds with 1.42 carat total, set in platinum case. ca 1962. Value varies according to size, quality and color of diamonds. . . . . $1,250—1,650

Hamilton "Diamond & Platinum Cord". 17J adjusted movement. 36 round brilliant, 16 baguette, and 2 marquise-cut diamonds with 1.23 carat total, set in platinum case. ca 1962. Value varies according to size, quality and color of diamonds. . . . . $1,150—1,400

Hamilton "Diamond & Gold Cord". 17J adjusted movement. 47 round brilliant, 10 baguette, and 2 marquise-cut diamonds with 1.34 carat total, set in 14K white gold case. ca 1962. Value varies according to size, quality and color of diamonds . . . . $650—875

Hamilton "Diamond & Gold Cord". 17J adjusted movement. 46 round brilliant and 4 baguette-cut diamonds with 1.27 carat total, set in platinum case. ca 1962. Value varies according to size, quality and color of diamonds . . . . $750—900

Hamilton "Diamond & Gold Cord". 17J adjusted movement. 40 round brilliant and 8 baguette-cut diamonds with 1.17 carat total, set in 14K white gold case. ca 1962. Value varies according to size, quality and color of diamonds. . . . . $900—1,100

Hamilton "Diamond & Gold Bracelet". 17J adjusted movement. 60 round brilliant and 8 baguette-cut diamonds with 1.30 total carat, set in 14K white gold case and bracelet. ca 1962 . . . . $550—700

Hamilton "Diamond & Platinum Cord". 17J adjusted movement. 36 round brilliant, 10 baguette and 6 marquise-cut diamonds, set in a platinum case. ca 1962. Value varies according to size, quality and color of diamonds. . . . . $2,000—2,450

Hamilton "Diamond & Gold Bracelet". 17J adjusted movement. 53 round brilliant and 6 marquise-cut diamonds with 1.12 total carat, in 14K white gold case and bracelet. ca 1962. Value varies according to size, quality and color of diamonds. . . . . $650—800

Hamilton "Diamond & Gold Cord". 17J adjusted movement. 34 round brilliant and 6 baguette-cut diamonds with .89 total carat. 14K white gold case. ca 1962 . . . . $600—750

Hamilton "Diamond & Gold Cord". 17J adjusted movement. 28 round brilliant and 6 baguette-cut diamonds with .66 carat total, set in 14K white gold case. ca 1962. . . $325—400

Hamilton "Diamond & Gold Cord". 17J movement. 38 round brilliant-cut diamonds with .68 carat total, set in 14K white gold case. ca 1962. . . . . $350—475

Hamilton "Diamond & Gold cord". 17J oval, adjusted movement. 32 brilliant-cut diamonds with .70 total carat. 14K white gold case. ca 1962 . . . . $350—450

Hamilton "Diamond & Platinum Cord". 17J adjusted movement. 30 round brilliant-cut diamonds with .97 total carat, in a platinum case. ca 1962 . . . . $575—700

Hamilton "Diamond & Gold Cord". 17J adjusted movement. 24 round brilliant and 4 baguette-cut diamonds with .72 total carat. 14K white gold case. ca 1962 . . . . $250—350

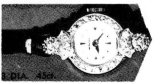

Hamilton "Diamond & Gold Cord". 17J adjusted movement. 28 brilliant-cut diamonds with .45 total carat. 14K white gold case. ca 1962. . . . . $300—375

Hamilton "Diamond & Gold Cord". 17J adjusted movement. 30 round brilliant-cut diamonds with .55 total carat. 14K white gold case. ca 1962 . . . . $325—450

Hamilton "Diamond & Gold Cord". 17J adjusted movement. 28 round brilliant-cut diamonds with .39 total carat. 14K white gold case. ca 1962 . . . . $275—350

Hamilton "Diamond & Gold Cord". 17J adjusted movement. 18 round brilliant-cut diamonds with .62 total carat. 14K white gold case. ca 1962 . . . . $225—300

Hamilton "Diamond & Gold Cord". 17J adjusted movement. 22 round brilliant-cut diamonds with .40 carat total. 14K white gold case. ca 1962. . . . . $275—350

Hamilton "Diamond & Gold Cord". 17J square, adjusted movement. 30 round brilliant-cut diamonds with .60 total carat. 14K white gold case. ca 1962 . . . . $225—300

Hamilton "Diamond & Gold Cord". 17J adjusted movement. 40 round brilliant and 22 baguette-cut diamonds with 1.18 carat total, set in platinum case. ca 1962. Value varies according to size, quality and color of diamonds. . . . . $1,000—1,250

Hamilton "Diamond & Gold Cord". 17J adjusted movement. 42 round brilliant and 10 baguette-cut diamonds with 1.19 total carat, in a 14K white gold case. ca 1962. Value varies according to size, quality and color of diamonds. . . . . $700—900

Hamilton "Diamond & Gold Cord". 17J adjusted movement. 40 round brilliant-cut diamonds with 1.01 total carat. 14K white gold case. ca 1962. Value varies according to size, quality and color of diamonds. $700—825

Hamilton "Diamond & Gold Bracelet". 17J adjusted movement. 72 round brilliant-cut diamonds with 1.36 carat total, set in 14K white gold case and bracelet. ca 1962. Value varies according to size, quality and color of diamonds. . . . . $750—900

Hamilton "Military Style". Glass enamel or luminous dial. 0 size, 17J round movement. Round, plain polish 20 Yr. gold-filled case. ca 1917....................$25—40
Silver .... 35—55

Hamilton "Military Cushion". Glass enamel or silvered metal luminous dial, subsidiary seconds. 0 size, adjusted 3 positions, Grade 981, round movement. Sterling silver cushion case with wire strap lugs, cased & timed at the factory. ca 1918. 14K gold ..... $150—200
Silver .... 40— 60

Same as above except 17J, 6/0 size, round movement. 14K gold .... $125—115
14K gold filled .... 35— 55
Silver .... 35— 55

Hamilton "Cushion Strap Watch". Luminous dial. 17J, 6/0 size 986-A movement. 14K gold or GF or silver cushion, man's case. ca 1922.
14K Gold . $50—80   14K GF .... $20—35
Silver ...... 15—30
Also made in 0 size, ¾ plate, 17J 981, which is a larger case.
14K Gold .$75—100 14K GF ....$25—40
Silver .... 20—35

Hamilton "Oval". Silvered dial with plain or luminous numerals, subsidiary seconds. Grade 987, 17J, 6/0 size round movement. Cased & timed at the factory in rectangular, square, cut-corner, oval, tonneau, cushion and barrel-shaped cases. ca 1926. Platinum. . . $150—200
14K green gold .... 125—150
14K white gold .... 110—140
14K gold-filled .... 30— 50
14K gold buckle............ 25— 50

Hamilton "Glendale". Radium or plain dial. Subsidiary seconds, 19J, 6/0 size 979 movement. 14K gold engraved case. ca 1929.

14K yellow gold........ . . . $150—200
14K white gold .... 100—135

Hamilton "Pinehurst". Radium dial. Subsidiary seconds, 17J, 987 movement. 14K gold case. ca 1929.

14K yellow gold............ $175—200
14K white gold .... 125—150

Hamilton "Meadowbrook". Radium or plain dial. Subsidiary seconds, 19J, 6/0 size 979 movement. 14K gold or platinum cushion case. ca 1929.

14K yellow gold............ $125—135
Platinum .... 175—225

Hamilton "Coronado". Hour numerals of gold set in black enamel on the bezel. Subsidiary seconds, 19J, 6/0 size 979 movement. 14K gold case. ca 1929

14K yellow gold. $350–400
14K white gold 300–350

Hamilton "Mount Vernon". Subsidiary seconds, Grade 987, 6/0 size, 17J movement. 14K WGF or YGF tonneau case with square hinged lugs. ca 1932 . . . . $75–100

Hamilton "Piping Rock". Hour numerals of gold set in black enamel on the bezel. Subsidiary seconds, 19J, 6/0 size 979 movement. 14K gold case. ca 1929.

14K yellow gold. $350–400
14K white gold 325–350

Hamilton "Wilkinson". Subsidiary seconds, Grade 401, 19J, 12/0 size movement. 14K white or yellow gold, faceted rectangular case. ca 1932. 14K white. $110–145
14K yellow 145–175

Hamilton "Spur". Hour numerals of gold set in black enamel on the bezel. Subsidiary seconds, 19J, 6/0 size 979 movement. 14K gold case. ca 1929 . . . . $450–550

Hamilton "Ericsson". Subsidiary seconds, Grade 401, 19J, 12/0 size movement. 14K yellow or white gold molded rectangular case. ca 1932. 14K white. $110–150
14K yellow 135–175

Hamilton "Andrews". Subsidiary seconds, Grade 401, 19J, 12/0 size movement. 14K yellow or white gold rectangular case. ca 1932.
14K white $100–135
14K yellow 135–165

Hamilton "Greenwich". Luminous numeral dial, subsidiary seconds. Grade 987, 6/0 size, 17J round movement. 14K WGF or YGF molded square case. ca 1933. . . . . . . $35–55

The Flintridge

A New Sports Watch in Two Popular Grades

Here it is—an altogether new sport model—the out-of-doors watch with a *cover!* This cover is operated by a spring in the upper right hand lug. Is serves as a protection against dust and dampness, jolts and jars, and *broken crystals!* Undoubtedly it will find favor with America's sportsmen!

It is available in two grades—Grade 979, Hamilton's finest 19-jewel strap watch, and Grade 987, the popular 17-jewel Hamilton. Case designs for both grades are of 14K solid yellow or white gold only.

Consumer prices:

Grade 979	Grade 987
$150.00	$125.00

Open

When the spring is released the cover flies shut.

Closed

At last there's a place for you to put a monogram !

Patent applied for.

Hamilton "Flintridge". Protective spring cover. Subsidiary seconds, 19J, 6/0 size, 979 movement. 14K gold case. ca 1934. . . . $650—800

Hamilton "Byrd". Raised gold figures or luminous dial. Subsidiary seconds, 19J, 12/0 size, 401 rectangular movement. 14K gold rectangular case. ca 1934 . . . . $135—175

Hamilton "Drake". Raised gold figure dial. Subsidiary seconds, 17J, 6/0 size 987 movement. 10K GF rectangular case. ca 1934. $35—55

Hamilton "Dixon". Raised gold figure or luminous dial. Subsidiary seconds, 17J, 6/0 size 987 movement. 10K GF square case. ca 1934 . . . . $35—55

Hamilton "Cushion B". Luminous, etched or aviation dial. Subsidiary seconds, 19J, 6/0 size 979 movement. 14K GF round case. ca 1934 . . . .$30—50

Hamilton "Langley". Raised gold figure or luminous dial. Subsidiary seconds, 19J, 6/0 size, 979 movement. 14K gold rectangular case. ca 1934. . . . .$135—175

Hamilton "Oakmont". Raised gold figures or luminous dial. Subsidiary seconds, 19J, 6/0 size, 979 movement. 14K gold case. ca 1934 . . . .$110—135

Hamilton "Grant". Raised gold figure or luminous dial. Subsidiary seconds. 19J, 6/0 size 979 movement. 14K GF bowed rectangular case. ca 1934 . . . .$35—55

Hamilton "Lee". Raised gold figure or luminous dial. Subsidiary seconds. 19J, 6/0 size 979 movement. 14K GF rectangular case. ca 1934 . . . .$35—55

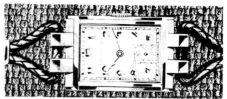

Hamilton "Donovan". Silvered dial with applied gold numerals, subsidiary seconds. 19J, 14/0 size, Grade 982, tonneau movement. Square 14K yellow gold, curved case, with cord lugs. ca 1935. . . . .$125—150

Hamilton "Livingstone". Raised gold hour markers. Subsidiary seconds, 19J, 12/0 size 401 rectangular movement. 14K GF rectangular case. ca 1934 . . . .$50—75

Hamilton "Custer". Silvered applied gold numeral, subsidiary second dial. 14/0 size, Grade 982, 19J tonneau movement. Rounded rectangular 14K gold curved case. ca 1935. . . . .$135—160

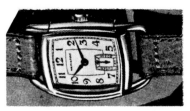

Hamilton "Dodson". Black enamel numeral dial, subsidiary seconds. 17J, 6/0 size, Grade 987 round movement. 10K YGF, molded square case with curved lugs. ca 1935 . $35—65

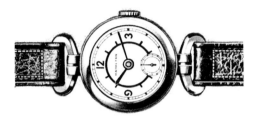

Hamilton "Ellsworth". Black or raised gold numeral dial, subsidiary seconds. Grade 987, 17J, 6/0 size round movement. 10K gold-filled round case, large molded loop lugs. ca 1935. . . . . $100—135

Hamilton "Clark". Silvered dial with applied gold numerals, subsidiary seconds. 17J, 14/0 size, Grade 980 tonneau movement. Slim tonneau, 14K YGF curved case with intergal lugs. ca 1936. . . . . $40—60

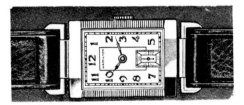

Hamilton "Pierre". Silvered dial with applied gold numerals, subsidiary seconds. 19J, 14/0 size, Grade 982 tonneau movement. Rectangular 14K yellow gold curved case with engraved bezel & large attached lugs. ca 1936 $135—175

Hamilton "Rutledge". 18K applied gold numeral dial and hands. Subsidiary seconds, 19J, 14/0 size 982 movement. 10% iridium platinum rectangular case. ca 1937 . $225—275

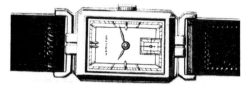

Hamilton "Taylor". Silvered dial with applied gold markers, subsidiary seconds. 17J, 14/0 size, Grade 980 tonneau movement. Rectangular, 14K YGF curved case with large attached lugs. ca 1936. . . . . $50—75

Hamilton "Harris". Applied gold or black enamel numeral dial, Subsidiary seconds, 17J, 6/0 size 987 movement. 10K GF square case. ca 1937 . . . . $35—55

Hamilton "Merritt". Applied gold or black enamel numeral dial. Subsidiary seconds, 17J, 6/0 size 987 movement. 10K GF rectantular case. ca 1937 . . . . $35—55

Hamilton "Dorsey". Applied gold on two-tone inlaid numeral dial. Subsidiary seconds, 19J, 14/0 size 982 movement. 14K gold bowed rectangular case. ca 1937. . . . . . $125—150

Hamilton "Seckron" (Doctor's Watch). Black enamel dial. Subsidiary seconds, 17J, 14/0 size 980-B movement. 14K GF rectangular case. ca 1936 . . . . $175—250

Hamilton "Sutton". Applied gold numeral or inlaid black enamel numeral dial. Subsidiary seconds, 17J, 14/0 size 980 movement. 14K GF rectangular case. ca 1937 . . . . . $75—100

Hamilton "Elliott". Applied gold or inlaid black enamel numeral dial. Subsidiary seconds, 17J, 14/0 size 980 movement. 14K GF square case. ca 1937 . . . . $35—55

Hamilton "Sidney". Applied gold or black enamel numeral dial. Subsidiary seconds, 17J, 6/0 size 987 movement. 10K GF rectangular case. ca 1937 . . . . $75—100

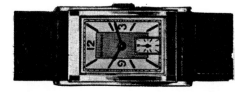

Hamilton "Boone". Applied gold on two-tone gilt inlaid enamel marker and numeral dial. Subsidiary seconds, 17J, 14/0 size 980 movement. 14K gold rectangular case. ca 1937. . . . . $135—165

Hamilton "Contour". (Driver's watch) introduced by Hamilton in Fall 1938. White dial, raised gold numerals. 17J movement. 14K yellow gold-filled, square, curved case. ca 1938. . . . . $75—100

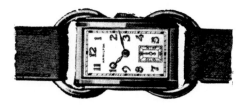

Hamilton "Bentley". Applied gold numeral dial. Subsidiary seconds, 19J, 14/0 size 982 movement. 14K gold rectangular case. ca 1937. $200—250

Hamilton "Dennis". 18K gold numerals on silver dial. 17J, 14/0 size, 980 movement. 10K GF case. ca 1949 . . . . $60—80

Hamilton "Piping Rock". Black enamel bezel with gold Roman numerals. Subsidiary seconds, 17J, round 747 movement. 14K gold bowed rectangular case. ca 1949

14K yellow gold. $375–425
14K white gold 325–375

Hamilton "Boulton". 18K gold numerals on silver dial. 19J, 14/0 size, 982 movement. 14K GF case. ca 1949 . . . . $85–110
Recently reissued and retailed at $295

Hamilton "Neil". 18K gold numerals on silver dial. 17J, 8/0 size, 747 movement. 14K GF round case. ca 1949. . . . .$30–50

Hamilton "Darrell". 18K gold numerals and markers on silver dial. 17J, 8/0 size, 747 movement. 10K gold square case. ca 1949 . .$35–55

Hamilton "Barton". 18K gold numerals on silver dial. 19J, 14/0 size, 982 movement. 14K gold rectangular case. ca 1949. . . . $135–165

Hamilton "Milton". 18K gold numerals and dots on silver dial. 19J, 14/0 size, 982 movement. 14K GF rectangular case. ca 1949. . . . .$35–55

Hamilton "Clinton". Various dials. 17J, 8/0 size, 747 movement. Stainless steel case. ca 1949 . . . .$10–25

Hamilton "Donald". 18K gold numerals on silver dial. 19J, 14/0 size, 982 movement. 14K gold rectangular case. ca 1949. . . . $125–150

Hamilton "Glenn". 11 diamonds on silver dial. 17J, 8/0 size, 747 movement. 14K gold case. ca 1949. . . . . $185–225

HAMILTON ELECTRIC

Hamilton introduced eight case styles in 1958. Seven are illustrated in the first pictures. These watches did not run well and were (and still are) hard to repair. The movement was railroad approved. Two grades, Grades 500 & 505, and later a 5/0 size movement, were used, the 505 being the better one. The chances are good that this watch will become highly collectible in the long run because of it being the world's first electric, low survival rate, and uniquely styled cases.

Hamilton "Sea-Lectric I". Waterproof. Yellow embossed numerals with pearl track dial. Grade 500 Hacking Sweep Seconds battery electric movement. 10K YGF round case, large bar lugs. ca 1958. . . . . $45–65
Bracelet 5–15

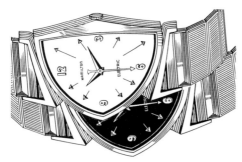

Hamilton "Pacer Electric". 14K gold numerals & markers on white or black sterling silver dial. Grade 500, Hacking Sweep Seconds battery electric movement. 10K tu-tone yellow gold-filled asymmetrical case & white gold-filled lugs. ca 1958. . . . . $100–125
Yellow gold-filled 65– 85
Bracelet 10– 20

Hamilton "Everest Electric". 14K raised gold numerals & dots. Grade 500, hacking sweep second battery electric movement. 10K YGF asymmetrical embossed, bright polished, gold center case. ca 1958 . . . . $35–55
With bracelet 45–65

Hamilton "Spectra Electric". Waterproof. 14K gold numerals & dots with fine black transfer on white dial, or gold lines on black sterling silver dial. Grade 500, hacking sweep second battery electric movement. 14K yellow gold round case. ca 1958. . . . . $175–225

Hamilton "Valiant". Hand applied 14K gold numerals and markers. 22J, adjusted 5 positions movement. Asymmetrical. 10K yellow gold-filled case. ca 1962 . . . . $35–65
Bracelet 3– 8

Hamilton "Titan Electric". Waterproof. 14K gold numerals & markers with pearled track on white or black dial. Grade 500, hacking sweep second battery electric movement. 10K YGF round case. ca 1958. . . . . $75–100
With bracelet 85–110

Hamilton "Van Horn Electric Masterpiece".
Waterproof. 14K gold numerals & markers with
pearled track on white or black sterling silver
dial. Grade 500, hacking sweep second battery
electric movement. 14K yellow gold round
case. ca 1958 . . . . $175—225
With 12-diamond dial. . . . . 250—300

Hamilton "Bradford Masterpiece". Rhodium
plated or black on sterling silver dial, 14K
raised gold dots & numerals, subsidiary seconds.
22J movement. 14K yellow or white gold,
round case. ca 1958. . . . . $125—150
With 11-diamond dial. . . . . 175—225

Hamilton "Golden Tempus Masterpiece". Rhodium plated, 14K gold numerals & markers on a
sterling silver dial with Eastern, Central,
Mountain & Pacific Time Zoned dial. Center
seconds, 18J movement. 14K yellow gold
round case, molded arrow-shaped lugs. ca
1958 . . . . $140—160
With 11-emerald cut diamond dial . 175—225

Hamilton "Astramatic I". Waterproof, luminous dots & pearled track, 14K gold numerals
& markers on a sterling silver dial. 25J movement. 18K yellow gold round case. ca 1958.
. . . . $125—150

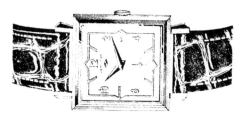

Hamilton "Aldrich Masterpiece". Embossed
markers & raised diamond-shaped rim on
silver dial, 14K gold numerals, subsidiary
seconds. 22J movement. 14K yellow gold
square case, 14K gold buckle. ca 1958.
. . . . $125—150

Hamilton "Sutton Masterpiece". 14K gold
numbers & markers on a sterling silver, tu-tone
dial, subsidiary seconds. 22J movement. 14K
yellow gold square case. ca 1958 . . $125—150

Hamilton "Sir Echo Masterpiece". Rhodium
plated, sterling silver dial. 14K raised gold markers, subsidiary seconds. 22J movement.
Round case with extended lugs. ca 1958.
14K gold. . . . . $125—150
With 2-diamond dial . . . . 150—175

Hamilton "Stormking IV Military". Waterproof, 24 hr. sterling silver dial, pearled track, luminous dots, black numerals & 14K gold markers. 18J movement. 10K YGF round case, stainless steel back ca 1958 ...... $35—60

Hamilton "Automatic K-576 Calendar". Waterproof, luminous markers & dots, embossed numerals, center seconds & date window, 17J movement. Round stainless steel case with heavy lugs. ca 1958 .... $20—35

Hamilton "Seabeach". Waterproof, luminous dial, center seconds, 17J movement. 10K yellow rolled gold plate, round case. ca 1958. .... $15—25

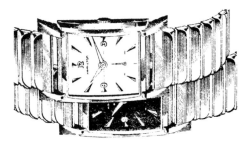

Hamilton "Ventura Electric". 14K gold dots (rhodium plated for white model) on white or black sterling silver dial. Grade 500, Hacking Sweep Second movement. ca 1959.
14K yellow gold. .... $275—350
14K white gold .... 200—300
Add for 6-diamond dial .... 75—100

Hamilton "Trent Medallion Series". Raised 14K gold markers & numerals on rhodium plated, or black on sterling silver dial, subsidiary seconds, 22J movement. 10K YGF or WGF rectangular case, stainless steel back. ca 1958 .... $30—55

Hamilton "Rotomatic III." Waterproof, yellow embossed numerals & markers, luminous dots & pearled track. 23J movement. 10K YGF round case & heavy molded lugs. ca 1958. .... $30—55

Hamilton "Savitar Electric". 14K raised gold numerals & markers. Hacking Center Seconds Grade 505 battery electric movement. 14K gold asymetrical case. ca 1961. .... $175—250

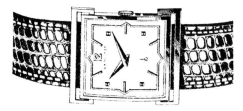

Hamilton "Baton". 14K gold numbers, squares & embossed markers with embossed raised rim on sterling silver dial, subsidiary seconds. 22J movement. 14K yellow gold square case with conforming lugs. ca 1958 . . . . . $150—175

Hamilton "Casino". Rhodium plated silvered dial, subsidiary seconds. 17J movement. 14K yellow or white gold round case. ca 1958. 14K gold . . . . $100—125
With 5-diamond dial . . . . 135—165

Hamilton "Tuxedo Masterpiece". 14K gold, rhodium plated markers on a sterling silver dial. 22J movement. 14K white gold round case with 44-diamond bezel. ca 1958 $450—525

Hamilton "Automatic K-302". Waterproof, yellow embossed numerals, luminous markers & dots with pearled track dial, center seconds. 17J movement. 10K yellow gold case. ca 1958. 10K gold . . . . $100—125
10K top . . . . 50— 75

Hamilton "Courtney Masterpiece". 14K gold, rhodium plated numerals & 6 diamonds on a sterling silver dial. Subsidiary seconds, 22J movement. 14K yellow or white gold square case. ca 1958 . . . . $125—150
With 6-diamond dial . . . . $150—175

Hamilton "Chanticleer Alarm". Waterproof, luminous dial, center seconds, alarm indicator hand & window & reserve power indicator window. 17J movement. 10K YGF round case, stainless steel back. ca 1958 . . . . . . $50—75

Hamilton "Victor Electric". Raised 14K gold dots & numerals on a white or black dial. Grade 500 Hacking Sweep Second battery electric movement. 10K, YGF asymmetrical case. ca 1958 . . . . $35—45
With bracelet . . . . 45—55

Hamilton "Coburn". Embossed dial, subsidiary seconds, 17J movement. 10K yellow rolled gold plated round case, molded extended lugs. ca 1958. . . . . $15—25

Hamilton "Polaris Electric". Silvered dial with gold numerals & markers. Hacking Center Second, Grade 505, 5/0 size, electric movement. 14K gold bezel on stainless steel back, asymmetrical case. ca 1961 . . . . . . $60—90

Hamilton "Vega Electric". Grade 505 Hacking Center Seconds, 5/0 size movement. 14K GF romboid-shape case. ca 1961 . . . . . $35—55
With Band . . . . 65—85

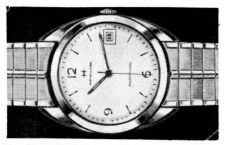

Hamilton "Thinline A-575". Silvered dial with **Calendar** window at 3 & sweep second. Round case. ca 1961. 14K gold . . . $60—95
Stainless steel . . . . 20—40

Hamilton "Thinline T-451". Silvered tutone dial with sweep second. Round case. ca 1961. 14K gold . . . . $60—90
Stainless steel . . . . 15—35

Hamilton "Flight II". Hand applied, 14K gold numerals. 22J, adjusted 5 position movement. 10K yellow gold-filled, asymmetrical case. ca 1962 . . . . $35—55

Hamilton "Dennis". Hand applied, 14K gold numerals and markers. 22J, adjusted 5 position movement. 14K yellow, multi-color gold, rectangle case. ca 1962 . . . . $100—125

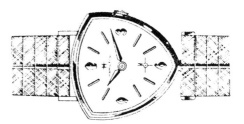

Hamilton "Thor II". Silvered dial. 17J, subsidiary second movement. 10K yellow rolled gold plate, asymmetrical case. ca 1963 . $25—45
Multi-color bracelet . . . . 3— 8

Hamilton "2001". Limited edition for Stanley Kubick's film, "2001: A Space Odyssey". Circular dial in a case of satin-finished chromium 1½ inches wide, with black plastic velcro closing band. Three small windows show month, day & Greenwich Mean Time. 12 Hour movable bezel. A red button at a corner controls the alarm. ca 1963. No sales recorded.
. . . . (?) $500—750

Hamilton "Thin-O-Matic T-403". Grey or gold dial. 17J, sweep second, thin movement. 10K gold-filled, asymmetrical case. ca 1963. $25—45

Hamilton "505 Railroad Special". Silvered full bold black numeral dial with outside 5/60 red minute track. Hacking Center Second Grade 505, 5/0 size electric movement. Round case with heavy lugs & milled bezel. ca 1963. 10K GF top . . . . $75—115
Stainless steel . . . . 65— 85

Hamilton "Natilus 500 Electric". Silvered black numeral dial. Hacking Center Second Grade 505, 5/0 size electric movement. Round stainless steel case. ca 1963 . $35—55

Hamilton "Calendar Automatic". Silvered sweep second dial with **Calendar** window at 6. Round, polished bezel, heavy lug case. ca 1967. 14K gold . . . . $75—100
Stainless steel . . . . 20— 40

Hamilton "Electric". Silvered dial with raised gold numerals. Hacking Center Second Grade 505, 5/0 size electric movement. Cushion case. In 1963 Hamilton was offering 43 differend models & variations of cases for the 505 electric movement. ca
1963. 14K gold . . . . $90—110
10K gold-filled top . . . . 45— 65
Stainless steel . . . . 40— 60

Hamilton "Thinline 2001". Silvered dial with subsidiary seconds. 22J movement. Round milled bezel case. ca 1967. 14K gold . . . . $75—100
14K gold-filled . . . . 25— 45
Stainless steel . . . . 20— 40

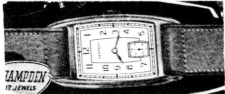

Hampden "Curved Gold Plate". Raised gold numerals, subsidiary seconds. 7J or 17J movement. 10K yellow rolled gold plate, tonneau case. ca 1941 . . . .$35–50

Hampden "Gold Plate". Raised gold numerals, subsidiary seconds. 17J movement. 10K yellow rolled gold plate, tonneau case. ca 1941 $20–35

Hampden "Black Beauty Automatic". Gold numerals on black dial, center seconds. Self-winding, 25J movement. 10K rolled gold plate, tonneau case. ca 1963 . . . . $3–5

Hampden "59 Jewel Automatic". Waterproof. Luminous dial with center seconds. Automatic, 59J movement. Round case. ca 1963.
Yellow gold plated $7–15
Stainless steel 5–10

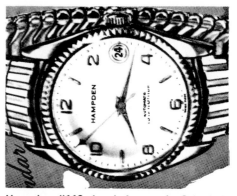

Hampden "110 Jewel Automatic Calendar". Waterproof. Raised markers on luminous dial. Center seconds, date window at 3. Self-winding, automatic, 110J movement. Round yellow gold plated case. ca 1963 . . . .$10–20

NOTE: See American-made Hampden on page 86.

Hampden "Time Tester Chronograph". Black dial, subsidiary seconds, 30 minute recorder with outer telemeter and tachometer rings. 17J movement. Round chrome case & stainless steel back. ca 1970 . . . .$25–50

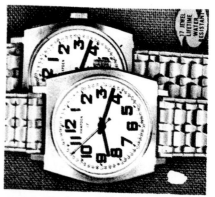

Hampden "Engineer 69". Waterproof. Center seconds. 17J movement. Cushion case. ca 1970. Steel or yellow plated $3–5

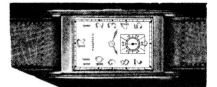

Hampden "Curved Gold Plate". Raised gold numerals, subsidiary seconds. 17J movement. 10K yellow rolled gold plate, rectangular case. ca 1941. . . . .$20—35

Hampden "Curved Gold-Filled". Raised gold numerals, subsidiary seconds. 17J movement. 10K rectangular yellow gold-filled case. ca 1941 . . . .$25—40

Hampden "Plated Top". Raised gold numerals, subsidiary seconds. 7J or 17J movement. 10K yellow rolled gold plate, tonneau case. ca 1941. . . . .$20—30

Hampden "Curved Gold". Raised numerals on dial, subsidiary seconds. 17J movement. 14K yellow gold tonneau case. ca 1941 . $110—135

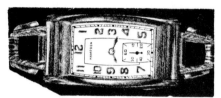

Hampden "Curved Rose Gold-Filled". Raised dial, subsidiary seconds. 17J movement. Rectangular, 10K rose gold-filled case. ca 1941. . . . .$35—50

Hampden "Curved Gold Plate". Raised gold numerals, subsidiary seconds. 17J movement. Rectangular 10K yellow rolled gold plate case. ca 1941. . . . .$25—40

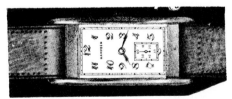

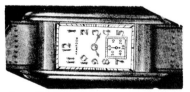

Hampden "Curved Gold-Filled". Raised dial, subsidiary seconds. 17J movement. Rectangular, 10K yellow gold-filled case. ca 1941. . . . .$35—50

Hampden "Curved Gold Plate". Raised gold numerals, subsidiary seconds. 7J or 17J movement. Rectangular 10K yellow rolled gold plate case. ca 1941 . . . .$30—45

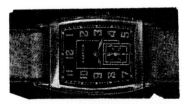

Hampden "Rose Gold-Filled". Raised gold numerals, black dial, subsidiary seconds. 17J movement. 10K rose gold-filled, tonneau case. ca 1941. . . . .$35—50

Hampden "Rose Gold Plate". Raised dial, subsidiary seconds. 7J or 17J movement. 10K rose rolled gold plate ,cushion case. ca 1941. . . . .$30—45

Hampden "Skindiver Calendar Automatic". Waterproof. Black dial, center seconds, date window at 3. Round stainless steel case, black calibrated revolving bezel. ca 1970 . . . . $3—5

Harvard "Chronograph". Silvered duo-dial, 12 hour & 30 minute recorders, center seconds with telemeter & tachometer. 15J movement. Round case. ca 1940. Gold-filled . . . $75—100 Stainless steel . . . . 40— 50

Hampden "Black Beauty Automatic". Gold numerals on black dial. 25J movement. Gold plated, tonneau case. ca 1970 . . . . . $20—35

Harvard "Chronograph". Tu-tone, duo-dial, 12 hour & 30 minute recorders. 15J movement. Round case. ca 1940. Gold-filled . . . . $75—100 Stainless steel . . . . 40—50

Happiness. Ladies, 14K asymmetrical horseshoe case. ca 1923 . . . . $50—85

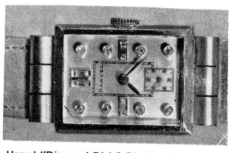

Harvel "Diamond Dial & Platinum". Subsidiary seconds. Platinum rectangular case with large hinged lugs. ca 1940 . . . . $175—225

Happiness. Ladies (Pat. April 10, 1923 by M. Seiger, N.Y.). 14K asymmetrical horseshoe case. ca 1923 . . . . $50—85

Harvel. Day, Date & Month Calendar, subsidiary seconds. Waterproof, 17J movement. Round stainless steel case. ca 1947 . . . $25—45

Harvel "Strap". Tu-tone dial, center seconds. 17J movement. Square, gold-filled case and lugs. ca 1947. . . . . $10—15

Harvel "Gold Strap". Subsidiary seconds. 17J movement. 14K gold, faceted tonneau case. ca 1947 . . . . $100—125

Harwood. Self-winding, luminous Arabic numerals & hands. 9K gold, 29mm. tonneau case. $200—250

Harwood. Self-winding, white matte dial, movement signed "Harwood Self-winding Watch Co., Ltd." Hands set by rotating bezel. 9K gold, 28mm. round case with beveled edges. . . . . $200—250

Harwood Luxor. Luminous Arabic numerals & hands. 9K gold, 29mm. cushion case. . . . . $200—250

Helbros "Lorelei". Ladies. 6J movement. 10K gold-filled, engraved octagonal case with matching band. ca 1930 . . . . $10—25

Helbros "Sophomore". Ladies. Oval dial, 6J movement. 10K gold-filled, enameled tonneau ribbon case. ca 1930 . . . . $20—30

Helbros. Ladies. Round dial. 17J movement. Gold-filled tonneau case. ca 1946 . . . . . $8—16

Helbros "Jack Mulhall". Luminous hands & numerals, subsidiary seconds. 6J movement. 10K gold-filled, engraved rectangular case. ca 1930. . . . . $25—45

Helbros "Milton Sills". Luminous numerals & hands, subsidiay seconds. 6J movement. 10K gold-filled, engraved rectangular case. ca 1930. . . . . $25—50

Heyworth "Automatic". Silvered dial, luminous hands & markers, center seconds. Yellow rolled gold plate round case. ca 1949 . . . . . $10—15

Heyworth "Date". Tu-tone dial. Raised gold numerals, luminous hands & dots, center seconds, date window at 3. 17J movement. Round case, chrome top, stainless steel back. ca 1949 . . . .$10—15

Heyworth "Alarm". Raised gold numerals, center seconds, red alarm hand. 17J movement. Round case with chrome top & stainless steel back. ca 1949 . . . .$20—35

Hoffres "Monterey". Ladies. Engraved silver dial. 6J or 15J, 6½''' movement. Tu-tone green and white gold plate, tonneau case. ca 1928. . . . .$25—35

Hoffres "18K White Gold, Diamond & Emerald Bracelet". Ladies. 15J, 5½''' movement. 10 diamonds and 12 emeralds set in an 18K white gold, tonneau case, with 14K pierced white gold bracelet. ca 1928 . . . . $160—220

Hoffres "18K White Gold & Platinum Diamond Bracelet". Ladies. 17J, 5½''' movement. 16 diamonds in case with 14K pierced white gold bracelet. ca 1928 . . . . $225—275

Hoffres "Diamond, Emerald, Gold & Platinum Bracelet". Ladies, 17J, 5½''' movement. 16 diamonds and 16 synthetic sapphires set in 18K white gold and platinum case, with a 14K white gold pierced bracelet. ca 1928. . . . $325—400

Hoffres "14K White Gold, Diamond & Sapphire Bracelet". Ladies, 15J, 5½''' movement. 14K white gold, tonneau case with attached pierced bracelet. ca 1928 . . . . $160—220

Hoffres "Marguerite". Ladies. Engraved silver dial, 15J, 6½''' movement. Red or green enamel inlay on white rolled gold plate, tonneau case with jeweled stem. ca 1928 . . . . . . $15—25

Huguenin "Ladies Diamond & Gold Cord". Rectangular case set with diamonds & single lugs. ca 1966. . . . . $175—225

Huguenin "Calendar". Center seconds & date window. 14K yellow gold round case. ca 1966.
. . . . $125—150

Huguenin. White dial, raised gold markers. Wide molded, 18K gold, square case. ca 1966.
. . . . $140—175

Hyde Park "Moonphase Calendar". Center seconds, day & month windows with outer date ring. 12''', 17J movement. Round stainless steel case. ca 1950 . . . . $80—120

Hyde Park "Chronograph". Radium silvered dial, subsidiary seconds & 30 minute recorder with outer tachometer ring. Round chrome case with steel back. ca 1953 . . . . $50—75

Hy. Moser & Cie "Sun and Moon Salto-Fix". Sun and moon indicates the hour through a window on a 12-Hour dial, beginning and ending at 6, with a conventional minute hand. Sweep second hand that beats seconds. Stop watch timing. By pushing the crown in, the sweep second hand stops without stopping the movement. ca 1955.
14K yellow gold. . . . . $300—400
Stainless steel . . . . 150—200

Hy. Moser & Cie "Jumping Second Salto-Fix". Silvered dial, sweep second hand that beats seconds. Stop watch timing. By pushing the crown in the sweep second hand stops without stopping the movement. Round stainless steel case. ca 1954 . . . . $50—75

HYDE PARK

Supplied to the trade by Emil Leichter Watch Co., New York, NY. a full line of designs and case metals for both men and women.

Hyde Park "Man's Gold". Subsidiary seconds. 17J movement. Square, 14K yellow gold case. ca 1946. . . . . $110—135

ILLINOIS WATCH COMPANY
Springfield, Illinois
1869 to 1927

Hamilton bought the Illinois Company in 1927 and continued to operate in Springfield until 1933, and was then moved to Hamilton's main plant at Lancaster, Pa.

Illinois entered the wrist watch market about 1914 with ladies watches converted from their line of pocket watches. The first two illustrations are two styles of many offered during this period (1914–1925), which consisted of square, round, cushion, decagon, hexagon, cut-corner, etc., in solid gold and gold-filled, silver and base metal. Illinois (like most all other watch companies in the U.S.A.) offered to the trade uncased movements. Slowly at first, Illinois cased, timed and boxed wrist watches at the factory. Later, as rectangle and baguette movements were developed, case styles changed.

After about 1934, Illinois wrist watch advertisements disappeared and did not reappear until the mid-1950's when Hamilton offered wrist watches with the Illinois name on them. Many Hamilton wrist watches in the 400 Grade Series were made with Illinois movements with Hamilton markings that were either made from unfinished stock or of new manufacture.

We have illustrated all of the factory cased Illinois case styles of which we are aware. As far as we can tell, there has not been any organized collecting of Illinois wrist watches at this time, and, as with all other companies, many Illinois wrist watches can be bought for less than the values shown here. There are some very high quality and beautiful Illinois movements.

Ron Starnes of Tulsa, Oklahoma gave us a lot of help with the Illinois section.

NOTE: The watches that were cased and timed at the factory were supplied with matching convertible bracelets and boxes but are not included in the values above. Illinois also sold movements only for custom cased watches.

Illinois "Ladies Ribbon". Dials various colors and finishes. Made in both 15J 6/0 size Grade 903, and 19J 6/0 size Grade 907, round movements. Open face with subsidiary seconds, hunting without. Case shapes include round, tonneau, cushion, decagon, hexagon and square, in various metals with matching ribbons and factory boxes. Ribbon & box not included in values. ca 1914 to 1925.

14K green gold	$60–80
14K yellow gold	60–80
14K yellow gold-filled	20–40
Silver	20–40

Illinois "Ladies Convertible". Dials various colors and finishes. Made in both 15J 6/0 size Grade 903, and 19J 6/0 size Grade 907. Round movements. Open face with subsidiary seconds, Hunting without. Case shapes are round, cushion, hexagon and decagon, in various metals. ca 1914 to 1925.

14K green gold	$60–80
14K yellow gold	60–80
14K green gold-filled	20–40
14K yellow gold-filled	20–40
Silver	20–40

Illinois "Redonda". Ladies. Hexagonal dial. Grade 807, 17J, 18/0 size movement. 14K gold-filled, tonneau case with black & light red enameling. ca 1928 . . . . $25–40

"Mary Todd". Ladies. Engraved dial. 807, 17J, 18/0 size movement. 18K w. .e gold, engraved tonneau case with black enamel. This watch was made in at least four similar case styles. ca 1928 . . . . . . $75–100

Illinois "Bar Harbor". Ladies. Square dial. Grade 807, 17J, 18/0 size movement. White gold, engraved tonneau case. ca 1928. . $45–65

Illinois "Berkshire". Ladies. Grade 807, 17J, 18/0 size movement. 14K white gold-filled, engraved rectangular case. ca 1928 . . . $20–30

Illinois "Berkeley". Ladies. Tu-tone hexagonal dial. Grade 807, 17J, 18/0 size movement. 14K white gold, tonneau case with green & black enameling. ca 1928 . . . . $35–55

Illinois "Long Beach". Ladies. Hexagonal dial. Grade 807, 17J, 18/0 size movement. 14K gold-filled, engraved tonneau case. ca 1928. . . . . $20–35

Illinois "Newport". Ladies. Engraved tonneau dial. Grade 807, 17J, 18/0 size movement. 14K white gold-filled, engraved tonneau case. ca 1928 . . . . $20–35

Illinois "Edgewater". Ladies. Square dial. Grade 807, 17J, 18/0 size movement. 14K white gold-filled, engraved tonneau case. ca 1928 . . . . $20–35

Illinois "Narragansett". Ladies. Engraved dial with inlaid enamel numerals. Grade 807, 17J, 18/0 size movement. Engraved tonneau case. ca 1928. . . . . $50–75

Illinois "Del Monte". Ladies. Square dial. Grade 807, 17J, 18/0 size movement. 14K white gold-filled tonneau case with white & black enameling. ca 1928 . . . . $25–40

Illinois "Biloxi". Engraved tonneau dial. Grade 807, 17J, 18/0 size movement. 14K gold-filled faceted tonneau case. ca 1928 . . . . . $25–35

Illinois "Beverly". Same as above except solid 14K gold case $50–75

Illinois "Lenox". Ladies. Grade 807, 17J, 18/0 size movement. 14K white or yellow gold, octagonal case. ca 1931 . . . . $40–60

Illinois "Biloxi". Same as above except 14K gold-filled $20–30

Illinois "Daytona". Hexagonal tu-tone dial. Grade 807, 17J, 18/0 size movement. 14K gold, engraved & polished tonneau case. ca 1928.
. . . .$45—65

Illinois "Fairport". Ladies. Oval dial. Grade 807, 17J, 18/0 size movement. Gold-filled, engraved tonneau case. ca 1931 . . . . . $20—35

Illinois "Coronado". Ladies. Tu-tone inlaid enamel dial. Grade 807, 17J, 18/0 size movement. 14K gold, tonneau case inlaid with black enamel. ca 1928. . . . .$45—75

Illinois "Avalon". Ladies. Grade 807, 17J, 18/0 size movement. 14K gold, plain rectangular case. ca 1931. . . . .$40—65

Illinois "Roslyn". Ladies. Rectangular dial. Grade 807, 17J, 18/0 size movement. Gold-filled tonneau case with engraving & black enameling. ca 1931 . . . .$20—35

Illinois "Brighton". Ladies. Oval dial. Grade 807, 17J, 18/0 size movement. 14K gold, tonneau case, engraved & enameled in black. ca 1931. . . . .$50—75

Illinois "Argyle". Ladies. Grade 807, 17J, 18/0 size movement. 14K gold, molded rectangular case. ca 1931 . . . .$45—65

Illinois "Claudette". Ladies. Grade 805, 15J, 18/0 size movement. 14K white or yellow gold, molded rectangular case. ca 1932 . . . . $20—30

Illinois "Glencoe". Ladies. Grade 807, 17J, 18/0 size movement. 14K gold-filled, engraved rectangular case with faceted corners. Also sold in a plain case. ca 1931 . . . .$40—60

Illinois "Suzette". Ladies. Grade 107, 17J, 21/0 size movement. 14K white gold-filled, vertically lined rectangular case. ca 1932.
. . . .$20—30

Illinois "Glenna". Ladies. Grade 805, 15J, 18/0 size movement. 14K white gold-filled, molded tonneau case. ca 1932. . . . . . $25—35
Bracelet . . . . 5—10

Illinois "Florette". Ladies. Rectangular dial. Grade 105, 15J, 21/0 size movement. 14K white or yellow gold-filled, molded tonneau case. ca 1932 . . . . $20—30

Illinois "Florentine". Ladies. Tu-tone dial. Grade 805, 15J, 18/0 size movement. 14K white gold-filled, molded & engraved tonneau case. ca 1932 . . . . $20—35

Illinois "Debutante". Ladies. Grade 805, 15J, 18/0 size movement. 14K white or yellow gold-filled, engraved & molded rectangular case. ca 1932. . . . . $20—35

Illinois "Constance". Ladies. Grade 807, 17J, 18/0 size movement. 14K gold-filled, tu-tone rectangular case. ca 1932. . . . . $20—30

Illinois "Babette". Ladies. Grade 105, 15J, 21/0 size movment. 14K white gold, engraved, rectangular case. ca 1933. . . . . $40—60

Illinois "Arlene". Ladies. Tu-tone dial. Grade 805, 15J, 18/0 size movement. 14K white gold, molded rectangular case. ca 1933. $45—65

Illinois "Rosette". Ladies. Grade 107, 17J, 21/0 size movement. 14K white gold-filled, molded rectangular case & matching bracelet. ca 1933. . . . . $20—35
Bracelet . . . . 5—10

Illinois "Muzette". Ladies. Grade 107, 17J, 21/0 size movement. 14K white gold-filled, vertically lined, molded rectangular case. ca 1933 . . . . $20—30

Illinois "Lady Mary". Ladies. Grade 805, 15J, 18/0 size movement. Plain pattern, molded sterling silver case. ca 1933 . . . . $20—30

Illinois "Juliette". Ladies. Grade 107, 17J, 21/0 size movement. 14K white or yellow gold-filled, engraved rectangular case with faceted corners. ca 1933 . . . . $20—30

Illinois "Vardon". Ladies. Grade 807, 17J, 18/0 size movement. 14K white gold, molded rectangular case & double lugs. ca 1932 $35—50

Illinois "Marilyn". Ladies. Grade 807, 17J, 18/0 size movement. 14K white or yellow gold-filled, molded rectangular case. ca 1932 $20—30

Illinois "Queen Anne". Ladies. Grade 805, 15J, 18/0 size movement. Sterling silver, molded & engraved rectangular case. ca 1932.
. . . . $25—40

Illinois "Lynette". Ladies. Grade 105, 15J, 21/0 size movement. 14K white gold-filled, carved rectangular case. ca 1932 . . . . $20—30

Illinois "Princess". Ladies. Rectangular dial. Grade 805, 15J, 18/0 size movement. White 14K gold, engraved tonneau case. ca 1932 $35—55

Illinois "Janette". Ladies. Rectangular dial. Grade 105, 15J, 21/0 size movement. 10K white gold-filled, faceted tonneau case. ca 1932 . . . . $20—30

Illinois "Patricia". Ladies. Grade 807, 17J, 18/0 size movement. 14K white or yellow gold-filled, engraved tonneau case with single lugs. ca 1932. . . . . $20—30

Illinois "Hollywood". Ladies. Grade 805, 17J, 18/0 size movement. 14K white or yellow gold-filled, engraved & faceted tonneau case. ca 1932. . . . . $20—30

Illinois "Joan". Ladies. Square dial. Grade 807, 17J, 18/0 size movement. 14K white gold-filled, molded & faceted tonneau case. ca 1932.
. . . . $25—35

Illinois "Gloria". Ladies. Grade 805, 17J, 18/0 size movement. 14K yellow or white gold-filled, vertically lined, molded rectangular case. ca 1932 . . . . $20—30

Illinois "Irene". Ladies. Grade 805, 15J, 18/0 size movement. Molded rectangular case with extended, molded large lugs. ca 1933. . $20—30
Bracelet . . . . 5—10

Illinois "Beverly". Ladies. Grade 805, 15J, 18/0 size movement. 14K or 10K white or yellow gold-filled, engraved rectangular case. ca 1933. . . . . $20—35

Illinois "Military Style". Glass enamel or luminous dial. 11, 15 or 17J, 0 size round movement. Round silver, 20 Yr. GF or 25 Yr. GF case. ca 1917 . . . . $25—40

Illinois "Admiral Evans". Luminous dial. 3/0 size, round movement. Octagon jointed silver case. ca 1918. 7J . . . . $25—40
15J . . . . 30—45

Illinois "Off Duty". Bold silvered dial, subsidiary seconds. 3/0 size, 17J, Grade 307 movement. Waterproof, 14K WGF round case, with stars on bezel. ca 1927 . . . . $25—45

Illinois "Marquis". Luminous or plain dial, subsidiary seconds. 6/0 size, 17J, Grade 607 movement. 14K GF tonneau case, plain or engraved bezel, oxidized WGF or tu-tone white & green gold filled case & matching buckle. ca 1927 . . . . $100—125
Gold Filled buckle . . . . 5—10

Illinois "Beau Brummel". Plain or radium dial. 6/0 size, 17J, round, Grade 607 movement. Plain or oxidized, 14K WGF or YGF, tonneau case, with engraved bezel & matching buckle. ca 1928. . . . . $45—65

Illinois "Bennett". Radium hands & numerals on a silvered dial with subsidiary seconds. 6/0 size, 19J, Grade 907, round movement. 14K WGF, square cut corner case. ca 1928 . $55—75

Illinois "Maxine". Luminous dial & hands, subsidiary seconds. 3/0 size, 17J, Grade 307 movement. Tivoli quality gold filled octagonal shaped case with matching buckle. ca 1928
.... $45—65
Gold filled buckle............. 5—10

Illinois "Biltmore". Plain or radium silvered dial. 18/0 size, 17J, rectangular, Grade 807 movement. Plain, rectangular, 14K green or white gold filled case. ca 1930..... $50—75

Illinois "Stephen". Silvered dial with radium hands & numerals. 6/0 size, 15J, Grade 605, round movement. Square, engraved Scepter, green or white gold filled case. ca 1928 $45—65

Illinois "Consul". Plain or radium silvered dial. 6/0 size, 21J, round, Grade 601 movement. 14K solid white oxidized gold tonneau case with engraved bezel & matching 14K buckle. ca 1930. 14K............... $150—200
14K buckle.............. 25— 45

Illinois "Ronald". Silvered dial with luminous numerals & hands. 3/0 size, 17J, Grade 24, round movement. Diamond shape green or white, Stellar, gold filled case. ca 1928. $45—65

Illinois "Frontenac". Radium silvered dial, subsidiary seconds. 12/0 size, 17J, Grade 207 movement. 14K WGF or YGF, plain rectangular case. ca 1930............. $45—65
With GF band.............. 55—75

Illinois "Beau Monde". Sterling silver, 18K applied gold numeral dial, subsidiary seconds. 6/0 size, 21J, round Grade 601 movement. 14K WGF or YGF, tonneau case with engraved bezel. ca 1930............... $55—80

Illinois "New Yorker". Luminous or plain silvered dial, subsidiary seconds. 6/0 size, 17J, Grade 607 movement. 14K white or yellow oxidized gold filled, engraved rectangular case with matching buckle. ca 1930.. $55—75
Gold Filled buckle........... 5—10

Illinois "Jolly Roger". Radium dial, subsidiary seconds. 3/0 size, 17J, Grade 307 movement. 14K plain white or oxidized white gold filled, molded cushion case. ca 1930 . . . . . $55–80
Gold Filled buckle   5–10

Illinois "Medallist". Radium or plain silvered dial, subsidiary seconds. 12/0 size, 17J, Grade 207 movement. 14K WGF or YGF faceted rectangular case. ca 1930. . . . .$45–65

Illinois "Manhattan". Radium silvered dial, subsidiary seconds. 6/0 size, 21J, Grade 601 movement. 14K WGF or YGF, engraved rectangular case & metal band. ca 1930 . .$45–65
Gold-filled band. . . . .$ 8–15

Illinois "Major". Luminous dial, subsidiary seconds. 3/0 size, 17J, Grade 307 movement. 14K oxidized WGF tonneau case, engraved or plain bezel. ca 1930. . . . .$45–60

Illinois "New Yorker". Luminous or plain silvered dial, subsidiary seconds. 6/0 size, 17J, Grade 607 movement. 14K YGF or WGF rectangular case with extended lugs & matching buckle. ca 1930 . . . . $45–65
Gold Filled buckle   5–10

Illinois "Speedway". Silvered luminous or plain dial, subsidiary seconds. 3/0 size, 17J, Grade 307 movement. 14K plain or oxidized WGF, engraved tonneau case & matching buckle. ca 1930 . . . .$45–65
Gold filled buckle.   5–10

Illinois "Mate". Radium dial, subsidiary seconds. 3/0 size, 17J, Grade 307 movement. 14K plain or oxidized WGF tonneau case with fancy engraved bezel & matching buckle. ca 1930 . . . .$40–60

Illinois "Skyway". Standard aeronautical dial, subsidiary seconds. 3/0 size, 17J, Grade 307 movement. Dust-proof screw back, 14K WGF, round case, star bezel & extra strength crystal. ca 1930. . . . .$45–60

Illinois "Ritz". Etched dial, subsidiary seconds. 6/0 size, 17J, Grade 607 movement. 14K, tutone, gold filled tonneau case, yellow bezel. ca 1930. . . . . $100—135

Illinois "Tuxedo". Ladies' or mens' watch, radium silvered dial. 18/0 size, 17J, Grade 807 movement. 14K green or white solid gold, curved & engraved, rectangular case. ca 1930.
14K White . . . . $150—200
14K Green . . . . 175—225

Illinois "Ensign". Silvered dial, subsidiary seconds. 6/0 size, 15J, Grade 607 movement. 14K gold filled, oxidized white or plain white tonneau case, with fancy engraved bezel & matching buckle. ca 1930 . . . . $45—65
Gold filled buckle. . . . . 5—10

Illinois "Blackstone". Plain or radium octagonal silvered dial. 6/0 size, 17J, round, Grade 607 movement. 14K WGF or YGF octagonal case with extended lugs. ca 1930 . . . . $50—75

Illinois "Piccadilly". Silvered dial, subsidiary seconds. 6/0 size, 17J, Grade 607 movement. 14K WGF, molded oval case, matching buckle. ca 1930. . . . . $75—115
Gold Filled buckle . . . . 10—15

Illinois "Chieftain". Plain or radium silvered dial, subsidiary seconds. 6/0 size, 15J, round, Grade 607 movement. 14K WGF or YGF, engraved tonneau case. ca 1930 . . . . $80—110

Illinois "Townsman". Radium silvered dial, subsidiary seconds. 6/0 size, 17J, Grade 607. 14K, **tu-tone** gold filled, engraved cushion case, yellow bezel. ca 1930 . . . . . . $75—100

Illinois "Special". Luminous dial & hands, subsidiary seconds. 3/0 size, 17J, Grade 307 movement. 14K gold filled cushion case. ca 1931 . . . . $30—45

Illinois "Viking". Luminous dial & hands, subsidiary seconds. 3/0 size, 17J, Grade 307 movement. 14K WGF, molded tonneau case. ca 1931. . . . .$35—55

Illinois "Cavalier". Silvered dial, subsidiary seconds. 6/0 size, 17J, round, Grade 607 movement. 14K WGF or YGF tonneau case. ca 1932. . . . .$40—55

Illinois "Ardsley". Snow white finished dial with black enamel numerals, subsidiary seconds. 12/0 size, 17J, Grade 207, rectangular movement. 14K WGF or YGF, curved rectangular case. ca 1931 . . . . $55—75

Illinois "Commodore". Etched silver dial with black numerals, subsidiary seconds. 6/0 size, 15J, round, Grade 607 movement. Square, 14K WGF or YGF case. ca 1932 . . . .$35—55

Illinois "Futura". Luminous dial, subsidiary seconds. 12/0 size, 17J, Grade 207, rectangular movement. 14K WGF or YGF, molded rectangular case. ca 1931 . . . . $75—100

Illinois "Ensign". Luminous dial, subsidiary seconds. 6/0 size, 17J, Grade 607 movement. 14K white or green gold filled, tonneau case with rope engraved bezel. ca 1932 . . .$45—65

Illinois "Arlington". Silvered dial, subsidiary seconds. 6/0 size, 15J, Grade 607 round movement. 14K WGF or YGF, molded rectangular case. ca 1932 . . . . $35—55

Illinois "Finalist". Silvered dial, subsidiary seconds. 12/0 size, 17J, Grade 207 movement. 14K white or natural yellow gold filled, faceted & engraved rectangular case. ca 1932. .$45—65

Illinois "Hudson". Applied figured dial, subsidiary seconds. 12/0 size, 17J, Grade 207 movement. 14K WGF or YGF, plain rectangular case. ca 1932 . . . . $45—65

Illinois "Beau Royale". Silvered dial, subsidiary seconds. 6/0 size, 15J, round, Grade 607 movement. 14K WGF or YGF tonneau case, with engraved bezel. ca 1932 . . . . . . $55—85

Illinois "Kenilworth". Silvered dial, subsidiary seconds. 12/0 size, 17J, Grade 207 movement. 14K WGF or YGF tonneau case. ca 1932. . . . . $65—85

Illinois "Wembley". Etched dial, subsidiary seconds. 12/0 size, 17J, Grade 207 movement. 14K WGF or YGF, faceted rectangular case. ca 1932. . . . .$45—65

Illinois "Trophy". Plain or luminous silvered dial, subsidiary seconds. 12/0 size, 17J, Grade 207 movement. 14K WGF or YGF, plain rectangular case. ca 1932. . . . . $45—65

Illinois "Chesterfield". Etched silver dial. 12/0 size, 17J, rectangular, Grade 207 movement. Tu-tone, 14K WGF and YGF, rectangular, trimmed case. ca 1933 . . . . $100—135

Illinois "Baronet". Sterling silver dial, subsidiary seconds, with 14K applied numerals. 6/0 size, 21J, round, Grade 607 movement. 14K White or yellow gold, molded rectangular case. ca 1932. 14K white. . . . . . . $125—175
14K yellow . . . . 155—190

Illinois "Derby". Silvered dial, subsidiary seconds. 17J, Grade 607 movement. 14K YGF tonneau case. ca 1933 . . . . $35—55

Illinois "Hawthorn". Silvered dial, subsidiary seconds. 17J, Grade 607 movement. 14K WGF or YGF, molded rectangular case & matching buckle. ca 1933 . . . . $35—55

Illinois "Gallahad". Luminous dial, subsidiary seconds. 12/0 size, 17J, Grade 207 movement. 14K WGF or YGF tonneau case. ca 1933. . . . . $75—100

Illinois "Larchmont". Silvered dial, subsidiary seconds. 17J, Grade 207 movement. 14K WGF, faceted rectangular case. ca 1933 . . . $35—55

Illinois "Rockliffe". Applied numeral dial, subsidiary seconds. 12/0 size, 17J, Grade 207 movement. 14K WG or YG' tonneau case. ca 1933. 14K white gold . . . . $150—200
14K yellow gold . . . . 175—225

Illinois "Vernon". Etched silvered dial, subsidiary seconds. 12/0 size, 17J, Grade 207 movement. 14K WGF or YGF, faceted rectangular case & wide link band. ca 1933 . . . . $40—60
Bracelet . . . . 8—15

Illinois "Potomac". Square dial, subsidiary seconds. 6/0 size, 15J, Grade 607 movement. 10K WGF or YGF, molded rectangular case. ca 1933. . . . . $45—60

Illinois "Bostonian". Silvered, bold numeral dial, subsidiary seconds. 6/0 size, 15J, round, Grade 607 movement. 14K WGF or YGF, square case with matching bracelet. ca 1933. . . . . $35—55
Head only . . . . 35—50

Illinois "Pimlico". Luminous or plain silvered dial, subsidiary seconds. 15J, Grade 607 movement. 14K white gold-filled or yellow gold-filled tonneau case. ca 1933 . . . . . . $45—65
Gold-filled bracelet . . . . 7—15

Illinois "Valedictorian". Etched dial, subsidiary seconds. 6/0 size, 17J, Grade 607 movement. 14K, **tu-tone** gold filled white bezel & back, tonneau case, open link band. ca 1933. . . . . $100—125
Bracelet only . . . . 8—15

Illinois "Westchester". Plain or radium silvered dial, subsidiary seconds. 12/0 size, 17J, Grade 207, rectangular movement. 14K WGF or YGF case with metal band. ca 1933. . . . $55—75
Bracelet only . . . .   8— 15

Illinois "Caprice" Purse Watch. Silvered dial, 6/0 size. 17J, round, Grade 607 movement. Gold filled inner case, covered with snake or ostrich . . . . $75—95

Illinois "Wentworth". Silvered luminous or plain dial, subsidiary seconds. 12/0 size, 17J, Grade 207 movement. 14K YGF or WGF. rounded rectangular case. ca 1933 . . . $55—75

Illinois "Coquette" by Hamilton. Ladies. Waterproof. White dial, 17J movement. Molded square gold-filled case, single molded lugs. ca 1954. . . . . $8—14

Illinois "Beau Geste". Etched silver dial, subsidiary seconds. 6/0 size, 15J, round, Grade 607 movement. 14K WGF tonneau case with engraved bezel. ca 1933. . . . . $45—65

Illinois "Lady H" by Hamilton. Waterproof. White dial, 17J movement. Molded square gold-filled case with single lugs. ca 1954 .$8—14

Illinois "Lady Gay B" by Hamilton. White dial, 17J movement. Square gold-filled, molded case with single fancy lugs. ca 1954 . . . . . $10—15

Illinois "Andover". Etched silver dial, subsidiary seconds. 12/0 size, 17J, Grade 207, rectangular movement. 14K WGF or YGF rectangular case. ca 1933. . . . . $55—80

Illinois "Lady Gay" by Hamilton. White dial, 17J movement. Molded, gold-filled square case with single lugs. ca 1954 . . . . . $10—20

Illinois "Career Girl" by Hamilton. Ladies. Waterproof. White dial, center seconds. 17J movement. Round, gold-filled case, single molded lugs. ca 1954 . . . . $10—15

NOTE: Read Page 6 before using this book to value your wrist watch.

Illinois "Automatic" by Hamilton. Waterproof. White dial, luminous hands & markers, center seconds. 17J movement. Round gold-filled case. ca 1954 . . . . $15—25

Illinois "Golden Treasure" by Hamilton. Ladies. White dial, 17J movement. Square gold-filled case, fancy molded single lugs. ca 1954. . . . .$7—15

NOTE: All values are given for the head only unless the bracelet is included in the description.

Illinois "Signamatic" by Hamilton. Automatic with reserve power indicator. Waterproof. White dial, center seconds. 17J movement. Round gold-filled case. ca 1954 . . . . .$20—35

Illinois "Career Girl" by Hamilton. Ladies. Round dial, luminous hands & markers, center seconds. 17J movement. Round gold-filled case. ca 1954. . . . . $10—15

Illinois "Debonair E" by Hamilton. Waterproof. White dial, center seconds. 17J movement. Heavy, round molded gold-filled case. ca 1954 . . . . $20—35

Illinois "Lady Gay G". by Hamilton. White dial, 17J movement. Molded, gold-filled square case with single lugs. ca 1954 . . . .$7—12

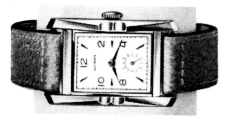

Illinois "Topper B" by Hamilton. Waterproof. White dial, 17J movement. Gold-filled, molded rectangular case. ca 1954. . . . .$20—35

Imperial "Doctors or Nurses". Luminous dial, center seconds. 10½''', 7J or 17J movement. Round case. ca 1940. Rolled gold plate $20–25
Stainless steel 15–20

Illinois "Debonair" by Hamilton. Waterproof. White dial, subsidiary seconds. 17J movement. Gold-filled, molded round case. ca 1954.
. . . . $15–25

Imperial "Doctors or Nurses". Luminous hands & numerals, center seconds dial. 10½''', 15J movement. Faceted rectangular case. ca 1940. 10K gold-filled $20–25
Stainless steel 15–20

Illinois "Nautilus" by Hamilton. Waterproof. White dial, center seconds, 17J movement. Round gold-filled case. ca 1954 . . . . . $15–30

Index-Mobile, Split-Second tachometer chronograph, 1000m. base. Silver dial, subsidiary seconds & 30 minute register. 34mm. round stainless steel case. $375–425

Illinois "Debonair" by Hamilton. Waterproof. White dial, subsidiary seconds. 17J movement. Molded square case, extended lugs. ca 1954.
14K gold $100–125
14K Gold-filled 20–35

Illinois "Topper A" by Hamilton. Waterproof. White dial, subsidiary seconds. 17J movement. Gold-filled, scalloped rectangular case. ca 1954.
. . . . $20–35

Ingersoll "Rist-Arch". Silvered dial, subsidiary seconds. 2J movement. Curved chromium-finished, molded tonneau case. ca 1940.
. . . . $ 7–10
With Box. 10–30

Ingersoll "Lassie". Ladies. Silvered dial, subsidiary seconds. Chromium-finished tonneau case, single lugs. ca 1940 . . . .$ 7—10
With box . . . . 10—35

Ingersoll "Midget". Plain or radiolite silvered paper or metal dial, subsidiary seconds. 6 size, round pin lever movement. Stainless chromium finished round case with plain bezel. ca 1930.
. . . .$20—30
With box . . . . 30—40

NOTE: Read Page 6 before using this book to value your wrist watch.

Ingersoll "Midget". Silvered paper or metal dial, subsidiary seconds. 6 size, round pin lever movement. Stainless chromium finish, round case. ca 1912 . . . .$20—30
With box . . . . 30—40

Ingersoll "Mite". Silvered dial. Ingersoll advertised "Every Mite Must Pass the 4 Position, 192 Hours of Dependable Timekeeping". 0S, round chromium finish case with wire lugs. ca 1930. . . . .$10—20
Complete mint watch & box . . . . . . 20—30

NOTE: All values are given for the head only unless the bracelet is included in the description.

Ingersoll "Radiolite". Radium hands & numerals on black or white dial. 6S, pin lever movement. Round nickel silver case with wire lugs. ca 1924. . . . .$20—35
Complete mint watch & box . . . . . . 30—50

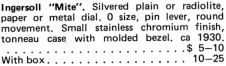

Ingersoll "Mite". Silvered plain or radiolite, paper or metal dial. 0 size, pin lever, round movement. Small stainless chromium finish, tonneau case with molded bezel. ca 1930.
. . . .$ 5—10
With box . . . . 10—25

Ingersoll "Alden". Radium silvered dial, luminous hands & numerals. 7J, 6/0 size movement. Green or white rolled gold plate, cushion case. ca 1927. . . . .$ 5—10
With box . . . . 10—20

Ingersoll "Climax". Plain or radiolite dial, subsidiary seconds. Chromium-plated cushion case. ca 1932 . . . . $ 7—10
With box . . . . 10—30

Ingersoll "Compact". Black dial, luminous hands & markers. Tu-tone enamel, chromium-finished case. ca 1936 . . . . $10—20
With box . . . . 25—45

Ingersoll "Mite". Luminous dial, subsidiary seconds. Chromium metal round case. ca 1932.
. . . .$ 7—10
With box . . . . 10—30

Ingersoll "Swagger". Silvered dial, subsidiary seconds. Chromium-finish, molded tonneau case. ca 1940 . . . . $ 7—10
With box . . . . 10—30

Ingersoll "Aero". Etched metal dial, subsidiary seconds. Chromium-finished, embossed bezel. ca 1936 . . . .$ 7—10
With box . . . . 10—30

Ingraham. Silvered dial. Pin lever rectangular movement. Engraved chromium tonneau case. ca 1931. . . . .$ 5—10
With box . . . . 10—35

Ingersoll "Topper". Round silvered dial. Chromium-finished tonneau case. ca 1936.
. . . .$ 7—10
With box . . . . 10—35

International W. Co. "Schaffhausen". Ladies, round, 18K gold case and applied dial indexes. ca 1951. . . . . $175—225

International Watch Co. Ladies. 18K gold, 23mm. round case with diamond bezel. ca 1970 . . . . $500—600

International W. Co. "Schaffhausen".. Round stainless steel case with 18K gold applied figures and indexes. ca 1951 . . . . . $75—100

International Watch Co. Curvex tank, white matte dial, gold numerals. 17J movement. 18K gold angular curvex case, 44mm. . . $500—550

International Watch Co., Geneve. Center seconds. 18K gold, 32mm. moulded square case. ca 1955 . . . . $500—600

International Watch Co. 18K gold, 36mm round case. ca 1950. . . . . $150—200

International Watch Co. 30mm. 18K gold moulded square case . . . . $450—550

International "Gold Automatic". Silvered dial with applied gold markers and hands. 21J, sweep second, self-winding movement, with 46 hour reserve. Round, 14K yellow gold case (Schaffhausen, Switzerland). ca 1952 $125—150

Itraco. Moonphase, calendar, center seconds, day & month windows with outer date ring. Round GF case with steel back . . . $150—175

Jacquet Droz. Tachometer chronograph base 1000m, subsidiary seconds & 30 minute register. Silver finished dial. 17J movement. Round GF case with steel back $35–45

Jaeger Le Coultre. Bi-coloured ladies, gold dial, 15J, 5½''' movement. 18K gold & platinum, 39x15mm. rectangular case. ca 1940. . . . . $500–600

Jaeger Le Coultre. Modern ladies 18K gold, 19x26mm. rectangular case with diamond shoulders. $1,000–1,100

Jaeger Le Coultre. Signed black dial, inscribed Duoplan. 14K gold, 36x17mm. rectangular moulded case with back winder . . . $250–350

Jaeger Le Coultre. Ladies, black dial, 18K gold oval case with double rowed diamond bezel. 25mm. ca 1975 . . . . $1,200–1,400

Jaeger Le Coultre "Reverso". Retailed by **Walser Wald.** Sweep second, black dial. 15J movement. Rectangular, 33mm. case. ca 1935. 18K gold $1,300–1,400
Stainless steel 350– 450

Jaeger. 18K gold rectangular case with moulded strap lugs, 16x35mm., winder on back plate. ca 1930. . . . . $400–600

Jaeger Le Coultre. Moonphase calendar. Silvered dial, subsidiary seconds, day & month windows with outer date ring. 18K gold, 35mm. round case. ca 1945 . . . . . $750–850

Jaeger Le Coultre. Moonphase, calendar, subsidiary seconds, day & month windows with outer date ring. Plain GF 45mm. tank case with red enameled bar numerals on bezel
. . . . $1,050—1,350

Jaeger Le Coultre & Vacheron & Constantin. Black dial signed "Le Coultre", with diamond studded bar numerals & diamond 'mystery' hour & minute indicators. 14K gold, 33mm. round case. ca 1960. . . . . $375—450

Jaeger Le Coultre. Automatic, center seconds with state of wind indicator. 9K gold 33mm. round case. ca 1953. . . . . $200—250

Jaeger Le Coultre, Automatic. Calendar, center seconds & date window. 18K gold, 34mm. round case. ca 1968. . . . . $225—250

Jaeger Le Coultre. Automatic, subsidiary seconds & state of wind. 18K gold round case with back wind. ca 1955 . . . . . . $350—450

Jaeger Le Coultre. 18K gold round case with mesh strap . . . . $700—800

Jaeger Le Coultre "Memovox". Black dial, center seconds, window date, 18K gold round case. ca 1955 . . . . $400—500

Jaeger Le Coultre. Modern wood veneer dial, 18K gold, 25x32mm. rectangular case. .
. . . . $350—400

Jovis. Ladies. 6''' movement. 14K gold, engraved oval case. ca 1924 . . . .$60–75

Junghans "Nobrk". Shockproof, luminous dial, octagon, nickeled case. ca 1928 . . . . . .$5–10

Junghans "Nobrk". Shockproof, luminous dial, round nickeled case. ca 1928 . . . .$5–10

Jules Jurgensen "Ladies Cord Platinum & Diamond". Art Deco design rectangular case. ca 1930. . . . . $300–375

Jules Jurgensen "Ladies Cord Platinum & Diamond". Art Deco design rectangular case. ca 1930. . . . . $350–400

Junghans "Nobrk". Shockproof, luminous dial, cushion, nickeled case. ca 1928 . . . . .$5–10

Jules Jurgensen "Ladies Cord Platinum & Diamond". Art Deco design rectangular case. ca 1930. . . . . $375–425

Jules Jurgensen "Diamond & Platinum". Ladies, 17J movement. Square platinum case and geometric lugs, set with diamonds. ca 1937. Value varies according to size, quality and color of diamonds $300–375

Junghans "Nobrk". Shockproof, luminous dial, barrel or tonneau, nickeled case. ca 1928 $5–10

Jules Jurgensen "Ladies Gold". 17J movement. 14K gold, molded rectangular case and single lugs. ca 1937. . . . .$30–50

Jules Jurgensen "Gold Cord". Ladies, 17J movement. 14K gold, rectangular case and single lugs. ca 1937 . . . . $30—50

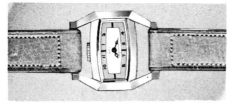

Jules Jurgensen "Ladies Gold". Tu-tone dial. 17J movement. 14K gold geometric case. ca 1937 . . . . $80—120

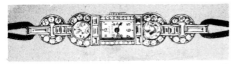

Jules Jurgensen "Diamond & Platinum". Ladies, 17J movement; Rectangular platinum case and lugs set with diamonds. ca 1937. Value varies according to size, quality and color of diamonds. . . . . $600—800

Jules Jurgensen "Minute Repeater". Brushed white dial, raised gold numerals, subsidiary seconds. 29J lever movement, repeating by a slide opposite the crown. 18K gold cushion case. . . . . $4,500—5,500

Jules Jurgensen "Gold Tank". 17J movement. 18K gold rectangular case. ca 1937 . $150—200

Jules Jurgensen. White matte dial with silver bars. 14K gold rectangular case set with diamonds on two sides. . . . . $200—225

Juvenia "Clover". Ladies. Gold-finished dial. Gold-filled, 22mm. cloverleaf-shaped case. ca 1957 . . . . $15—20

Juvenia "Jumper". Silvered dial with raised gold numerals. Rectangular, 14K gold, ladies case, with massive hinged strap lugs. ca 1949. $150—200

Juvenia "Sweep Second". Silvered dial. 14K gold tonneau case. ca 1949 . . . . . $125—150

Juvenia "Mystere". Transparent face & back. Red hands on jet black center rim. 17J movement. Thin, yellow gold-filled round case, 3 sizes. ca 1957. 30mm. . . . . $40—45
28mm. . . . . 35—40
22mm. . . . . 30—35

Juvenia "Gentry". Black dial, center seconds. Veri-thin 33mm., round stainless steel case. ca 1957. . . . . $20—25

Juvenia "Planete". Dial with three multi-color discs to mark hours, minutes & seconds. Round rolled gold plate, 19mm. case. ca 1957. $35—50

Juvenia. Champagne dial. 14K gold square, 22mm., case, with woven gold band. ca 1980.
. . . . 20% over gold

Juvenia Watch Co. Skeletonized, 16J gold movement exposed through glazed back. Numbers on bezel. 18K, 33mm round case.
. . . . $1,200—1,300

Kelbert "Claire". Ladies, 17J movement. Square case, molded lugs set with oriental rubies. ca 1942. Platinum . . . . . . $100—120
Gold . . . . 80—100
Gold-filled . . . . 25— 40
Polished steel . . . . 20— 35

Kelbert "Sweetheart". Ladies, 15J movement. Heart shaped case with single lugs. ca 1942. Platinum . . . . $100—120
Gold . . . . 80—100
Gold-filled . . . . 25— 40
Polished steel . . . . 20— 35

Kelbert "Kelomatic". Center seconds. Round steel case. ca 1951 . . . . $10—20

Koehn, Ed. Ladies. 18J movement. Rectangular platinum & diamond case. ca 1928 . $250—350 Value varies according to size & quality of stones.

Kelton "Dexter" (by Ingersoll). Subsidiary seconds, 2J movement. 10K rolled gold plate tonneau case & stainless metal back. ca 1940. . . . . $ 5—10
With box. . . . . 10—25

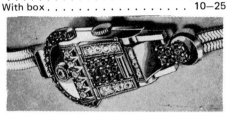

Koehn, Ed "Platinum, Diamond & Emerald". Ladies, 18J movement, 5 adjustments. Platinum rectangular case & lugs set with 70 diamonds & 8 Oriental emeralds. ca 1928. . . . . $800—1,200

Kingston. Ladies Hunting. Platinum "Art Deco" designed case set with diamonds and rubies. ca 1945 . . . . $800—1,000

Koehn, Ed "Platinum, Diamond & Emerald Bracelet". Ladies, 18J movement, 7 adjustments. Platinum tonneau case & lugs, set with 6 square, 4 baguette, 2 pentagon, 2 triangle-cut diamonds, and 20 Oriental emeralds. ca 1928. . . . . $6,500—7,500

Kingston "14-Diamond Dial". Subsidiary seconds. 17J movement. 14K gold square case and large link mesh bracelet. ca 1947. . $60—75

Koehn, Ed "Platinum & Diamond Bracelet". Ladies, 18J movement, 5 adjustments. Platinum tonneau case and lugs, set with 284 round and 2 triangle-cut diamonds. ca 1928.$4,250—5,250

Kingston "Date-O-Fix Moonphase Calendar". Subsidiary seconds, day & month windows with outer date ring. Round 14K gold case. ca 1959 600-700
Gold-filled top. . . . . 100—150

Kody "Multi". Ladies interchangeable bracelet watch, illustrated with 14K gold flexible snake band. Also could be converted to chatelaine, purse, or pocket, and a choice of wrist bands. 14K gold head, with heavy, arched crystal. ca 1949. 14K head only . . . . . . $150—200

Koehn, Ed "Platinum, Diamond & Sapphire". Ladies, 18J movement, 7 adjustments. Rectangular case set with 58 round and 2 marquise-cut diamonds & 40 Oriental sapphires. ca 1928. . . . . $1,750—2,000

Koehn, Ed "Platinum, Diamond & Sapphire". Ladies, 18J movement, 5 adjustments. Platinum rectangular case set with 58 diamonds and 24 Oriental sapphires. ca 1928 . . . $1,600–2,200

Koehn, Ed "Platinum, Diamond & Emerald". Ladies, 18J movement with 5 adjustments. Platinum rectangular case and lugs, set with 80 diamonds and 36 Oriental emeralds. ca 1928. . . . . $2,600–2,900

Koehn, Ed. Ladies. Plain round dial. 18J movement. Platinum, skeleton-type tonneau case. Roman numerals inlaid in round enamel bezel. ca 1929. . . . . $225–275

Koehn, Ed. Ladies. 18J movement. Platinum rectangular case. ca 1929. . . . . . . $125–150

Koehn, Ed "Sport". Ladies. Silvered dial. Platinum horseshoe case, stirrup lugs. ca 1930. . . . . $135–175

Koehn, Ed. "Man's Enamel". Plain dial. 18J movement. Square platinum case, numerals enameled on bezel. ca 1928 . . . . . $375–475

Koehn, Ed, Geneva. Silvered dial (various styles), subsidiary seconds. 18J rectangular movement. 46x24mm. platinum, unmarked, American contract case. ca 1928 . . $375–450

Koen, E., Geneva. Hunting case, subsidiary seconds. 18K gold, 28x42mm. rectangular case. ca 1930. . . . . $900–1,200

Kreisler & Co. Ladies rectangular platinum case set with diamonds, with matching band. ca 1928. Price varies according to size & quality of diamonds.

Kreisler & Co. Ladies. Rectangular platinum case set with diamonds & emeralds, matching band. ca 1928. Price varies according to size & quality of diamonds.

LaFond "Platinum & Diamond". Ladies, 17J movement. Platinum tonneau case, set with 24 diamonds. ca 1930 . . . . $250–350

Lamont "Automatic Lieutenant's Lady". Waterproof. Subsidiary seconds. 17J, self-winding movement. Round stainless steel case. ca 1946. . . . . $10—20

Lathin "Ladies Diamond & Gold". 14K gold square case, heavy cord lugs. ca 1946. Value varies according to size, quality and color of diamonds. . . . . $125—150

Lamont "Compensamatic". Luminous numerals & hands, subsidiary seconds. 17J, self-winding movement. Round stainless steel case. ca 1943. . . . . $10—20

Lathin "Ladies Diamond & Gold". 14K gold square case with extended lugs. ca 1946. Value varies according to size, quality and color of the diamonds. . . . . $150—200

Lamont. Silvered dial with radium hands & numerals, center seconds. 17J movement. Round, 14K yellow gold case. ca 1945. . . . . 10% over gold value

Lathin "Automatic". Luminous hands & numerals. Center seconds. 14K yellow gold round case. ca 1946 . . . . $100—125

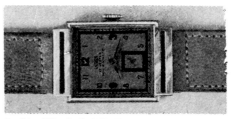

Lathin "Man's Gold". Tu-tone gold finish dial, subsidiary seconds. 14K yellow gold rectangular case. ca 1946 . . . . $125—150

Landeron-Hahn "Chronograph". White dial, radium hands, subsidiary seconds, 30 minute recorder, with outer tachometer ring. 17J movement. Round stainless steel case. ca 1949. . . . . $25—40

LeCoultre. Ladies, 5½''', 15J movement. 19½K white gold rectangular case and single lugs set with 8 diamonds. ca 1930 . $100—125

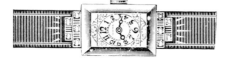

LeCoultre. Ladies. Engraved dial. 5½''', 15J movement. 19½K gold rectangular case and graduated lugs set with 10 diamonds. ca 1930.
. . . . $125—150

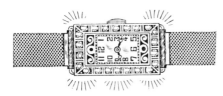

LeCoultre. Ladies, 5½''', 15J movement. 19½K gold rectangular case set with 22 diamonds & 18K gold mesh bracelet. ca 1930 . . $200—250

LeCoultre. Ladies. Engraved dial. 5½''', 15J movement. 14K white gold, enameled and engraved rectangular case. ca 1930 . . .$40—60

LeCoultre. Ladies. 5½''', 15J movement. 19½K white gold, engraved and enameled rectangular case. ca 1930 . . . . $60—85

LeCoultre. Ladies. Engraved dial, 5½''', 15J movement. 19½K white gold, engraved and enameled rectangular case and lugs set with 2 diamonds. ca 1930 . . . . $75—100

LeCoultre. Ladies. 5½''', 15J movement. 19½K white gold, engraved and enameled rectangular case. ca 1930 . . . . $75—100

Le Coultre "Ladies Strap". Black arched dial with gold numerals. Unusually high arched crystal. 17J movement. 14K yellow gold rectangular case with heavy lugs. ca 1939.
. . . . $250—350

LeCoultre. Ladies. Silvered dial with raised gold numerals. 17J movement. 14K white or yellow gold rectangular case with heavy cord lugs. ca 1939. . . . . $150—175

LeCoultre. Ladies. Silvered dial with applied gold numerals. 17J round movement. 14K yellow or white gold, round case, with attached 14K gold bracelet. ca 1939.
. . . . 10% to 25% over gold value

LeCoultre "Irma". Ladies. 14K gold rectangular case with engraved diamond design & single lugs. ca 1950. . . . 10% to 20% over gold value

LeCoultre "Duchess". Ladies. Faceted gold-filled rectangular case with single lugs. ca 1950.
. . . .$30—50

LeCoultre "Flair". Ladies. 14K gold geometric design, rectangular case. ca 1952.
. . . . 15% to 25% over gold value

LeCoultre "Backwind". Ladies. Round platinum or 14K gold case and braided bracelet. ca 1952.. 10% to 20% over gold or platinum value

LeCoultre . Silvered dial. 6¾''', 15J movement. Oxidized 14K white gold-filled, Wadsworth rectangular case, and gold-filled Kreisler mesh bracelet. ca 1930. Head only . . . . . $25—35
Bracelet . . . .   4— 8

LeCoultre "World's Smallest Watch in 1952". Ladies. Less than one-third the width of a dime. Rectangular platinum strap case. ca 1952.
. . . . $400—600

LeCoultre. Silvered dial with plain or radium numerals. 9¼''', 15J movement. Enameled 14K white gold-filled, Wadsworth tonneau case. Gold-filled Kreisler mesh bracelet. ca 1930. Head only . . . . $30—45
Bracelet . . . .   4— 8

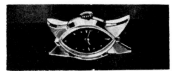

LeCoultre "Marquise". Ladies. Black or white dial. 14K gold, marquise case with bow-style lugs. ca 1952. . . . 10% to 20% over gold value

"LeCoultre "Caprice". Ladies. 14K gold swirl design case. ca 1952 10% to 20% over gold value

Le Coultre "Reverso". Silver dial, subsidiary seconds, 17J, 8''' movement. 38x23 polished steel rectangular case. ca 1935. . . . $225—325

LeCoultre "Judy—Hunting". Ladies. 14K gold round case. ca 1952 10% to 20% over gold value

LeCoultre "Coral Hunting". Ladies. 14K gold square case. ca 1952 10% to 20% over gold value

Le Coultre. Tu-tone gold tinted dial with black numerals. 14K yellow gold square case with raised lugs. ca 1939 . . . . $175—250

LeCoultre "Moonphase Calendar". Subsidiary seconds, day & month windows with outer date ring. 18K gold round case. ca 1952 . $800–900
Gold filled 225–275

LeCoultre "Aristocrat". Silvered dial, man's with subsidiary seconds. Gold-filled, wedge-shaped case. ca 1952. Man's $45–65
Ladies 35–50

LeCoultre "Beau Brummell". Plain white dial. 14K gold round case with hour markers on bezel. ca 1950 . . . . $175–250

LeCoultre. Black dial, man's with subsidiary seconds. Molded, gold-filled rectangular case. ca 1952. Man's $45–65
Ladies 35–50

Le Coultre "Automatic". Silvered dial with gold markers and hands. Round, 17J, 493 movement. Round, 27mm. case. ca 1957. GF . . . . $ 25– 40
14K gold 125–150

LeCoultre "Automatic H". Tu-tone silvered dial, center seconds. Gold-filled square case. ca 1952. . . . .$55–75

LeCoultre "Automatic". Center seconds & re-serve power indicator window. Round 14K gold case. ca 1950 . . . . $150–200
Gold-filled 35– 50

LeCoultre "Royale Automatic". Tu-tone silvered dial. Center seconds. 18K gold round case with engraved bezel. ca 1952. . $150–200

LeCoultre "Automatic Mark 7". Silvered tu-tone dial, center seconds, applied markers & power indicator window at 12. 17J, self-winding movement. Round case with molded and raised, heavy lugs. ca 1952. 14K .$175—225
Gold-filled . . . .   50— 70

LeCoultre "Pomp and Circumstance". Silvered dial, man's with subsidiary seconds. Gold-filled square case. ca 1952. Man's . . . .$45—65
Ladies . . . .   35—50

LeCoultre "Coronet". Silvered tu-tone dial, man's with subsidiary seconds. Round gold-filled case. ca 1952. Man's . . . .$50—70
Ladies . . . .   35—50

Le Coultre "Memovox Alarm". Silvered dial with a turning-disc alarm indicator. Round, 814 or 489, 17J nickel, sweep second movement. Round, 35mm. case. ca 1955. GF. . $ 50— 75
Stainless steel . . . .   40— 60
14K gold . . . . 250—300

LeCoultre "Alarm". Tu-tone silvered dial with rotating disc to set alarm. Two crowns on a round case with heavy molded lugs. ca 1952.
18K gold . . . . $300—375
Gold-filled . . . .   50— 75

LeCoultre "Moonphase Calendar". Subsidiary seconds, day & month windows and date ring. Gold-filled rectangular case with hours calibrated on bezel. ca 1950 . . . . $1,100—1,400

Le Coultre "Powermatic". Silvered dial with polished raised markers, reserve power indicator window at 12. Sweep second, self-winding movement. Round case with heavy lugs. ca 1954. 14K yellow gold . . . . $200—250
14K gold-filled . . . .   60— 85
Stainless steel . . . .   50—100

Le Coultre. 14K gold cufflinks . . . $600–800

Le Coultre. Black dial signed "Duoplan". 18K gold, 22x35mm. rectangular case with moulded sides $275–350

Lemania "Chronograph". This gold chronograph was sold with a rating certificate from the Observatory at Neuchatel. In 336 hours of testing in 7 positions, the watch must not vary more than a fraction of a minute, to be awarded the certificate. Sweep second tachometer base 1 mile. 1/5 second chronograph with subsidiary seconds, 30 minute & 12 hour recorders. Round case with heavy lugs. ca 1947. 14K yellow gold $300–375
Stainless steel 100–125

Le Coultre "Futurematic". Silvered dial with gold hands & hour markers. Subsidiary seconds & reserve power indicator. 12 ligne, round, nickel, 497 self-winding movement, with back set and hacking device. Round, 35mm. case. ca 1956. GF . . . . $ 60– 85
14K gold 250–300

LEONARD BY NEW HAVEN

Le Coultre & Co. "Coin-Form". Matte white dial, 18J movement, folding into a 1904 U.S. $20 gold piece, 1-3/8" $1,200–1,500

Leonard. Radium, bold numeral dial. 6S, pin lever movement. Round, silver nickel or gun metal case with wire lugs. ca 1922. Complete mint watch & box. $30–50

Le Coultre & Vacheron Constantin, Orbital model. Dial signed Le Coultre, with diamond set bar numbers & diamond stud minute & hour indicators. 14K gold, 33mm. round case. ca 1960 . . . . $375–450

Leonard "Strap". Silvered dial. 6S, pin lever movement. Round, silver nickel or gun metal case with wire lugs. ca 1922 . . . . . . $20–35
Complete mint watch & box. 30–50

Leonidas. Moonphase calendar, chronograph. Day and month windows, with outer date ring. Round case. ca 1949. 18K gold . . . $550—650
Gold-filled . . . . 125—150
Stainless steel . . . . 100—125

Leonidas. Calendar, chronograph, subsidiary seconds, 30 minuted & 12 hour register. Day & month windows with outer date ring. 18K gold 37mm. round case . . . . $200—250

Le Shan "Diamond & Platinum". Ladies, 18J movement. Platinum rectangular case & lugs, set with 2 large and 10 small, square-cut diamonds, and 90 round diamonds. ca 1930.
. . . . $2,250—2,500

Levy-Wander "Duo-Style Purse". Luminous numerals on dial. Rectangular case with faceted corners. ca 1926. Chrome plated . . . . $15—20
Rolled gold plate . . . . 15—20

Lip "Man's Strap". Subsidiary seconds. Tonneau case. ca 1930. 14K gold . . $175—250
Gold-filled . . . . 20— 30
Silver . . . . 15— 25
Nickel . . . . 5— 10

Locust. Subsidiary seconds. 10½''', 15J movement. White rolled gold plate, tonneau case. ca 1930. . . . . $8—16

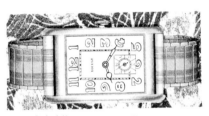

Locust. Subsidiary seconds. 9¾''', 15J movement. Curved rectangular, white rolled plate case. ca 1930 . . . . $15—30

Locust. Center seconds. 10½''', 15J movement. White rolled plate, tonneau case. ca 1930.
. . . . $10—20
White woven mesh bracelet . . . . 2— 3

Locust. Round dial, subsidiary seconds. 10½''', 15J movement. Rectangular skeleton-type, white rolled gold plate case, round black enameled bezel with Roman numerals. ca 1930.
. . . . $35—55
White mesh, adjustable bracelet . . . . . 2— 3

Longines. Ladies. 14K gold & diamond rectangular case, semi-precious stone-set lugs. ca 1929. . . . . $200—250

Longines. Ladies. Rectangular engraved, platinum & enamel case. ca 1929. . . . . $100—150

Longines "Ladies Platinum & Diamond". Rectangular case set with 16 baguette-cut diamonds. ca 1930 . . . . $600—800

Longines. Ladies. Rectangular platinum case set with diamonds and semi-precious stones, hinged lugs. ca 1928. . . . . $550—650

Longines "Ladies Presentation Watch". Round dial, 17J movement. 14K gold tonneau case, 6-diamond set single lugs. ca 1936 . $125—175

Longines "Delilah". Ladies 17J movement. 14K gold-filled tonneau case. ca 1936 . $10—20

Longines "Miramar L". Ladies. White dial, 18K gold applied markers. 14K gold square case & large linked bracelet. ca 1954.

. . . . $275—350

Longines "Diamond Coronation". Ladies. White dial, 18K gold applied figures. 18K white gold case. 34-diamond bezel. ca 1954 $150—175

Longines "Starlight Sonata". Ladies 18K white gold reound case and "V" lugs set with 28 round and 4 baguette diamonds. ca 1957. . . . . $325—400

Longines "Eldorado, Gold Bracelet". Ladies. 14K gold square case with semi-bracelet. ca 1957 . . . . 10% to 20% over gold value

Longines "Starlight Concerto". Ladies. 14K gold square case and triangular lugs set with 4 diamonds. ca 1957 . . . . $75—95

Longines "Fashion, Gold". Ladies. 14K gold round lugs and molded leaf lugs. ca 1957. . . . . $50—75

Longines "Starlight Splendor". Ladies. 14K white gold oval case with extended lugs set with 24 diamonds. ca 1957 . . . . . $200—250

Longines "Starlight Serenade". Ladies. 14K white gold round case, swirl lugs, set with 6 diamonds. ca 1957 . . . . $100—125

Longines. 14K gold rectangular case with faceted corners & thin lugs. ca 1919. . .$50—75

Longines. Luminous hands & numerals, subsidiary seconds. Square tank case. ca 1923.
18K gold . . . . $150—175
14K gold . . . . 110—125
Gold-filled . . . . 20— 25

Longines Watch Co., retailed by Tiffany & Co. Silvered dial, luminous numerals. 18K gold, tonneau case. ca 1925 . . . . $250—275

Longines. Subsidiary seconds. 17J movement. 14K yellow gold, round case. ca 1928.
. . . . $160—200

Longines. Subsidiary seconds. 17J movement. 18K yellow gold, faceted rectangular case. ca 1928. . . . . $150—175

Longines. Silvered radium dial. 15J movement. White or green gold square case. ca 1928.
18K gold . . . . $140—180
14K gold . . . . 115—135

Longines. Silvered radium dial, subsidiary seconds. 15J movement. White or green gold rectangular case with faceted corners. ca 1928.
18K gold . . . . $140—170
14K gold . . . . 125—155

Longines. Luminous hands & numerals, subsidiary seconds. 14K gold rectangular case with hidden lugs. ca 1928 . . . . $135—165

Longines. Luminous hands & numerals, subsidiary seconds. 15J movement. Cushion case. ca 1928. 14K gold . . . . $85—125
Gold-filled . . . . 15— 25

Longines. Silver finish diamond numeral and baguette cut diamond dial, 17J movement. **Platinum,** curved rectangular, unmarked, 20x50mm., American contract case. ca 1928. . . . . $475—525

Longines. Silvered radium dial, subsidiary seconds. 15J movement. 14K white gold, curved tonneau case. ca 1928 . . . . $150—175

Longines. Silvered baguette diamond dial, 17J movement. **Platinum,** 25x33mm. round, unmarked American contract case, with pyramid form extended lugs. ca 1928. . . . . $350—400

Longines. Silvered radium dial, subsidiary seconds. 15J movement. 14K white or green gold rectangular case. ca 1928. . . . . $135—175

Longines. Gold finished dial, subsidiary seconds. 17J movement. **Platinum,** 20x41mm. moulded rectangular, unmarked American contract case. ca 1928 . . . . $300—350

Longines. Silvered radium dial, subsidiary seconds. 15J movement. 14K white gold, rectangular case with faceted corners. ca 1928. $135—175

Longines "Aero Bremen". Luminous hands & numerals, subsidiary seconds. 10/0 size movements. 14K white gold curved tonneau case. ca 1928. . . . . $150—175

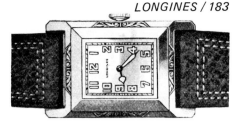

Longines. Luminous hands & numerals. 14K gold molded, embossed rectangular case. ca 1929 . . . . $150—200

Longines. Silver radium dial, subsidiary seconds. 15J movement. 14K white or green gold, curved rectangular case. ca 1928 . . $150—200

Longines. Doctors Watch. Subsidiary seconds, 18K rose gold rectangular case with chamfered sides. 19x33 mm . . . . $700—800

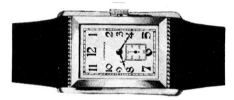

Longines. Subsidiary second. 14K gold molded rectangular case. ca 1929. . . . . . . $135—175

Longines "George Washington". Subsidiary seconds, 17J movement. 14K gold, hand-made tonneau case. ca 1936 . . . . $135—175

Longines. Subsidiary seconds. 14K gold rectangular case set with semi-precious stones on two sides. ca 1929 . . . . $250—300

Longines "David Crockett". Tu-tone dial, subsidiary seconds. 17J movement. 14K gold-filled, molded rectangular case. ca 1936. . . . .$35—55

Longines. Luminous hands & numerals. 14K gold rectangular case with corners faceted into lugs. ca 1929. . . . . $150—175

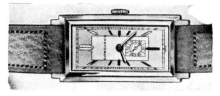

Longines "Men's Presentation Watch". Tu-tone dial, subsidiary seconds. 17J movement. 14K gold, molded rectangular curved case. ca 1936. . . . . $160—190

LONGINES—WEEMS SECOND—SETTING WATCH

It is practically impossible to build a commercial timepiece which will keep time to the exact second under the conditions met in a ship or in an airplane. The unavoidable variation in the chronometer from true time has necessitated an extra calculation in navigation to compensate for this chronometer error. Lt. Commander P.V.H. Weems, U.S.N. (Retired), and formerly instructor in navigation at Annapolis, saw that in an airplane moving at speeds of 200 to 300 miles an hour or more the time required for calculating chronometer error was a hazard that should be eliminated. Since it is impractical because of high gear ratio to set the second hand to the dial, Commander Weems hit upon the idea of setting the dial to the hands. The seconds dial in the center of the large watch is rotated by the small stem. On the small watch the second-setting dial is marked on the outer bezel which is rotated by hand and then locked into position by an outer stem.

USE: The hour and minute is set on the watch in the usual way. For navigation purposes the Greenwich Civil time is set directly on the watch face. When being set with a radio time signal which comes in on the minute, the seconds dial is rotated to keep the 60 mark continuously under the second hand. The dial is stopped the instant the signal is heard. For serious navigation, a record should be kept of the errors and of the daily rate as indicated by movement of the seconds dial. The Longines-Weems Second-Setting Watch is made in two styles.

The smaller model is useful not only for sea and air navigators and airline pilots, but particularly for those working in radio broadcasting and others, such as civil engineers requiring exact time.

(1940 Longines Advertisement)

The small Weems Second-Setting watch is shown at the top of the next column.

Longines—Weems Second—Setting Watch. 15J movement. **Large Model, 47mm.,** stainless steel round case. ca 1940. . . . Estimate—$600—800

Longines—Weems Seconds—Setting Watch. (See description above). 15J, sweep second movement, with rotatable bezel. **Small Model, 30mm.** case. ca 1940.

14K yellow gold.	Estimate—$300—400
14K yellow gold-filled . .	Estimate— 150—200
Stainless steel	Estimate— 100—150

LINDBERG—LONGINES HOUR ANGLE WATCH

HISTORY: During his study of navigation under Commander P.V.H. Weems, Col. Charles A. Lindbergh conceived the idea of adding new features to the Weems Second-Setting watch to simplify finding the Greenwich hour angle of an observed celestial body. The Lindbergh-Longines Hour-Angle Watch eliminates three steps in navigation—1. compensation for chronometer error; 2. conversion of hours into degrees and minutes of arc; 3. calculation of the equation of time of the observed body.

DESCRIPTION: The main dial of the watch is marked in units of both time and arc (1 o'clock—15 deg.; 2 o'clock—30 deg. etc.); the center "second-setting dial" is read in seconds of time or minutes of arc (4 sec.= 1 min. of arc.; 8 sec.=2 min. of arc. etc.). This center dial is rotatable by means of a second stem. The outer bezel, rotatable by hand, covers 15 degrees of arc with 15 min. subdivisions.

USE WITH THE SUN: The watch is regulated and set to Greenwich Civil time to the second by rotating the center seconds dial as necessary. The plus or minus value of the sun's equation of time is determined from the nautical almanac and set on the watch face as follows: The outer bezel is rotated to the left for a plus and to the right for a minus equation of time. The inner seconds dial is rotated to left or right to increase or decrease seconds to set the proper seconds for the equation of time. The Greenwich hour angle is then read directly from the watch face as follows: read from the hour hand on the fixed dial increments of 15 deg.; add to this the degrees and increments of 15' read from the minute hand on the outer movable bezel.

Add to these two values the minutes read from position of second hand on inner dial.

USE WITH STARS: The watch is rated and set to the exact Greenwich Sidereal time which gains 3' 56.6s. per day on Civil time. Then read the Greenwich Sidereal time in arc from the watch face as described for the sun. Apply to this reading the right ascension in arc of the observed star and this gives the Greenwich Hour Angle of the Star. If the watch is rated to Greenwich Civil time a conversion table is necessary to convert the readings into Sidereal time.

The Lindbergh-Longines Hour-Angle watch is illustrated in its original large, 48mm. form below. This watch has been the most popular working watch of aviators in day-in and day-out flying.

The smaller model shown below was designed for daily use as a personal timepiece and may be used, as well, as a navigating instrument in the most exacting service.

(1940 Longines Advertisement)

Longines "Lindbergh Hour-Angle Watch". 15J pin set movement. Sweep second hand. The silvered inner circle dial can be set by pulling out the crown. The bezel with engraved calibrations moves for setting. Outer chapter ring is enameled, with Roman numerals. 180 degrees is in blue. **Large Model, 47mm.** round case. ca 1940. 18K yellow gold Estimate—$2,000—2,500
Silver . . . . Estimate— 1,200—1,400
Stainless steel . . . . . Estimate— 1,000—1,200

Longines "Lindbergh Hour-Angle Watch". (See full description above). 15J movement. **Small Model, 30mm.** round case. ca 1940.
18K yellow gold. . . . Estimate—$1,000—1,200
14K yellow gold-filled Estimate— 400— 500
Stainless steel . . . . . Estimate— 200— 300

LONGINES NAUTICAL STOPSECOND WATCH (HACKING)

The Longines Nautical Watch is constructed on the Longines Stopsecond Flyback movement and was developed in cooperation with the U.S. Lighthouse Service for use in connection with the Distance Finding Stations of the Radio Beacon System. These stations during thick weather send out audible horn or whistle signals in synchrony with their radio signals. By measuring the time interval between receiving the radio signal and hearing the sound signal, the approximate distance of a ship from the beacon can be estimated. The operation of the watch is as follows. The side push piece is fully depressed and the center sweepsecond hand flies flies back to zero. When the radio signal is heard the push piece is released and the sweepsecond hands starts in motion. When the sound signal is heard the push piece is depressed half way and the hand stops. The position of the sweepsecond hand on the outer scale shows the approximate distance from the beacon in nautical miles.

The Longines Nautical Watch may be used as a second-setting master watch for chronometer comparison, or second-setting navigation timepiece. (1940 Longines Advertisement)

Longines "Nautical Stopsecond" (Hacking). 15J non-magnetic movement. Stainless steel, 33mm. case. ca 1940 . . . .$50—75

Longines "Stopsecond Flyback". (One Button). Silvered dial with subsidiary seconds and sweep second flyback. 15J non-magnetic movement. Round 30mm. case. ca 1940.
14K yellow gold-filled . . . . $75—100
Stainless steel . . . . 40— 60

Longines "1/5—Second Chronograph". Silvered telemeter-tachymeter dial with subsidiary seconds and 30 minute recorder. 17J non-magnetic movement. Stainless steel round, 34mm. case. ca 1940 . . . .$50—75

Longines "1/5 Second Chronograph". Silvered 60 second sweep second dial with subsidiary seconds and 30 minute recorder. 17J non-magnetic movement. Stainless steel round, 34mm. case. ca 1940 . . . .$50—75

Longines "Starting Time Indicator Chronograph". Black dial with white radium coated figures and hands. Chronograph with subsidiary seconds and 30 minute recorder. For counting of a period of time longer than 30 minutes, the rotatable bezel is provided with an indicator which can be set to the starting time. 17J non-magnetic movement. Stainless steel round, 38mm. case. ca 1940 . . . .$75—100

Longines "Stopsecond with Elapse-Time Register". (One button) inside conventional hour, minute and subsidiary seconds dial with an additional outer hours rotatable by a second winding crown. The outer bezel, rotatable by hand, is an additional minute dial. Sweep stopsecond hand is stopped by a half push on the push piece and returns to zero with a full push and starts instantly when the push piece is released. 15J non-magnetic movement. Round stainless steel, 33mm. case. ca 1940.
. . . . $150—200

The 1940's section on Longines-Wittnauer watches was taken from a 1940 catalog in the library of Roland Thomas "Rod" Minter. Our thanks to Rod for the use of this material.

Longines "Grand Prize Chronograph". 18K gold applied dial markers, subsidiary seconds, 30 minute recorder with date telemeter & tach-ometer rings. 1/5 second, time-out timing mechanism. 14K gold round case. ca 1954.
. . . . $200—275

Longines "Revere Sweep". Tu-tone dial, 18K raised gold markers, center seconds. 14K white gold round case with sweeping polished lugs. ca 1954. . . . . $175—200

Longines "Nobel Sweep". Engine-turned dial in classic wave pattern, 18K gold applied numerals, center seconds. 14K gold round case. ca 1954 . . . . $125—150

Longines "Fleming Sweep". 18K gold applied Roman numerals, center seconds. 14K gold round case. ca 1954 . . . . $115—150

Longines "Windsor". 18K gold applied markers on dial, subsidiary seconds. 14K gold round case. ca 1954 . . . . $100—150

Longines "Hopkins Sweep". 18K gold applied markers on dial, center seconds. 14K gold round case. ca 1954 . . . . $125—150

Longines "President McKinley". 18K gold applied markers on dial, subsidiary seconds. 14K gold round case. ca 1954 . . . . $125—150

Longines "Windsor". Black dial, 18K gold applied markers, subsidiary seconds. 14K gold, tu-tone square case, white gold bezel & yellow gold body. ca 1954 . . . . $350—450

Longines "Farragut Sweep". Brush-finished dial, 18K gold applied markers, center seconds. 14K gold round case, large molded lugs. ca 1954 . . . . $125—165

Longines "Carter". Engine-turned dial, 18K raised gold markers, subsidiary seconds. 14K gold square case. ca 1954 . . . . . . $225—275

Longines "Bradford". White dial, 18K gold applied markers, subsidiary seconds. 14K gold hand-lapped square case, stirrup lugs. ca 1954.
. . . . $175—225

Longines "Hastings". Brush-finished dial, 18K gold applied markers, subsidiary seconds. 18K gold, molded rectangular case & swirl lugs. ca 1954 . . . . $200—250

Longines "Sherwood". Tu-tone dial, 18K gold applied numerals & markers, subsidiary seconds. 14K gold round case. ca 1954 $125—150

Longines "Cromwell". Engine-turned dial, 18K gold applied markers, subsidiary seconds. 14K round case with large molded lugs. ca 1954.
. . . . $150—200

Longines "Wellington". Engine-turned dial, 18K gold applied numbers & markers, subsidiary seconds. 14K gold round case. ca 1954.
. . . . $125—150

Longines "Pearey". Waterproof. Tu-tone dial, 18K gold applied markers, subsidiary seconds. 14K gold round case, large molded lugs. ca 1954 . . . . $125—150

Longines "Barcelona Sweep". Self-winding. White dial, 18K gold applied markers, center seconds. 14K gold round case. ca 1954.
. . . . $200—250

Longines "Advocate". White dial, 18K gold applied markers, subsidiary seconds. 14K white gold rectangular case with two ends paved with 16 diamonds. ca 1954 . . . . $300—350

Longines "Consul". Silvered dial, 18K gold raised markers, 6-diamond dial, subsidiary seconds. 14K yellow or white gold, faceted rectangular case. ca 1954. . . . . . $225—275

Longines "Emissary". Silvered 18K gold applied markers, subsidiary seconds. 14K white gold round case with bar lugs set with 16 diamonds. ca 1954 . . . . $250—300

Longines "Continental". Brushed, 13-diamond dial, subsidiary seconds. 14K white or yellow gold, faceted rectangular case. ca 1954.
. . . . $250—300

Longines "Lord". White, 8-diamond dial, subsidiary seconds. 14K gold rectangular case with faceted lugs. ca 1954 . . . . $225—275

Longines "Advocate Deluxe". Silvered, 17-diamond dial, subsidiary seconds. 14K white gold rectangular case with two ends paved with 16 diamonds. ca 1954 . . . . $400—500

Longines "Chancellor". Silvered dial, 18K gold applied markers, subsidiary seconds. 18K white gold round case, 44-diamond bezel. ca 1954 . . . . $400 -500

Longines "Sovereign". Silvered, 17-diamond dial, subsidiary seconds. 14K gold round case, square lugs with 2 diamonds. ca 1954.
. . . . $350—375

Longines "Viscount". Silvered, 33-diamond dial, subsidiary seconds. 14K gold round case with sweeping polished lugs. ca 1954 $325—375

Longines "Paris Sweep". Self-winding, water-proof. White dial, 18K gold applied markers, center seconds. 14K gold round case with wide bezel. ca 1954 . . . . $150–200

Lonville "Gold Strap". Subsidiary seconds. 14K yellow gold, square case and lugs. ca 1940. . . . . $110–135

LONVILLE
Trademark of Langendorf Watch Co.
Switzerland – ca 1940

LORRAINE WATCH CO.
12 John St., New York

Importers of movements 5½''' to 13'''
In all shapes, in 1928.

Lonville "Ladies Gold Strap". 14K gold rectangular case and engraved cylinder lugs. ca 1940. . . . . $40–65

Lorraine. Ladies engraved tonneau case. ca 1926. Gold filled & Silver $20–30

Lonville "Ladies Gold Strap". Tu-tone dial, subsidiary seconds. 14K yellow gold, round case. ca 1940 . . . .$50–70

Lonville "Ladies Strap". Black dial. 14K yellow gold, molded tonneau case. ca 1940. . . . .$30–50

Lorraine "Ultra-Modern". ca 1926. Gold filled $35–55
Nickel 15–25

Lonville "Gold Strap". Black dial, subsidiary seconds. 14K yellow gold, rectangular case. ca 1940 . . . . $125–150

Lorraine. Silvered dial, subsidiary seconds. 15J movement. 18K white gold tank-style case. ca 1927. . . . . $125–165

LOUIS WATCH CO.

Supplied watches to the trade in 1947 from 580 5th Avenue, New York, NY U.S.A.

Louis "6-Diamond Dial" set in palladium with 18K yellow gold markers. 17J movement. Rectangular, 14K yellow gold case with molded lugs. ca 1947. . . . . $125—150

Louis "6-Diamond Dial" set in palladium with 18K gold markers. 17J movement. Square, 14K yellow gold case with heavy lugs. ca 1947. . . . . $145—175

Lucien Picard "Ladies Diamond & Citrine Bracelet". 14K gold rectangular case, flanked by a row of diamonds, fancy cut citrines and pearls, with a double row, gold link bracelet. . . . . $400—600

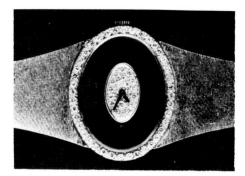

Lucien Piccard "Diamond & Gold Bracelet". Blue enamel and diamond pave'd dial. 14K gold, oval case, with diamond set bezel and tapered, textured band . . . . . . $1,000—1,200

Lucien Piccard "Palladium, Diamond & Emerald". Man's strap watch with palladium, diamond-set dial. ca 1963 . . . . . . $400—500

Lucien Piccard "Palladium Dial, Case & Bracelet". ca 1963 . . . . $350—450

Lyceum "Doctors". Center seconds. 10½''', 17J movement. 10K yellow rolled gold plate round case. ca 1938. . . . . $10—20

Lyceum. Raised gold-filled numerals on dial. 17J movement. Curved, elongated rectangular case. ca 1938. 14K gold . . . . $125—150
10K gold-filled . . . . 25— 35

Lyceum "Medical". Tu-tone dial, center seconds. 6¾''', 17J movement. 10K yellow rolled gold plate, molded rectangular case. ca 1938. . . . . $20—30

Lyceum. Raised gold-filled numerals on dial, subsidiary seconds. 17J movement. 14K gold, rectangular case. ca 1938. . . . . . . $100—125

Lyceum "Chronograph". Silvered dial, subsidiary seconds, 30 minute recorder with fly-back. 6¾''', 15J movement. Plain rectangular case. ca 1938. Gold-filled. . . . . $150—175
Stainless steel . . . . 110—135

MARVIN WATCH CO.
Chaux-De-Fonds, Switzerland

Manufacturers of the "Winton" and "Marvin" movements, in all sizes from 3¾''' to 10½''', etc. ca 1932.

Marvin "Jumping Figures". Ladies. 4¼''' movement. Solid rectangular case with hour & minute windows. ca 1932. Chrome .$20—35
Rolled gold plate . . . . 25—40

Marvin. Ladies. White dial. 14K gold square case, single molded cord lugs. ca 1946.
. . . . 10% to 20% over gold value

Marvin. Tu-tone dial, center seconds. 14K gold square case. ca 1946 . . . . $135—165

Mathey-Tissot "Ladies Diamond & Gold Cord". 14K gold square case & single lugs, set with 2 diamonds. ca 1944 . . . . $150—175

Mathey-Tissot "Ladies Gold Cord". 17J movement. 20mm., 14K gold round case with single lugs. ca 1947. . . . .$50—70

Mathey-Tissot "Captive". 17J movement. 40mm., sterling silver purse watch. ca 1947. . . . .$75—100

Mathey-Tissot "One Button Chronograph". Subsidiary seconds, 30 minute recorder. 14K yellow gold, cushion case. ca 1929
. . . . $400—450

Mathey-Tissot "Gold Strap". Silvered dial with subsidiary seconds. Square, 18K yellow gold case with cylinder lugs. ca 1944. . . $125—150

Mathey-Tissot "Calamatic". Moonphase calendar chronograph. Subsidiary seconds, day & month windows with outer date ring. 34mm., 14K gold round case. ca 1947. . . . $600—700

Mathey - Tissot. Tachometer chronograph, brown matte dial, subsidiary seconds, 30 minute & 12 hour recorders and outer tachometer ring. 14K gold, 39mm. round case. $300—350

Mathey-Tissot . Self-winding, moonphase calendar, white brushed, sweep second dial, day & month windows with outer date ring. 14K gold, 32mm. round case . . . . . . $750—850

Mathey-Tissot. Gold plated dial, black Arabic numerals. Hidden in a 36mm., 1904 U.S. gold piece. 17J movement . . . . $1,200—1,500

Mathey-Tissot. Moonphase calendar, chronograph. Subsidiary seconds, 30 minute & 12 hour recorders, day & month windows with outer date ring. 18K gold, round case. . . . . $1,100—1,300

L. & C. MAYERS CO.
New York

Sold goods manufactured and supplied by others.

Mayers "Gold, Diamond & Topaz Bracelet". Ladies. Black dial. 17J movement. 14K yellow gold round case with molded swirl surrounding one side and set with 5 diamonds and 8 topaz, with double row snake bracelet. ca 1942. . . . . $400—500

Mayers "Tu-Tone Gold Bracelet". Ladies. 17J movement. 14K yellow and rose gold, horn shaped case and matching flexible link case, 5 rubies set in clasp. ca 1942. . . . . 10% to 20% over gold value

Mayers "Gold Ladies Reverso". Black dial. 17J movement. 14K yellow gold, molded rectangular case, tapered lugs set with 2 Garnets, and flexible bracelet. ca 1942.
. . . . 10% to 20% over gold value

Mayers "Gold Bracelet". Ladies, 17J movement. 14K rose gold, square case, matching flexible link attachment. ca 1942.
. . . . 10% to 20% over gold value

Mayers "Diamond, Rubies & Gold Art Deco Bracelet". Ladies. 17J movement. 14K rose gold, horn shaped case set with 2 diamonds and 5 rubies, and snake link bracelet. ca 1942.
. . . . $300—375

Mayers "Diamond, Rubies & Gold Geometric Bracelet". Ladies. 17J movement. 14K rose gold rectangular case and geometric clasp, with double row snake link bracelet. ca 1942.
. . . . $600—750

Mayers "Gold Geometric Bracelet". Ladies, 17J movement. 14K rose gold, molded geometric case with double row snake link bracelet. ca 1942. . . . . $250—300

Mayers "Thin Gold Strap". Waterproof. Subsidiary seconds. 17J movement. Square case. ca 1942. 14K gold . . . . $100—125
Stainless steel . . . . 10— 15

Mayers "Gold Strap". Ruby markers on dial, subsidiary seconds. 17J movement. 14K rose gold, molded rectangular case. ca 1942.
. . . . $120—140

Meister. Moonphase calendar , chronograph. Gilt dial, subsidiary seconds, 30 minute & 12 hour recorders, day & month windows, with outer date ring. 18K gold round case.
. . . . $1,000—1,200

Mercier "Diamond, Sapphire & Platinum". Silver dial. 17J adjusted movement. Rectangular platinum case with 24 diamonds and 8 sapphires. ca 1927 . . . . $250—300

Meylan "Diamond, Emerald & Platinum". Silver dial. 18J adjusted movement. Rectangular platinum case set with 54 diamonds and 24 emeralds. ca 1927 . . . . $900—1,200

Mido "Automatic Multifort". Waterproof. Black dial, center seconds. 17J, self-winding movement. Round case. ca 1946.
14K gold . . . . $100—125
Gold-filled . . . .   20— 35
Stainless steel . . . .   15— 25

Mido "Ocean Star". Waterproof. 18K gold applied markers, center seconds. Round case. ca 1961. 14K yellow gold . . . . . $125—150
Yellow gold-filled . . . .   35— 50

Mido "Multi-Centerchrono". Waterproof. 24 & 12 hour & 60 minute chapter rings. Telemeter & tachometer rings. 17J movement. Round case. ca 1948. 14K gold . . . . . . $150—200
Gold-filled . . . .   80—110
Stainless steel . . . .   50— 75

Mido "Ocean Star Powerwind". 14K gold markers on black or white dial, center seconds. 17J, self-winding movement. Round case. ca 1962. 14K yellow gold . . . . $125—150
14K yellow gold-filled . . . .   45— 70
Stainless steel . . . .   15— 30
With calendar, add . . . .   20— 30

Mido Split Second. mile base tachometer chronograph with center 60 minute recorder. 17J in a round stainless steel case. ca 1949.
. . . . $400—450

Mido "Winnetka Stainless Powerwind". Waterproof. Etched markers on dial, center seconds. Round stainless steel case. ca 1962 . . .$15—30

MIMO

Made by Graef & Co., Chaux-de-fonds, Switzerland. Sold through wholesale distributors only. ca 1930.

Mimo "Calendar". Subsidiary seconds, date window. 14K yellow gold rectangular case. ca 1931. . . . . $110—140
Yellow gold-filled . . . .   35— 55

NOTE: Read Page 6 before using this book to value your wrist watch.

Mimo "Ladies Baguette". Molded, white gold-filled baguette case with graduated lugs. ca 1931 . . . . $20—30

Mimo "Calendar". Luminous hands & numerals, subsidiary seconds, date window at 3. Molded rectangular case. ca 1930.
14K gold. . . . . $125—150
Gold-filled . . . .   35— 55

Mimo "8-Day". Subsidiary seconds. Molded and engraved, 14K gold rectangular case. ca 1931 . . . . $110—140

NOTE: All values are given for the head only unless the bracelet is included in the description.

Mimo "Calendar". Luminous hands & numerals, subsidiary seconds, date window at 3. Tonneau case. ca 1930. 14K gold . . $125—150
Gold-filled . . . . : . . . .   35— 55

Mimo "Jump Hour". Hour, minute & seconds windows. Chrome rectangular case and matching band. ca 1931 . . . .$50—65

Mimo "Calendar". Luminous hands & numerals, subsidiary seconds, date window at 3. Rectangular case. ca 1930.
14K gold . . . . $125—150
Gold-filled . . . .   35— 55

Mimo. Tu-tone dial with luminous hands & numerals, subsidiary seconds. 12''', 17J, 30 Hour movement. 14K white gold-filled rectangular case, yellow lugs. ca 1932 . . .$25—40

Mimo "8 Day". Luminous hands & numerals, subsidiary seconds. 10½''', 17J movement, with two mainsprings. White chromium finish, tonneau case. ca 1932 . . . . $85—115

Mimo "8 Day". Luminous hands & numerals, subsidiary seconds. 10½''', 17J movement, with two mainsprings. 14K yellow gold-filled, molded tonneau case. ca 1932. . . . . $85—115

Mimo "Man's Gold-filled Strap". Luminous hands & numerals, subsidiary seconds. 12''', 17J, 30 Hour movement. 14K white gold-filled tonneau case. ca 1932 . . . . $20—30

Mimo "Ensign Curvette". Raised gold numerals, subsidiary seconds dial. 15J movement. Nickel silver case. ca 1935 . . . . $15—25

Mimo "Pilot Curvette". New "Stix", tu-tone dial, subsidiary seconds. 15J movement. Faceted, rectangular chrome case. ca 1935. . . . . $10—20

Mimo "Duo-Dial" (Doctor's). Tu-tone upper dial for hours, lower dial for seconds. 15J movement. 14K white or yellow gold-filled case. ca 1935 . . . . $175—225

Minerva "Chronograph". Waterproof. Black dial, subsidiary seconds, 30 minute recorder with outer tachometer ring. 13''', 17J movement. Round stainless steel case. ca 1959. . . . . $25—40

Minerva "Calendar Chronograph". Waterproof. Black dial, subsidiary seconds, 30 minute & 12 hour recorder, day & month windows with outer date ring. 17J movement. Round stainless steel case. ca 1959 . . . . $40—65

Minerva "Chronograph". Waterproof. Subsidiary seconds, 30 minute recorder, with outer ring base 100. 13''', 17J movement. Round stainless steel case. ca 1959 . . . . . . $25–40

Minerva "Chronograph". Waterproof. Subsidiary seconds, 30 minute & 12 hour recorder, with outer ring base 100. 14''', 17J movement. Round stainless steel case. ca 1959 . . . $30–45

Moeris. Moonphase calendar, chronograph. Matte silver dial. Subsidiary seconds, 30 minute recorder, day & month windows, with outer date ring. 17J movement. 18K gold round case. $700–800

Moeris. Moonphase calendar chronograph. Self-winding & waterproof. Day & month windows with outer date ring. 23J movement. 18K white gold, 37mm round case $650–750

Moser & Co., Henry. Ladies. Platinum, 15mm. octagonal case with a diamond-set bezel. ca 1925 . . . . $175–225

Movado. "Purse Watch". 18K gold, 31x45mm. sliding case, engraved with a geometric design and linked to winding mechanism. ca 1930. $550–700

Movado "Ladies Gold Cord". Black dial. 14K gold rectangular case. ca 1940 . . . . . $30–50

Movado "Ladies Gold & Emerald Hunting" Bangle style. ca 1940. . . . . 10% to 20% over gold value

Movado "Ermeto" Purse Watch. Sliding case is linked to winding mechanism. ca 1940. $100–125

Movado "Ladies Diamond". Square dial. Rectangular case set with 10 diamonds & 2 large semi-precious stones, large link lugs. ca 1943.
. . . . $250—275

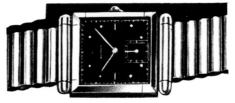

Movado "Man's Gold Bracelet". Black dial, subsidiary seconds. Gold square case and cylinder style lugs, matching band. ca 1940.
. . . . 10% to 20% over gold value

Movado. Black enamel dial. 14K gold and enamel, 47mm. case. Watch winds by closing case . . . . $400—450

Movado. Sweep second dustproof, water tight round case with heavy lugs. ca 1941
14K yellow gold. . . . . $150—200
Stainless & gold . . . . 75—100
Stainless . . . . 35— 65

Movado Ermeto. Divided in center and linked to winding mechanism, engraved with geommetric designs, 47mm. ca 1927.
9K yellow gold . . . . $300—400
Sterling silver . . . . 75—125

Movado "Chronacvatic". Chronograph base 1000m. with subsidiary seconds, 60 minutes and 12 hour recorder. 17J, round case, ca 1940
14K yellow gold. . . . . $350—425
Stainless steel . . . . 100—125

Movado. Moonphase calendar, subsidiary seconds, day & month windows with outer date ring. 33mm. 18K gold round case.
Gold . . . . $750—850
Steel . . . . 175—225

Movado. Calendar with outer date ring, window day & month, subsidiary seconds. Round case. ca 1941. 18K yellow or pink gold. . $350—450
14K yellow gold. . . . . 250—325
Stainless & gold . . . . 75—100
Gold-filled . . . . 50— 75
Stainless steel . . . . 25— 50

Movado. Date calendar on middle date chapter ring, window day & month. Round case. ca 1945. . . . 14K yellow gold $250–300
Stainless steel 35– 50

Movado "Sweep Second". Tu-tone dial, luminous hands & numerals, center seconds. Round case. ca 1943. Stainless steel. $25–35
14K gold . . . . 10% to 20% over gold

Movado "Astronic". Gilded & black dial, center seconds & 24 hour chapter ring, day time hours shown in black. Waterproof round case in 14K gold or stainless steel. ca 1944.
Stainless steel . . . . $ 50– 75
14K gold 175–200

calendermeto
OPEN IT, CLOSE IT—IT'S WOUND

Full calendar dial

Movado "Calendarmeto". Purse or pocket watch. Moonphase calendar, day & month windows, center seconds & inner date ring. Leather covered case. ca 1950. . . . $400–450

Movado "Calendomatic". Self-winding, center seconds, day & month windows with outer date ring. Round case, extended lugs. ca 1950.
14K gold $200–275
Stainless steel & 14K gold 100–15
Stainless steel 50– 75

Movado. Automatic, silver finished dial. Subsidiary seconds. Round GF case. $35–50

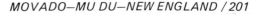

Movado "Calendoplan". Center seconds, date window at 3. Round case. ca 1952.
14K gold . . . . $110—135
Stainless steel & 14K gold . . . . . . 55— 75
Stainlless steel . . . . 25— 35

Movado, retailed by Van Cleef & Arpels. Calendar, chronograph, gold finished dial, subsidiary seconds, 30 minute & 12 hour recorders, date windows with outer tachometer ring. 18K gold, 40mm. tonneau case . . . . $350—475

Movado, Astronic. Moonphase, calendar, chronograph. Waterproof screw-down crown. Subsidiary seconds, 30 minute & 12 hour register; day, date & month windows, with outer tachometer ring, base 1000m. Stainless steel, bowed rectangular case. 36mm. $325—375

Self-winding
CALENDAR WATCH
the timeliest watch!

Tells:
DATE
DAY
HOUR
MINUTE
SECOND

WATER RESISTANT

calendolux
Stainless steel . . . . $110.

*Stainless steel and
14K Gold* . . . .$140.
14K Gold . . . .$245.

Prices in U. S. . . . . Fed. Tax incl.

MOVADO
WINNERS OF 168 OBSERVATORY AWARDS
SOLD AND SERVICED BY LEADING JEWELERS ALL OVER THE WORLD

Movado "Calendolux". Silvered dial. 17J self-winding movement. Subsidiary seconds, with windows for day & date near the seconds bit. Round case. ca 1953. 14K gold . . . $125—150
Stainless steel & 14K gold . . . . . . 75— 90
Stainless steel . . . . 25— 35

MuDu, marked Doublematic. Moonphase, calendar, center seconds, window day & month, white outer date ring. Waterproof plated case with steel base, Swiss lever movement.$125—175

New England "Alden". Glass enamel, subsidiary seconds dial. 10 ligne, 7J, round lever movement. ca 1913. 20 Yr. GF . . . .$20—35
14K gold . . . . 40—65
Add for colored dial . . . . 15—35

New England "Cavour". Glass enamel or metal dial. 15 ligne, 7J round lever movement. ca 1913. Silver . . . . $20—35
20 Yr. GF . . . . 20—35
Gun metal . . . . 10—20

New England "Cavour". Glass enamel dial. 15 ligne, 7J round lever movement. Round 20 Yr. GF case. ca 1913 . . . . $20—35

New England "Hale". Glass enamel, subsidiary seconds dial. 6S, round 7J lever movement. Round nickel converted pocket watch case. ca 1913. . . . . $25—40

New England "Waterbury". Glass enamel subsidiary seconds dial. 10 ligne, 7J round lever movement. ca 1913. 20 Yr. GF . . . . $20—35
14K gold . . . . 40—65
Add for colored dial . . . . 15—35

New Haven "Elf". Ladies. Silvered dial, etched golden numerals. Jeweled pin lever movement. Chromium-finished tonneau Wadsworth case. ca 1933. . . . . $ 5— 7
With box . . . . 10—25

New Haven "Duchess". Ladies. Silvered dial with etched gold numerals. 8/0 size, 7J movement. Yellow gold plated, engraved & molded tonneau case with chromium plated back. ca 1936 . . . . $ 5—10
Tu-tone strap . . . . 5—10
With box. . . . . 10—35

New Haven "Countess". Ladies. Oval, tu-tone silvered dial. 7J, 8/0 size movement. Yellow gold plated, engraved tonneau case with chromium plated back. ca 1936 . . . . $ 5—10
With box . . . . 10—30

New Haven "Tommy-Ticker". Silvered dial, sunken subsidiary seconds. 6/0 size movement. Nickel-plated cushion case with chromium plated back. ca 1930 . . . . $10—15
With box . . . . 15—40

New Haven "Tip-Top". Silvered dial, sunken subsidiary seconds. 6 size movement. Nickel-plated cushion case with chromium plated back. ca 1930 . . . . $20—30
With box . . . .   25—40

New Haven "Jerome Jr.". Designed by Wadsworth. Raised markers on silvered dial. Chromium-finished tonneau case. ca 1936. . . . .$ 3—5
With box . . . .$10—25

New Haven "Tip Top Par". Silvered dial, subsidiary seconds. Pin lever movement. Chromium plated tonneau case. Black enamel bezel with raised numerals. ca 1932 . . . .$10—20
With box . . . .   10—35

New Haven "Wales". 7J movement. YGF rectangular case. ca 1936 . . . .$ 3—5
With box . . . .   10—25

New York Standard Watch Co. came under the control of the Keystone Watch Case Co. just after the turn of the century. At first, wrist watches were made for ladies only and it was considered "sissy" for a man to wear one. During World War I, many soldiers began to wear them and you know the rest of the story. New York Standard were selling movements to jobbers and wholesalers to case according to the styles they could sell. These movements can be found in all of the popular wrist case styles of the day (1912—20). Examples are round (sky light, queen & open face), cushion, tonneau, square, decagon & hexagon, for ribbon, strap & bracelet. New York Standard usually made only 7 jewel, inexpensive movements, and are not popular with collectors at this time, even though they offered some of the first wrist watches made in the U.S.A.

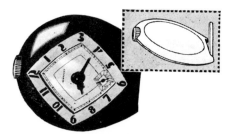

New Haven "Hand Bag". Diamond-shaped dial, black enamel numerals, subsidiary seconds. Black enamel case. ca 1936 . . . .$ 5—10
With box . . . .   20—40

New Haven "Brownie". Silvered dial, white metal tonneau case. ca 1936 . . . .$ 3— 5
With box . . . .   10—25

New York "Standard". Various color metal dials, with & without seconds. The movements with glass enamel dials were made for use in pocket watches, and are some of the earliest 7J, 0 size, round nickel movements. Cases in all of the styles popular at the time. ca 1912—20
20 Yr. gold-filled . . . .$10—20
Sterling silver . . . .   10—20
Silveroid . . . .   5—10

Niton "Ladies Diamond & Platinum Cord". 18J movement. Rectangular case. ca 1930. Value varies according to size, quality and color of diamonds. $600–800

Niton "Platinum Cord". Ladies rectangular platinum case, large link lugs. ca 1930.$75–100

Niton "Jump Hour". Engraved center on dial, hour window & minute recorder. 18J movement. Platinum & diamond tonneau case. ca 1930 . . . . $375–450

Niton "Jump Hour". Doctor's watch. Hour window, minute recorder, subsidiary seconds. 18J movement. Platinum rectangular case. ca 1930 . . . . $350–450

Nivada. Silver finished dial. Subsidiary seconds, 17J movement. 14K gold rectangular case. ca 1950. . . . . $100–110

Nivada "Chronomaster". Black dial, subsidiary seconds, 30 minute recorder with outer tachometer ring. 17J movement. Round, stainless steel case with calibrated revolving bezel. ca 1963 . . . .$40–60

Oberon. Calendar chronograph, painted & silvered dial, subsidiary seconds & 45 minute recorder, window date with outer tachometer ring, 1000m. base, 17J movement. Round steel case secured by screws $25–35

Octo "Man's Gold Strap". Tu-tone dial, center seconds. 14K gold round case. ca 1946. . . . . $100–135

Octo "Ladies Gold Bracelet". Square case, matching large linked bracelet. ca 1946. 14K gold . . . . . 10% to 20% over gold value

Ollendorff. Ladies. Rectangular, platinum & diamond case & matching band. ca 1929.
. . . . $800–1,000
Value will vary according to size & quality of stones.

Ollendorff "Kit-Kat". Subsidiary seconds. 14K gold-filled hexagonal case. ca 1929.
14K green gold-filled. $20–30
14K white gold-filled 15–25

Ollendorff "Honora". Ladies. Silvered dial. 15J movement. Engraved tonneau case. ca 1929.
14K gold $40–60
14K Gold-filled 15–25

Ollendorff "Sportsman". Subsidiary seconds. 15J movement. 14K white gold-filled, tonneau case and bracelet. ca 1929 . . . .$15–25
Bracelet 2– 4

Ollendorff "Princess". Ladies. 17J movement. 14K gold tonneau case, engraved and set with 4 diamonds. ca 1929 . . . . $125–175

Ollenforff "Timer". Subsidiary seconds. 15J movement. 14K white gold-filled rectangular case and gold-filled mesh band. ca 1929.
. . . .$15–25
Bracelet 3– 5

Ollendorff "Osborne". Subsidiary seconds, 17J movement. 14K gold, engraved rectangular case. ca 1928 . . . . $110–140

Ollendorff "Ossian". Subsidiary seconds. 17J movement. 14K gold, engraved tonneau case. ca 1928. . . . . $100–130
Gold-filled 20– 30

Ollendorff "Ogden". Silvered dial, subsidiary seconds. 17J movement. Engraved tonneau case. ca 1929. 14K gold $100–125
Gold-filled 20– 30

Ollendorff "Celtic". Luminous hands & numerals, subsidiary seconds. 17J movement. 14K gold, engraved tonneau case. ca 1929. . . . . $100–125

Ollendorff "Immar". Subsidiary seconds. 15J movement. Engraved octagonal case. ca 1929. 14K white gold-filled . . . . $15–25 14K green gold-filled 20–30

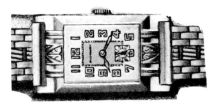

Ollendorff "Mark, Gold". Subsidiary seconds. 17J movement. 14K white gold, molded and engraved, rectangular case and matching bracelet. ca 1929 . . . . $125–150 14K bracelet. . . . . 10% over gold value

Ollendorff "Chevalier". Tu-tone dial, subsidiary seconds. 15J movement. Gold-filled, square engraved white case & lugs. ca 1930 . . $20–30 With bracelet 30–40

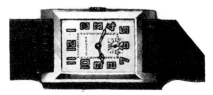

Ollendorff "Lucian, Gold". Subsidiary seconds, 17J movement. 14K white gold rectangular case with drop lugs. ca 1929 . . . . . . $100–125

Ollendorff "Swordsman". Silvered dial, subsidiary seconds. 15J movement. White gold-filled, curved back tonneau case. ca 1930. . . . . $20–30 With bracelet 30–40

Ollendorff "Robin". Subsidiary seconds. 15J movement. 14K tu-tone white and green gold-filled, engraved, faceted rectangular case. ca 1929 . . . . $15–25

Ollendorff "Knight". Silvered dial, subsidiary seconds. 15J movement. Hand-carved, white gold-filled tonneau case. ca 1930 . . . . $20–30 With bracelet 30–40

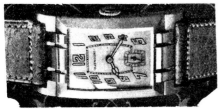

Ollendorff "Oceana". Radium dial, luminous hands & numerals, subsidiary seconds. 17J movement. 14K gold rectangular case with hinged lugs. ca 1927 . . . . $200—250

Olma. Silvered dial, center seconds, 15J movement. Gold plated square case. ca 1950 $10—15

Olympic Chronograph. Subsidiary seconds, 30 minute recorder with outer tachometer ring, 1000m. base. 17J movement. 18K gold round case. . . . . $175—200

Omega. "Nurse's Gold-Filled". Center seconds. 17J movement. 14K round, yellow gold-filled case. ca 1940 . . . . $15—20

Omega "Diamond & Gold Hunting". Ladies. 14K gold belt buckle designed case set with diamonds & rubies. ca 1943 . . . . $800—1,000

Omega "Diamond & Gold". Ladies. 14K gold square case, single lugs set with diamonds & precious stones. ca 1944 . . . . . . $150—200

Omega "Gold Ladies Bracelet". 14K gold square case & matching link bracelet. ca 1947 . . . . 10% to 20% over gold value

Omega "Diamond & Platinum Bracelet Hunting". Ladies. Round case and band set with 178 diamonds. ca 1957. Value varies according to size, quality & color of diamonds. . . . .$10,000—12,000

Omega "Diamond & Platinum Bracelet Hunting". Round case & band set with 177 diamonds. ca 1957. Value varies according to size, quality & color of diamonds. . . . . $8,000—10,000

Omega "Tank". Subsidiary seconds. 17J movement. 18K gold square case. ca 1929.$150—175

Omega "Marine". Silvered dial with subsidiary seconds. 15J, 8½''' movement. Rectangular double case (by sliding open to reveal the Hidden Crown at 12), 24x27mm. closed. ca 1937. 18K gold . . . . $800—1,000
Stainless steel . . . . 275— 300

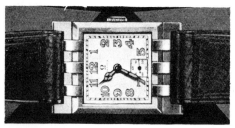

Omega. Luminous hands & numerals, subsidiary seconds. 14K gold square case with lugs. ca 1929. . . . . $100—125

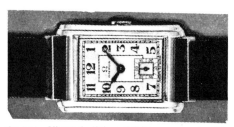

Omega. Silvered dial, subsidiary seconds. 15J tonneau case. Silver, molded rectangular case. ca 1931. . . . .$30—50

Omega. Subsidiary seconds. 18K gold, molded rectangular case. ca 1930. . . . . . . $125—150

Omega. Silvered dial, subsidiary seconds. 15J tonneau movement. Rectangular case. ca 1931. Gold-filled . . . .$30—50
Stainless steel . . . . 10—20

Omega. Silvered dial, subsidiary seconds. 15J tonneau movement. 14K gold rectangular case. ca 1931 . . . . $125—165

Omega. Silvered dial, subsidiary seconds. 15J tonneau movement. Gold-filled tonneau case. ca 1931 . . . .$25—45

Omega. Subsidiary seconds. 17J movement. 14K rose gold rectangular case. 14K gold hinged lugs. ca 1940 . . . . $150—175

Omega. Subsidiary seconds. 17J movement. 14K yellow gold-filled, tonneau case. ca 1940. . . . . $30—40

Omega. Subsidiary seconds. 15J movement. 10K yellow gold-filled case. ca 1940 . . $15—20
Stainless steel . . . . 10—15

Omega "Man's Gold Strap". Subsidiary seconds. 14K gold rectangular case. ca 1944. . . . . $125—150

Omega "Chronometer". Subsidiary seconds. 14K gold round case. ca 1947 . . . . $150—200

Omega Watch Co. Moonphase calendar, silvered dial, subsidiary seconds, day & month windows with outer date ring. 17J movement. 14K gold, 35mm. round case. ca 1950 . . $700—750

Omega "Centenary". 18K yellow gold dial, with 18K applied figures. 18K round gold case with heavy molded strap lugs, in sterling silver presentation case. ca 1951. Head only. . . . . $350—450

Omega. Luminous dial, center seconds. 17J movement. Waterproof case. ca 1942. 14K gold . . . . $100—135
Stainless steel . . . . 10— 20

Omega "Stainless Man's Strap". Subsidiary seconds. Stainless steel, rectangular case. ca 1947 . . . . $30—55

Omega "Ultra-Thin". 18K gold applied figures on silver-white dial, subsidiary seconds. 17J movement. 14K yellow gold, rectangular case. ca 1956. . . . . $100—125

Omega "Automatic Square". 18K gold applied figures on black or silver-white dial. Self-winding, sweep second, 17J movement. 18K yellow gold, square, heavy lug case. ca 1956. $250—315

Omega Seamaster. Automatic, silvered dial, 17J, waterproof & shockproof movement. Round steel case with gold bezel . . $100—125

Omega "Duet". Ladies or Men's. Subsidiary seconds on men's. Round, 14K gold case.
Men's 14K gold . . . . $150—175
Ladies 14K gold. . . . .   75— 95

Omega, retailed by Bourcheron. Champagne dial with vertical bars & dot numerals. 18K gold 20x37mm. rectangular case with horizontal bar design. Case signed. ca 1970 . . . . . $300—400

Omega "Ultra-Thin". 18K gold applied figures on silver-white dial, subsidiary seconds. 17J movement. 14K yellow gold round case. ca 1956 . . . . $90—125

Omega Speedmaster Professional. Tachometer chronograph, gold dial, subsidiary seconds, 30 minute & 12 hour recorder. 18K gold round case with red calibrated bezels. 200 limited edition. Back inscribed Omega Speedmaster Apollo XI, The First Watch Worn on the Moon. . . . . $1,500—2,000

OPTIMA

Trademark of Untermeyer, Robbins & Co., 20 West 47th St., New York, offering an extensive line of diamond mounted watches in 1928.

Oris "Bermuda". Ladies. Center seconds. Round chrome case. ca 1961 . . . . . . $3—5

Optima "Ladies Platinum & Diamond". Silvered dial, 5''' tonneau movement. Tonneau case. ca 1924 . . . . $50—85

Oris "Jacqueline". Ladies. Round dial. Molded chrome tonneau case. ca 1961. . . . . . . $3—5

Optima. Ladies. Geometric dial. Rectangular "Art Deco" designed, platinum ribbon case, set with diamonds & semi-precious stones. ca 1929 . . . . $225—300

Oris "Adorne". Ladies. Chrome tonneau case. ca 1961. . . . . $3—5

Optima. Ladies. Rectangular platinum ribbon case, set with diamonds. ca 1929 . . $200—300

Optima. Ladies. Rectangular platinum ribbon case, set with diamonds. ca 1929 . . $175—250

Optima. Silvered dial. 16J movement. 14K gold, embossed tonneau case. ca 1924. . . . . $150—200

Optima. Ladies. Rectangular "Art Deco" designed, platinum ribbon case, set with diamonds & semi-precious stones. ca 1929. . . . . $250—350

Optima. Silvered dial. 16J movement. 14K gold, embossed faceted rectangular case. ca 1924 . . . . $150—200

Oris "Ladies Strap". 7J movement. Stainless steel tonneau case. ca 1961 . . . .$8—16

Oris "Hyannis". Waterproof. Center seconds. 7J movement. Round chrome case. ca 1961 $5—10

Oris "Hyannis". Waterproof. Luminous hands & dots. Center seconds. Round stainless steel case & matching expansion band. ca 1961. . . . .$8—16

ORLAM
SOCIETE DES MONTRES
Orlam, 11, Rue La Fayette
Paris, France — ca 1935

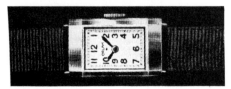

Orlam "18". Ladies. White dial, 14K gold faceted rectangular case. ca 1935 . . . .$40—75

Orlam "21". Ladies. White dial. Stainless steel, faceted rectangular case with single lugs. ca 1935. . . . .$10—20

Orlam "19". Ladies. White dial. Faceted, curved rectangular case. ca 1935.
14K gold . . . .$40—75
Stainless steel . . . . 8—18

Orlam "8". Ladies. White dial, faceted rectangular case, tapering into lugs. ca 1935.
14K gold . . . .$50—85
Stainless steel . . . . 10—20

Orlam "10". Ladies. Round white dial, polished tonneau case. ca 1935. 14K gold . . . .$40—75
Stainless steel . . . . 7—15

Orlam "31". Silvered dial, subsidiary seconds. Polished rectangular case. ca 1935.
14K gold . . . . $100—145
Stainless steel . . . . 10— 25

Orlam "9". Ladies. Tu-tone dial. Faceted rectangular case. ca 1935. 14K gold . $75—125
Stainless steel . . . . 10— 25

Orlam "7". Ladies. White dial. 14K gold, faceted rectangular case. ca 1935 . . . . $50—85

Orlam "20". Ladies. White dial. Faceted tonneau, stainless steel case. ca 1935 . . $10—20

Orlam. Silvered dial, subsidiary seconds. Faceted rectangular case. ca 1935.
14K gold . . . . $100—145
Stainless steel . . . . 10— 25

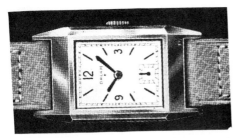

Orlam "30". White dial, subsidiary seconds. Faceted rectangular case. ca 1935.
14K gold . . . . $100—145
Stainless steel . . . . 10— 25

PACKARD

A full line for both men and women, in all case metals, supplied to the trade by Emil Leicher, New York, NY.

Packard "Man's Gold". Subsidiary seconds. 17J movement. 14K yellow gold square case. ca 1946. . . . . $100—135

PATEK PHILIPPE
Geneve, Switzerland

Patek Philippe has left a deeper impression on the history of watchmaking than any other watch company. They are considered the "Cadillac" of wrist watches and are sought after by those who "know" and can afford them. All factory cased Pateks were trademarked on the dial, movement, case, bracelet and buckle. They were made in 18 karat yellow or white gold, platinum, silver, and occasionally stainless steel. Like most all other companies, Patek sold movements to firms who then custom-cased them. Many original Patek cases have been scrapped or otherwise destroyed, and you will find many recased, and occasionally a watch with only a marked Patek dial.

Traders try to take advantage of the desirability of the Patek name on a watch and will "marry up" all kinds of case, dial and movement combinations. Watch out for these because they have far less value than the original. All values in this book for Patek watches are for originals only.

Patek is one of the three or four companies left in the world still making mechanical watches in limited numbers.

Most all Patek strap wrist watches were sold with a marked 18 karat buckle and a man's size will usually bring $65 to $75.

All other wrist watches in this book have been compared to a Patek when the current market value was being determined.

Patek Philippe & Co., Geneva, retailed by **Albert Hansen, Seattle, Washington.** Ladies, white enamel dial, 18K gold, 28mm. round case. ca 1913 . . . . $400—450

PATEK PHILIPPE
ca 1914

NOTE: This is an exact copy of an original advertisement by Shreve and Company, ca 1914. Original values are at the bottom of the page and the current values are set at 45 degree angle.

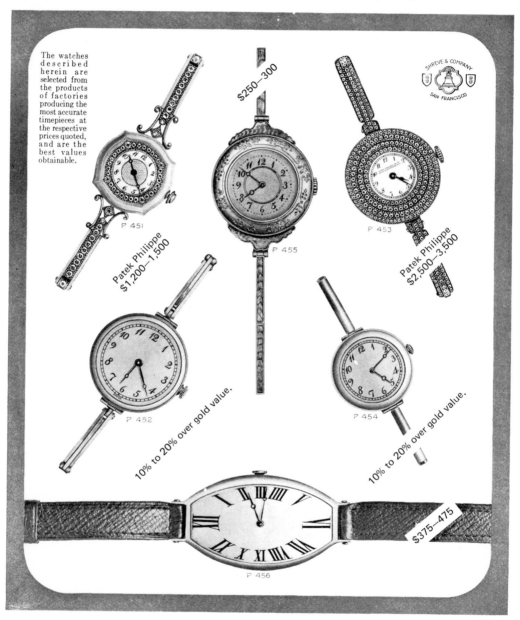

The watches described herein are selected from the products of factories producing the most accurate timepieces at the respective prices quoted, and are the best values obtainable.

$250–300

P 451

Patek Philippe $1,200–1,500

P 455

P 453

Patek Philippe $2,500–3,500

P 452

10% to 20% over gold value.

P 454

10% to 20% over gold value.

$375–475

P 456

ACTUAL SIZE

WATCHES

P 451 Extension bracelet watch; platinum with diamonds................................ $ 700.00
P 452 Extension bracelet watch; 14K........... 100.00
P 453 Extension bracelet watch; platinum and rose diamond paved case.................. 1250.00

P 454 Extension bracelet watch; flat; 18K........ $225.00
P 455 Extension bracelet watch; 14K; enameled front................................... 145.00
P 456 Bracelet watch; 14K; with leather strap..... 135.00

Patek Philippe & Co., Geneva. Ladies, round white enamel dial. 18K gold, oval, 23mm. case, set with single cut diamonds. Signed movement & dial $600–700

Patek Philippe & Co., Geneva. Ladies, white matte dial. Platinum rectangular case engraved with scrolls, onyx & diamond-set bezel and lugs. ca 1928. . . . . $1,400–1,725

Patek Philippe & Co. Ladies, platinum matte dial, platinum tonneau case with diamond-set bezel $1,200–1,400

Patek Philippe & Co., Geneva. Ladies, white matte dial, 18J movement. Platinum, oval shaped case, bezel set with old mine diamonds. Ends set with sapphires & centered by old mine diamonds. 31mm. signed case. ca 1930.
. . . . $1,400–1,750

Patek Philippe & Cie, Geneva. Ladies. Square face. Platinum and 14K gold, rectangular case and extended lugs, with numerous pavé-set single-cut diamonds, weave band. Value varies according to size, quality and color of diamonds. ca 1920 . . . . $3,000–3,600

Patek Philippe & Co. Ladies, silvered dial, platinum rectangular case, diamond-set bezel. 25x14mm. ca 1930 . . . . $900–1,050

Patek Philippe & Co. Ladies. Platinum, square case and band set with 250 diamonds. Value varies according to the size, quality and color of diamonds. (Very hard to give value).
. . . .$14,000–18,000

Patek Philippe "Ladies Platinum & Diamond". Tiny silvered dial. Rectangular case. ca 1933.
. . . . $2,000–2,500

Patek Philippe & Co., Geneva. Ladies, silvered dial. 18K gold, rectangular, 23x13mm. case. ca 1924. . . . . $600–675

Patek Philippe "Ladies Diamond & Gold". Silvered dial with black markers and hands. 18K yellow gold, rectangular case, with heavy raised ends. 18 brilliant diamonds in bezel and cord lugs. ca 1940. . . . . $1,500–1,800

Patek Philippe. Ladies, round platinum case with extended lugs set with full-cut round & baguette diamonds. ca 1940. Diamond size & quality will affect value . . . . . $1,500—2,000

Patek Philippe & Co., Geneve. Ladies, round white matte dial, 18J movement. Platinum, round case with filagree extensions set with diamonds & diamond bezel. Pearl & diamond band. ca 1940 . . . . $1,200—1,500

Patek Philippe "Ladies Cord". Round silvered dial, raised 18K gold numbers. 18J movement. Round case with large molded cord lugs. ca 1940. 18K yellow gold . . . . $400—500
Platinum . . . . 400—500

Patek Philippe & Co., Geneve. Ladies, silvered dial. 18K gold round, 29mm. case. Signed case, dial & movement. ca 1950 . . . . . $400—500

Patek Philippe & Co., Geneva. Ladies, silvered matte dial, 18K gold round case with rose-cut diamond-set bezel & extended diamond lugs. 14K gold cord band. ca 1962 . . . $850—1,000

NOTE: The 1967 Patek Philippe catalog used in this book was from the library of Bob Nelch, Modesto, California.

Patek Philippe "Diamond & Sapphire Ladies Platinum Bracelet". Brilliant and baguette-cut diamonds totaling 14.32 carats, mixed with 9.87 carats of choice sapphires in the head and bracelet of this one-of-a-kind watch. Any substitution of stones would reduce its value. ca 1967 . . . .$30,000—40,000

Patek Philippe "Diamond & Ruby Ladies Platinum Bracelet". This one-of-a-kind wrist watch is made up of 18.20 carats of rubies and 14.42 carats of various cut diamonds. Any substitution of precious stones or damage to the watch would reduce its value. ca 1967.
. . . .$35,000—45,000

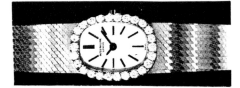

Patek Philippe "Diamond Ladies Gold Bracelet". Silvered dial with black markers and hands. 18K white gold, Golden Ellipse, case with 26 brilliant-cut diamond bezel, attached to a flexible, slanted, rectangular pattern bracelet. ca 1967 . . . . $1,800—2,200

Patek Philippe "Diamond Ladies Gold Bracelet". Midnight-blue dial with stick markers and hands. 18K white, oval case with 30 graduated, brilliant diamond bezel and integral, flexible gold bracelet. ca 1967 . . . . . $2,000—2,400

Patek Philippe "Diamond Ladies Gold Bracelet". White geometric dial with black Roman numerals and hands appear to be a part of the band. 18K white gold, Golden Circle, case, with 26 pear-shaped, graduated, diamond bezel, attached to a flexible, textured gold bracelet. ca 1967. . . . . $2,600–3,000

Patek Philippe "Diamond Ladies Gold Bracelet". Silvered dial with black markers and hands. 18K white gold, round case with 22 diamonds (3 carats) forming an oval-appearing bezel, with an integral, wave-pattern, flexible gold bracelet. ca 1967 . . . . . $2,800–3,400

Patek Philippe "Diamond Ladies Gold Bracelet". Florentine finish gold dial with black markers and hands with the dial appearing to be a part of the band. 18K white gold, Golden Circle, case, with 26 graduated brilliant diamonds forming a Golden Ellipse bezel. 18K white gold, florentined, flexible, attached bracelet. ca 1967 . . . . $1,800–2,200

Patek Philippe "Gold Ladies Bracelet". Florentine finish, yellow gold dial with black markers and hands. 18K yellow gold, Golden Ellipse, case, with florentine bezel and integral, checkerboard pattern, flexible gold bracelet. ca 1967. . . . . $1,200–1,600

Patek Philippe "Diamond Ladies Gold Bracelet". Silvered dial with black numerals and hands. 18K white gold, Golden Circle, case with 30 diamond bezel and integral, textured, flexible white gold bracelet. ca 1967.
. . . . $2,000–2,500

Patek Philippe "Diamond Ladies Gold Bracelet". Florentine finish, white gold dial with black markers and hands. 18K white gold, Golden Circle, case with 40 graduated, baguette diamond bezel, and matching attached, flexible gold bracelet. ca 1967 . . . . . . $2,000–2,500

Patek Philippe "Diamond Ladies Gold Bracelet". Gold textured dial with black markers and hands. 18K yellow gold, round case, with 16 graduated brilliant diamonds forming a Golden Circle bezel. Attached yellow gold, flexible, textured bracelet. ca 1967. . . . $3,000–3,600

Patek Philippe "Diamond Ladies Gold Bracelet". Yellow or white gold dial with black markers and hands. 18K gold, square case, with two rows of 7 graduated brilliant diamonds forming the side bezels, with a textured, flexible, attached, 18K gold bracelet. ca 1967.
18K yellow gold. $2,300–2,700
18K white gold 1,900–2,300

Patek Philippe "Gold Ladies Bracelet". Yellow gold dial with black numerals and hands. 18K yellow gold, Golden Circle, case, with florentine bezel and attached, flexible, gold bracelet. ca 1967. . . . . $1,100–1,500

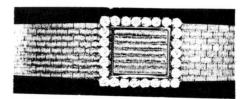

Patek Philippe "Diamond Ladies Gold Hunting Bracelet". The textured gold lid opens when a tiny spring is released. 18K yellow gold square case, with 28 brilliant diamond bezel, with attached, 18K yellow gold, flexible bracelet. ca 1967 . . . . $2,800–3,400

Patek Philippe "Diamond Ladies Gold Bracelet". Yellow gold dial with black markers an and hands. 18K yellow gold, oval case, with 40 brilliant diamond bezel and integral, flexible, gold bracelet. ca 1967 . . . . . $2,200–2,800

Patek Philippe "Diamond Ladies Gold Bracelet". Yellow gold dial with black markers and hands. 18K yellow gold, round case, with 14 graduated, brilliant diamond, oval bezel and attached flexible, textured, gold bracelet. ca 1967 . . . . $3,000–3,500

Patek Philippe "Gold Ladies Bracelet". Bark finish yellow gold dial with black Roman numerals and hands. 18K yellow gold, squared, Golden Ellipse, case, with polished bezel and matching integral, flexible, bark finish bracelet. ca 1967. . . . . $1,200–1,600

Patek Philippe "Gold Ladies Bracelet". Gold dial with polished gold markers and hands. 18K yellow gold, oval case, with polished bezel and matching integral, textured, flexible bracelet. ca 1967. . . . . $1,100–1,500

Patek Philippe "Gold Ladies Bracelet". Gold dial with thin black markers and hands. 18K yellow gold, rectangle case, with textured bezel and integral, flexible bracelet. ca 1967. . . . . $1,200–1,600

Patek Philippe "Gold Ladies Bracelet". Geometric lined gold dial with thin black markers and hands. 18K yellow gold, round case, with textured gold bezel and bracelet. ca 1967. . . . . $1,100–1,500

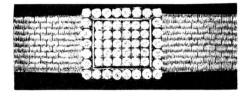

Patek Philippe "Diamond Ladies Gold Hunting Bracelet". 18K white, rectangle case, with 28 brilliant diamond bezel and 30 diamond checkerboard lid. Matching textured, integral, flexible, 18K white gold bracelet. ca 1967.
. . . . $3,400—4,000

Patek Philippe "Diamond Ladies Gold Bracelet". Florentine, white gold dial with black markers and hands. 18K white gold, Golden Circle, case, with 30 diamond bezel and integral, textured, flexible gold bracelet. ca 1967.
. . . . $1,800—2,100

Patek Philippe "Diamond Ladies Gold Bracelet". Black dial with white gold markers and hands. 18K white gold, rectangular cushion case, with 40 brilliant diamond bezel and integral, textured, flexible, white gold bracelet. ca 1967. . . . . $1,700—2,400

Patek Philippe. Ladies. Satin dial. 18K gold square case with molded lugs . . . . $400—500

Patek Philippe & Co. Ladies, blue metal dial, 18K gold, rectangular shaped case, signed 18K band & box. Modern . . . . . . $1,000—1,250

Patek Philippe "Diamond Ladies Platinum Bracelet". The 64 baguette diamonds in the head and bracelet were especially matched and cut for this watch, and totals 23.65 carats. Substitution of any diamond would reduce its value. ca 1967 . . . .$25,000—35,000

Patek Philippe & Co., Geneva. White matte dial. Platinum tonneau, 28mm. case. Signed case, dial & movement. ca 1913 . $1,250—1,350

Patek Philippe "Diamond Ladies Gold Bracelet". White gold dial with black markers and hands. 18K white gold, round case, with 36 brilliant diamond bezel and integral, flexible, textured gold bracelet. ca 1967 . $1,700—2,100

Patek Philippe & Cie, Geneve. Gold dial, 18J, 9¾''' movement. 18K gold, 25x33mm. rectangular case. ca 1913 . . . . . . $950—1,050

Patek Philippe & Co., Geneve, retailed by Shreve, Crump & Low. Silvered matte dial, 18J movement. 18K gold, 28mm. octagonal case stamped "A.W.C. Co." ca 1915.
. . . . $950–1,050

Patek Philippe & Co., Geneva. Curvex, gold plated dial. 18K gold tonneau case. Signed dial & movement. $1,100–1,200

Patek Philippe & Co., Geneva. Tu-toned, silvered dial, sweep second, 19J movement. Stainless steel & GF cushion, 32mm. case. Signed movement & dial.   . $400–500

Patek Philippe & Co., Geneve. Silvered dial, subsidiary seconds, 18J movement. 18K gold rectangular case. ca 1920. . . . . $1,200–1,250

Patek Philippe & Co., Geneva, retailed by Tiffany & Co. Gold dial, 18J movement. 18K gold, 25mm. hexagonal case, fully signed. ca 1918 . . . . $650–750

Patek Philippe & Co., Geneva. Curvex, gold plated dial. 18K tonneau, 45mm. case. Signed case, dial & movement. ca 1920. $1,150–1,250

Patek Philippe & Co., Geneva. Curvex, oval shaped, silvered dial. Elongated tonneau, 27mm. case. ca 1918 . . . . . . $1,200–1,250

Patek Philippe & Co., Geneva. Gold dial. 18K gold square tank, 28mm. case. Signed case, dial & movement. ca 1920 . . . . $1,000–1,200

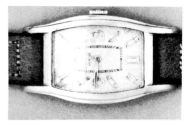

Patek Philippe & Co., Geneva. White gold finished dial with diamond baguette numerals. 18J rectangular movement. 18K gold, 44mm. tonneau, unmarked American contract case. Signed movement & dial. ca 1921. $800—1,000

Patek Philippe & Co., Geneva. Curvex silvered dial, diamond numbers. 18J movement. Platinum, tonneau, 38mm. case. Signed dial & movement. Unmarked American contract case. ca 1925. . . . . $800—900

Patek Philippe & Co., Geneva. White enamel dial, sweep seconds. 18K gold, 33mm. round case, solid lugs. Signed case, dial & movement. ca 1923. . . . . $700—800

Patek Philippe & Co., Geneva. Curvex, silvered dial. 18K gold, hinged rectangular, 43mm. case. Signed case, dial & movement. ca 1925. . . . . $1,350—1,450

Patek Philippe & Co., Geneva. Silvered dial, subsidiary seconds. 18K gold, 22mm. rectangular tank case, with C shaped angular lugs. ca 1925. . . . . $1,150—1,250

Patek Philippe & Co., Geneva. Black dial, subsidiary seconds, 18J movement. 18K gold rectangular case. Signed case, dial & movement. . . . . $1,300—1,500

Patek Philippe & Co., Geneva. Silvered dial, subsidiary seconds. 18K gold, 22mm. rectangular case. Signed case, dial & movement. ca 1936. . . . . $1,100—1,200

Patek Philippe & Co., Geneva, "Curvex". White brushed dial. 18K gold, chased engraved, 25mm. case. ca 1928 . . . . . . $1,250—1,350

Patek Philippe & Co., Geneva. Curvex, silvered dial. Subsidiary seconds, 18J movement. 18K gold tonneau, 35mm. case. Signed case, dial & movement. ca 1928. . . . . $1,150—1,250

Patek Philippe & Co., Geneva, "Curvex".
White matte dial, unusually heavy, black
Roman numerals. Subsidiary seconds, 18J
movement. Platinum, 40mm. rectangular case.
Signed case, dial & movement. ca 1928.
. . . . $1,275—1,350

Patek Philippe. Subsidiary seconds. 18K gold,
29x30mm. rectangular case with bowed sides.
ca 1935. . . . . $1,100—1,250

Patek Philippe. Subsidiary seconds. 18J movement. 18K yellow gold, cushion case. ca 1928.
. . . . $1,050—1,150

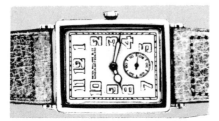

Patek Philippe. Subsidiary seconds. 18J movement. 18K yellow gold, rectangular case, black
enameled bezel. ca 1928 . . . . . $1,200—1,275

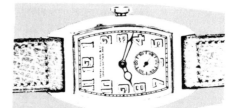

Patek Philippe. Subsidiary seconds. 18J movement. 18K yellow gold, tonneau case. ca 1928.
. . . . $1,250—1,325

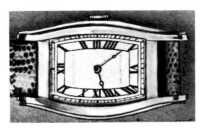

Patek Philippe. Silvered dial, 18J rectangular
movement. **Platinum** tonneau, unmarked,
26x44mm., American contract case. ca 1928.
. . . . $700—800

Patek Philippe & Co., Geneva, "Curvex".
Matte dial, platinum numbers, subsidiary
seconds, 18J movement. Platinum, 41mm.
rectangular case. Signed case, dial & movement.
ca 1930. . . . . $1,300—1,400

Patek Philippe & Co., Geneva. Quarter Repeater, silvered dial, subsidiary seconds at
9 o'clock. 18K gold round case.. $6,500—8,500

Patek Philippe & Co., Geneve. Matte dial, oval
movement. 18K gold, 36mm., slightly curved
rectangular case. ca 1930. . . . . $1,150—1,250

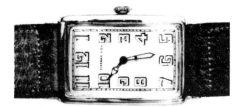

Patek Philippe & Co., Geneve. Silvered dial. 18K gold, curved rectangular case. ca 1930. . . . . $1,325—1,425

Patek Philippe & Co., Geneve. Silvered dial, subsidiary seconds, rectangular platinum case. . . . . $1,300—1,400

Patek Philippe & Co., Geneva, retailed by Spaulding & Co., Chicago. Silvered dial, rare "two-color", 18K white & yellow gold rectangular case with angled lugs . . $1,600—1,700

Patek Philippe & Co., Geneve. White dial.18K gold, square case . . . . $950—1,050

Patek Philippe & Co., Geneva. White matte dial, subsidiary seconds, 18J movement. 18K gold rectangular case with moulded borders. ca 1938. . . . . $1,200—1,275

Patek Philippe & Co., Geneve. Silvered dial. subsidiary seconds. 18K rose gold rectangular case with moulded lugs. . . . . . $1,200—1,300

Patek Philippe & Co., Geneve. Silvered dial, subsidiary seconds, 18K gold, 25mm. square case . . . . $900—1,000

Patek Philippe & Co., Geneve. Silvered dial, subsidiary seconds, tu-tone gold & platinum square case. . . . . $1,600—1,800

Patek Philippe & Co., Geneva. Silvered dial, subsidiary seconds, 18J movement. 18K gold, round moulded, 30mm. case with extended moulded lugs. ca 1940 . . . . . . $1,200—1,400

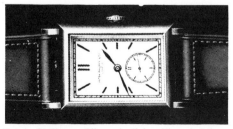

Patek Philippe. Silvered dial with subsidiary seconds. 18J movement. Rectangular case with polished bezel. ca 1933. . . . . . $1,100—1,200

Patek Philippe "Gold Man's Strap". Silvered dial with black markers, hands, and subsidiary seconds. 18K yellow gold, curved rectangular case with hidden lugs. ca 1940 . $1,200—1,400

Patek Philippe "Faceted Gold Strap". Black dial with applied gold markers and hands, subsidiary seconds. 18K yellow gold, rectangular faceted case with tapered ends. ca 1940 . . . . $1,200—1,300

Patek Philippe & Co., Geneva. Silvered dial, subsidiary seconds, 18J movement. 18K gold, 43mm, long rectangular case. ca 1940.
. . . . $1,200—1,300

Patek Philippe. Chronograph, tachometer base 1,000m. Tu-tone dial with subsidiary seconds & 30 minute recorder. Round 18K gold, 33mm. case. ca 1940. Chronograph . . . $2,800—3,200
Split seconds. . . . . 6,000—8,000

Patek Philippe "World Time". Silvered dial with black enamel 12 and 24 hour chapter rings, with sliding rim that tell at a turn the time in the major cities of the world's 24 time belts. Round case with heavy lugs. ca 1940.
18K yellow gold. . . . . $2,000—2,400
Platinum . . . . 2,000—2,400

Patek Philippe (case by Brock in Los Angeles, Ca.) Silvered dial with black markers and subsidiary seconds. 18K yellow gold rectangular case with heavy lugs, with screws to hold band. ca 1941. . . . . $700—900

Patek Philippe. Silvered dial, diamond numerals, subsidiary seconds, 18J movement. Platinum, 20x43mm. rectangular case. ca 1941.
. . . . $1,300—1,400

Patek Philippe. Subsidiary seconds. Rectangular 18K square gold case with moulded lower edge. ca 1945 . . . . $950—1,000

NOTE: Read Page 6 before using this book to value your wrist watch.

Patek Philippe & Co., Geneva. Silvered dial. Subsidiary seconds. 18K gold rectangular, 39mm. case. Signed case, dial & movement. ca 1945. . . . . $1,000—1,100

Patek Philippe & Co., Geneva, retailed by Freccero, Montevideo. Rose gold dial, subsidiary seconds, 18J movement. 18K gold, 37mm. rectangular case with extended lugs. ca 1945 . . . . $1,275—1,350

Patek Philippe & Co., Geneve. Silvered dial, subsidiary seconds, 18J movement. 18K gold, 36mm. round case. Signed case, dial & movement. ca 1945. . . . . $600—700

Patek Philippe & Co., Geneva. Gold matte dial, subsidiary seconds, 18J movement. 18K gold rectangular case. ca 1945. . . . . $1,100—1,200

Patek Philippe & Co., retailed by Tiffany & Co., New York. Silvered dial, 18J movement. Stainless steel, round case with moulded lugs. $350—450

Patek Philippe. Subsidiary seconds. 18K gold, 20x38mm. rectangular case with moulded ends. ca 1945. . . . . $1,150—1,250

NOTE: All values are given for the head only unless the bracelet is included in the description.

Patek Philippe & Co., Geneva. Silvered dial, brilliant & baguette diamond numerals, subsidiary seconds. 18K gold, square-form, 34mm. case. Signed case, dial & movement. ca 1946. . . . . $1,350—1,450

Patek Philippe & Co., Geneve. Silvered dial, subsidiary seconds. 18K gold, 34mm. round case. Signed case, dial & movement. ca 1946. . . . . $600—700

Patek Philippe, Geneva. Silvered dial, subsidiary seconds, 18K gold rectangular case. ca 1948 . . . . $1,100—1,200

Patek Philippe & Co., Geneva. Silvered dial, subsidiary seconds. 18J movement. 18K gold square case with moulded lugs. Signed case, dial & movement. ca 1948 . . . . $1,000—1,100

Patek Philippe & Cie, Geneva. Moonphase, calendar. Silvered dial, subsidiary seconds, red chapter ring with black Arabic numerals, day & month windows & outer date ring. 18J movement. Round platinum case. (Not perpetual calendar) . . . . $7,500—9,500

Patek Philippe. Black dial, subsidiary seconds. 18K gold, 20x42mm. rectangular case with arched front. ca 1949. . . . . . . $1,200—1,300

Patek Philippe & Co. White gold brushed dial with raised 18K gold numerals, subsidiary seconds. 18K gold, 34mm. round case with moulded sides swirled into lugs. Signed case, dial & movement. ca 1949 . . . . . $650—750

Patek Philippe & Co., Geneve. White matte dial, center seconds, 18K gold, 33mm. round case. Signed case, dial & movement. ca 1949. . . . . $600—700

Patek Philippe & Co., Geneve. Rose gold dial, subsidiary seconds. 18K gold, 28mm., wide, rectangular case with moulded lugs. Signed case, dial & movement. ca 1950. $1,000—1,100

Patek Philippe & Co., Geneve. Silvered dial, subsidiary seconds. 18K gold, 25mm. square case. Signed case, dial & movement. ca 1954.
. . . . $900—1,000

Patek Philippe & Co. Split-second chronograph, silvered dial, subsidiary seconds, 30 minute recorder & outer seconds ring, 25J movement. 18K gold, round case with extended lugs. Signed case, movement & dial . . $7,000—8,000

Patek Philippe & Co., Geneva. Retailed by **Gubelin.** Gold, engine-turned dial, Subsidiary seconds, 18J movement. 18K gold, 28mm. square case with matching engine-turning. Signed case, dial & movement. ca 1955.
. . . . $1,000—1,100

Patek Philippe & Co., Geneve. Silvered dial, center seconds, 18K gold, shaped square, 35mm. case. ca 1950 . . . . . . $1,100—1,200

Patek Philippe & Co., Geneva. Matte dial, subsidiary seconds, 18J, tonneau movement. 18K gold rectangular, 30mm. case, extended lugs. Signed case, dial & movement. ca 1955.
. . . . $1,250—1,350

Patek Philippe & Co., Geneva. Gold matte dial, subsidiary seconds. 18K gold, 30mm. rectangular moulded case. ca 1956 . . . . $1,150—1,225

Patek Philippe & Co., Geneva. Gold matte dial. Subsidiary seconds. 18K gold rectangular case with triangular sides. Signed case, dial & movement. ca 1955 . . . . $1,200—1,300

Patek Philippe & Co., Geneva. White matte dial, center seconds, 18K gold round case. ca 1956 . . . . $600—700

Patek Philippe & Co., Geneva. Silvered dial, 18J movement. 18K gold square, 33mm. case. Signed case, movement & dial. ca 1960.
. . . . $800—900

Patek Philippe & Co., Geneva. Self-winding calendar, silvered dial, date window, 36J movement. 18K gold, round case. Signed movement, case & dial . . . . $1,200—1,400

Patek Philippe. Automatic calendar, subsidiary seconds & window date. 18K gold circular 35mm. case with moulded lugs . $1,000—1,200

Patek Philippe. 18K gold slim, 28mm. square case. ca 1980 . . . . $1,000—1,200

Patek Philippe & Co., Geneva. White gold marbeled face. 18J movement. 18K gold square case, with matching marbled 18K gold Patek band. ca 1962 . . . . $1,900—2,300

Patek Philippe & Co., Geneve. Moonphase perpetual calendar, chronograph. White matte dial, subsidiary seconds, 30 minute & date recorders, day & month windows with outer tachometer ring, base one mile. 23J movement. 18K gold Patek round case. . .$13,000—14,000

Patek Philippe & Co., Geneva. Blued steel dial with gold bars* for markers. 18J movement. 18K gold, cushion case. ca 1964 . $950—1,050

Patek Philippe. Silvered dial, 18J movement. Rectangular case with **convex sides (or hour glass shape)** extending into lugs. ca 1957.
. . . . $1,300—1,450

Patek Philippe & Co., Geneva, "Curvex".
Silvered dial, subsidiary seconds, tonneau movement. 18K gold, 39mm. slightly curved, rectangular case. Signed case, dial & movement.
ca 1966. . . . . $1,200—1,300

Patek Philippe & Co., Geneva. Gold Matte dial,
subsidiary seconds, 18J tonneau movement.
18K gold rectangular curved, 29mm. case with
angular lugs. Signed case, dial, & movement.
ca 1966. . . . . $1,200—1,300

Patek Philippe. Unusual asymmetrical , 18K
gold, 29x34mm. case. . . . . . . $1,200—1,400

Patek Philippe & Co., Geneva. Retailed by
Beyer, Zurich. Blue gold enamel dial. 18J
movement. 18K gold, 34mm. cushion case. 18K
gold basket weave band. Signed case, strap,
movement & dial . . . . $1,800—2,200

Patek Philippe. 18K gold, 37mm. round case,
with a fitted gold bracelet. ca 1967. $600—700

Patek Philippe, Geneve. Steel blue dial, 18K
gold, 31mm. oval case, with marked 18K gold,
open link band. Man's size, Modern.
. . . . $2,700—3,100

**Patek Philippe "Man's Gold Automatic Calen-
dar Bracelet".** Black dial with polished white
gold numerals and hands, subsidiary seconds
and date window at 3. Self-winding movement.
Round, 18K white gold case with textured
bezel and integral flexible bracelet. ca 1967.
. . . . $1,500—1,700

**Patek Philippe "Ultra-Thin Man's Gold
Bracelet".** Slate finish dial with white gold
Roman numerals and hands. 18K white gold
square case with distinctive milled sides and
integral textured flexible bracelet. ca 1967.
. . . . $1,700—2,100

Patek Philippe "Diamond Ultra-Thin Man's Gold Bracelet". White gold dial with thin black markers and stick hands. 18K white gold, cushion rectangular case with 62 brilliant diamond bezel and matching textured flexible integral bracelet. ca 1967 . . . . $2,800—3,400

Patek Philippe "Diamond Bezel Ultra-Thin Man's Gold Bracelet". Silvered dial with thin black hands and markers. 18K white gold rectangular case with 30 baguette diamond bezel and integral flexible, checkerboard pattern, gold bracelet. ca 1967 . . . . . $3,500—4,500

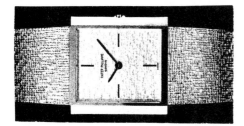

Patek Philippe "Ultra-Thin Man's Gold Bracelet". Black stick hands and markers on a florentine texture dial that appears to be a part of the bracelet. 18K white gold square case with beveled bezel and matching integral flexible, florentine finish, bracelet. ca 1967. . . . . $1,700—2,100

Patek Philippe "Ultra-Thin Man's Gold Strap". Gold dial with black markers and hands. Square 18K yellow gold case. ca 1967 . $1,200—1,500

Patek Philippe "Ultra-Thin Man's Gold Strap". White gold dial with thin markers and hands. 18K white gold round case. ca 1967 $800—900

Patek Philippe "Man's Gold Automatic Calendar". Florentined white gold dial with thin black stick markers and hands, subsidiary seconds, with date window at 3. Self-winding movement. Round, 18K white gold case with polished bezel. ca 1967. . . . . . $1,000—1,100

Patek Philippe "Thin Man's Gold Strap". Black Roman numerals on gold dial. Polished bezel and lugs. Golden Ellipse, 18K yellow gold case. ca 1967. . . . . $1,200—1,400

Patek Philippe "Thin Man's Gold Strap". Thin gold markers and hands, blue dial with polished yellow gold bezel. 18K yellow gold, Golden Ellipse case, with hidden lugs. ca 1967. . . . . $1,200—1,400

Patek Philippe "Automatic Man's Gold Strap". Silvered dial with black numerals and hands and subsidiary seconds. Self-winding movement. 18K yellow gold cushion case with round polished bezel. ca 1967. . . . . . $1,400—1,600

Patek Philippe "Ultra-Thin Man's Gold Strap". Silvered dial with gold markers and hands. Round, 18K yellow gold case. ca 1967. ca 1967 . . . . $800—900

Patek Philippe "Thin Man's Gold Strap". Rhodium dial with gold markers. Round, 18K yellow gold case. ca 1967 . . . . . . $700—800

Patek Philippe "Thin Man's Gold Strap". Silvered dial with thin gold stick markers and hands, subsidiary seconds. Round, 18K yellow gold case of classic, simple lines. ca 1967. . . . . $700—800

Patek Philippe "Moonphase Calendar". Silvered dial with gold markers and hands. Day and month windows below 12. Perpetual calendar date ring around colorful moonphase at 6. Round, 18K yellow gold case with polished bezel. ca 1967 . . . . $8,000—9,000

Patek Philippe "Thin Gold Man's Bracelet". Silvered dial with applied gold markers and hands. Identical satin textured gold on intergal bracelet and round 18K yellow gold case. ca 1967 . . . . $1,600—2,000

Patek Philippe "Ultra-Thin Man's Gold Bracelet". Case, dial and bracelet display the identical textured gold look in this rectangular design. ca 1967. 18K yellow gold $2,500—2,800
18K white gold . . . . 2,200—2,500

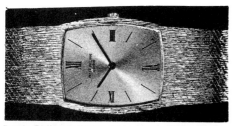

Patek Philippe "Ultra-Thin Man's Gold Bracelet". White or gold dial with black markers and hands. integral bracelet and case with continuous striated pattern on both. ca 1967. 18K yellow gold . . . . $2,200—2,600
18K white gold . . . . 1,800—2,200

Patek Philippe "Thin Man's Gold Bracelet". Dial and bracelet have matching yellow gold texture on this 18K yellow gold ,Golden Ellipse case with polished bezel. ca 1967 $2,000—2,400

Patek Philippe, Geneve. Self-winding, white gold matte dial. 18K gold, 36mm. round case, diamond-cut mesh bracelet . . . $1,500—1,750

Patek Philippe "Ultra-Thin Man's Gold Bracelet". White or yellow gold dial. integral textured bracelet and bezel. ca 1967. 18K yellow gold. . . . . $1,700—2,100
18K white gold . . . . 1,500—1,750

NOTE: Read Page 6 before using this book to value your wrist watch.

Patek Philippe "Man's Gold Automatic Calendar Bracelet". Gold dial with polished gold markers and hands, subsidiary seconds, and date window at 3. Self-winding movement. Round, 18K yellow gold case with florentined bezel and integral matching, gold textured, bracelet. ca 1967 . . . . $2,200—2,600

NOTE: All values are given for the head only unless the bracelet is included in the description.

Patek Philippe "Thin Man's Gold Bracelet". Gold dial with polished gold markers and hands. Golden Circle, 18K yellow gold case and integral bracelet with textured finish. ca 1967 . . . . $2,000—2,300

PERPETUAL SELF-WINDING WATCH COMPANY OF AMERICA INC., 485 Madison Ave., New York, NY, was offering 25 round and rectangular styles at prices from $29.75 to $125.00 in 1931. Large spreads of advertising was done in Vogue, Post, New Yorker and Vanity Fair magazines in the fall of 1930.

"Perpetual" marked on silvered dial. Red reserve power indicator visible through hole above 6. 15J round, Harwood movement. Hands are bezel set. 14K YGF, 29x36mm. tonneau case. ca 1931 . . . . $75–125

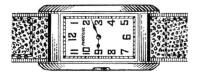

"Perpetual" marked on silvered dial. 15J self-winding movement. Crown at 9 sets hands only. 20x36mm. 14K WGF rectangular case. ca 1931 . . . . $125–200

"Perpetual" marked on silvered dial. Red reserve power indicator visible through hole above 6. 15J round Harwood self-winding movement. Hands are bezel set. 14K white gold 29x36mm. tonneau case. ca 1931. . $225–300

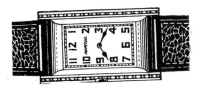

"Perpetual" marked on silvered dial. 15J self-winding movement. Crown at 9 sets hands only. 20x36mm., 14K yellow gold rectangular case. ca 1931 . . . . $350–425

Piaget. Ladies, gold dial, 18K gold, 23mm. round case, bezel set with 20 marque-cut diamonds. $800–1,000

Piaget. Ladies, black dial with 4 diamonds for numerals. 18K gold, 23mm. round case with engraved 18K gold band $700–900

Piaget. Ladies, gold matte dial, 18K gold round case, bezel set with two rows of 88 diamonds. $800–1,000

Piaget. Ladies 18K gold, enameled, rectangular case with green & blue enameled leaves. $1,200–1,400

Piaget. Ladies. Egg-shaped lapis lazuli dial, woven 18K gold mesh bracelet, 45mm. $2,200–2,600

Piaget. Ladies, white dial. 18K gold, 22mm. rectangular case, bezel set with 36 diamonds. 14K gold, engraved mesh band . . $800—1,000

Piaget. Steel blue dial, 18K gold, 32mm. round case, with 18K gold mesh band . . $800—1,000

Piaget. 18K gold, 22mm. rectangular case with rounded corners & link chain bracelet.
. . . . $2,500—2,800

Piaget "Man's Gold Strap". 18K white or yellow gold dial & wafer thin, oval case. ca 1964 . . . . $400—500

Piaget. 18K gold rectangular case with a bark finish, 23x28mm. . . . . $1,600—1,800

Piaget. Black dial, 18K gold rectangular case with milled borders, 33x25mm. . . . $300—375

Piaget, Asprey. Black dial with 4 diamond numerals. 18K, 23x28mm. rectangular gold case . . . . $400—450

Piaget. Automatic, lapis-lazuli dial signed Piaget Automatic Asprey, Swiss. 18K gold, 32mm. square case with bowed sides and milled bezel. ca 1970. . . . . $1,000—1,400

Piaget "Man's Gold Bracelet". Crocadolite dial, white gold hands. 18K white gold, rectangular case and mesh band. . . . . $2,500—3,000

Piaget. 18K gold, rectangular dial, case & bracelet, with synthetic sapphire crystal. ca 1978 . . . . $400—500

Piaget. Rectangular, 18K gold dial & case, with synthetic sapphire crystal. ca 1978.
. . . . $400—500

Piaget "Diamond & Gold Bracelet". 18K yellow gold dial, case & bracelet. 44-diamond bezel. ca 1978 . . . . $800—1,000

Piaget. Round, 18K gold dial & case, with synthetic sapphire crystal. ca 1978.
. . . . $400—500

Piaget. Modern black & diamond dial, with mystery diamond hour indicator. 18K gold square case with rounded edges & diamond bezel . . . . $1,400—1,600

Piaget. Modern diamond-set center on a mother-of-pearl background. 18K gold square case with rounded corners. 18K yellow & white gold band . . . . $3,000—4,000

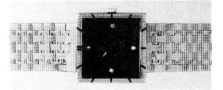

Piaget. Onyx dial, 4 diamonds for numerals. 18K gold square case, 25mm., bezel inset with bars for hour numerals, Piaget, 18K gold band.
. . . . 20% over gold

Pierce Chronograph. Subsidiary seconds & 60 minute recorder. Telemeter & tachometer. 15J movement. Round case. ca 1939.
Gold-filled top. . . . . $30—65
Stainless steel . . . . 25—45

Pierce "Four-in-One Chronograph". Subsidiary seconds, stop watch, telemeter, tachometer & time out feature. 17J or 7J movement. Round chrome case. ca 1941 . . . . $25—40
Gold-filled top, steel back . . . . 40—75

Post "Ladies Gold Cord". 17J movement. 14K gold square case and large link lugs. ca 1947. . . . . 10% to 20% over gold value

Post "Ladies Gold Cord". 17J movement. 14K gold square case with fancy single lugs. ca 1947 . . . . $60—80

Pulsar "Auto-Time". A twist of the wrist flashes the time. Date & seconds by pressing a button. ca 1975. Made in a variety of case & bracelet styles. 18K YG . . . . $450—550
14K YG . . . . 400—500
14K gold-filled . . . . 100—125
Stainless steel . . . . 45— 60

Precimax. Automatic, moonphase, calendar, center seconds, day & month windows, outer date ring. 18K gold, 36mm. round case. ca 1950 . . . . $575—675

Pulsar "Pulse/Time Computer". Limited edition of 100 serial numbered watches. The regular Pulsar watch, plus displaying your pulse rate on the data screen by placing your finger on the two jeweled dots in the black circle. 14K solid gold. ca 1977 . . . . (?) $850—950

Pulsar "Time Computer". ca 1972. Made in a variety of case and bracelet styles. Values include bracelet and must include battery & keeping time. 18K gold. . . . . $450—550
14K gold . . . . 400—500
14K gold top . . . . 200—250
14K gold-filled . . . . 100—125
Stainless steel . . . . 45— 60

Quarter Repeater. Gold finished dial, red numerals. 14K gold, 37mm. round case.
. . . . $2,000—2,200

Racine, Lady Sterling Silver Bracelet Watch. (one of the first wrist watches introduced in the U.S. to the public nationwide from 1908 to 1915). Glass enamel dial. 6 or 10J, pin set, Swiss cylinder movement with pigskin leather band . . .6J . . .$15—20 . . .10J . . .$30—35

Racine, Jules "Quick Train". Subsidiary seconds. 14K yellow gold, square case. ca 1929 . . . . $125—145

Racine. Round dial, subsidiary seconds. 15J, 10½''' movement. Stainless steel tonneau case. ca 1934 . . . .$15—25

Recta "Diamond, Emerald and Platinum". Rectangular case and hinged lugs. ca 1928. Value varies according to the size, quality and color of the diamonds and other precious stones. . . . . $250—350

Racine "Reserve Power Indicator". Self-winding, radium dial, center seconds. Stainless steel round case with moulded lugs. ca 1957. . . . .$25—50

Recta "Diamond, Emerald & Platinum Bracelet". "Art Deco" design. ca 1928. Value varies according to size, quality and color of the diamonds and other precious stones. . . . . 20% to 30% over diamond, emerald and platinum value.

Renaud "Diamond & Gold Bracelet". Ladies. Silvered dial. 18K gold, cushion case, diamond bezel & freeform gold link bracelet. ca 1966. . . . . .10% to 20% over diamond & gold value

Racine "Braille". Round enameled dial. Nickel tonneau case, stainless steel back, waterproof. . . . .$50—100

Renaud "Ladies Gold Bracelet". Silvered dial. 18K gold oval case & matching textured bracelet. ca 1966 . . . . 10% to 20% over gold value

ROCKFORD WATCH CO.
Rockford, Illinois
1876 to 1915

Rockford closed their factory in 1915, about the time wrist watches began to be sold in the United States. Only a few American-made Rockford wrist watches have shown up. About 1970, Swiss wrist watches wearing the Rockford name were marketed in the U.S.A.

Rockford "Commander Calendar". Waterproof. Silvered dial with date window at 3. Center seconds. 17J, Swiss movement. Round, yellow top, stainless steel back case. ca 1970 . $10—20

Rockford "Viking Automatic Calendar". Waterproof. Silvered grey or white dial with luminous markers and date window at 3, center seconds. 17J, Swiss movement. Yellow top or stainless steel round case. ca 1970. . . . .$10—20

Rockford "Meteor". Waterproof. Luminous silvered dial, center seconds. 17J movement. Round yellow top and stainless steel back. ca 1970. . . . .$7—18

Rockford "Arlene Automatic Ladies Calendar". Waterproof. Silvered or blue luminous dial, center seconds and date window. 17J movement. Stainless steel tonneau case. ca 1970. . . . .$10—20

Rockford "Lowell Calendar". Waterproof. Silvered dial with luminous hands and dots, center seconds, and date window. Round yellow top and stainless steel back. ca 1970 . . . .$7—18

Rockford "Saturn". Waterproof. Luminous silvered dial, center seconds. 17J movement. Round yellow top and stainless steel back. ca 1970 . . . .$7—18

Rockford "Executive Automatic Calendar". Waterproof. Silvered dial with gold markers and date window at 3. Center seconds. 17J, Swiss movement. 18K yellow gold round case. ca 1970 . . . . $100—125

Rockford "Nelson Calendar". Waterproof. Luminous silvered dial, center seconds and date window. 17J movement. Round yellow top and stainless steel back. ca 1970 . . . .$7—18

Rockford "Nassau Automatic Calendar". Waterproof. Luminous silvered or blue dial, with date window at 3. Center seconds. 17J, Swiss movement. Stainless steel florentine-finish tonneau case. ca 1970 . . . . . $10—20

Rockford "Admiral". Waterproof. Silvered luminous dial, center seconds. 17J movement. Round yellow top with stainless steel back. ca 1970 . . . .$7—18

Rodania "Tachometer Chronograph". Subsidiary seconds, 30 minute recorder with outer tachometer ring. 13¾''', 17J movement. Round chrome case with steel back. ca 1957. . $40—60

Rodania "Chrome Up-Down". Tu-tone gold & white luminous dial with center seconds, reserve power indicator at 12. 17J, 11½''' movement. Chrome top, steel back, round case. ca 1957. . . . . $20—30

Rodania "Moonphase Calendar". Luminous hands & dots, subsidiary seconds, day & month windows with outer date ring. 11½''', 17J movement. Round rolled gold plate case with steel back. ca 1957 . . . . $75—100

Rolex. Ladies. Silvered dial, 15J movement. 9K gold plain round case, lugs for ribbon band.
. . . . $100—150

Rolex. Silvered dial, subsidiary seconds. 14K gold tonneau case with engraved bezel. ca 1920 . . . . $375—450

Rolex. Ladies. Square white dial. 18K white gold, 15x29mm. rectangular case set with lines of diamonds & sapphires. ca 1924.
. . . . $450—600

Rolex "Ladies Ring". White enamel dial. 14K gold, bright-cut, engraved, 18mm. round case. Red enamel bezel with rose-cut diamonds. ca 1925. . . . . $350—450

Rolex. Ladies Prima movement. 18K gold, 15x40mm. oval case with diamond border & strap lugs. ca 1926 . . . . $400—500

Rolex. Silvered dial with engine-turned center. 15J movement. Silver man's cushion, 29mm. case. ca 1926 . . . . $250—350

Rolex. Ladies Prima movement. 18K white gold, 15x45mm. rectangular case, molded lugs, all inlaid in diamonds, and 9K gold bracelet. ca 1928. . . . . $1,200—1,500

Rolex. Ladies prima movement. 14K white gold, 15x24mm. tonneau case with diamond bezel . . . . $400—500

Rolex "Viceroy". Small tu-tone gold & silver finished dial. Ladies rectangular case with heavy cord lugs and arched top. ca 1935.
18K yellow gold. . . . . $300—375
9K yellow gold. . . . . 250—300
9K yellow gold top . . . . 100—150
Gold-filled . . . . 50— 75

Rolex "Duchesse". Silvered dial. Ladies strap tonneau case, with polished wide beveled edges. ca 1935. 9K yellow gold . . . . $300—350
9K yellow gold top . . . . 200—275
Gold-filled . . . . 150—200

Rolex "Princesse". Small silvered dial. Ladies rectangular movement and case with stepped sides and lugs. ca 1935.

18K yellow gold.	$300—375
18K yellow gold top	100—150
9K tu-tone	375—450
9K gold top	100—175
Gold-filled	50— 75

Rolex "Marquise". Silvered dial with bold black markers. Ladies strap tonneau case with narrow beveled edges. ca 1935.

18K yellow gold.	$400—450
9K yellow gold top	200—275
Gold-filled	150—200

Rolex "Princesse Egyptienne". Ladies. Small silvered dial. Rectangular movement and case with stepped cord lugs. ca 1936.

18K yellow gold.	$300—375
18K yellow gold top	100—150
Gold-filled	50— 75

Rolex "Rochettina". Small silvered dial. Ladies rectangular movement and ribbon case with polished beveled ends. ca 1936.

18K yellow gold.	$200—275
Gold-filled	50— 75

Rolex. Ladies. Hidden white dial, raised gold chapters. 18K gold fancy-shaped case. Lid shaped like a buckle, set with diamonds & synthetic rubies & behive link bracelet.
. . . . $1,200—1,800

Rolex. Ladies, self-winding, silvered dial. Subsidiary seconds. 18K gold square, 25mm. case. ca 1940. . . . . $600—700

Rolex Ladies. 14K gold square case, molded lugs set with diamonds & rubies. ca 1943.
. . . . $400—475

Rolex "Ladies Gold Bracelet". Silvered dial with 18K applied gold markers. 14K square head with integral 14K flexible snake band. ca 1949. . . . . $450—550

Rolex. Ladies. White dial, raised gold dots for numerals. Gold rectangular, 11x15mm. case with molded lugs. ca 1950 . . . . . . $150—200

Rolex Ladies Gold Oyster. 23mm. case. ca 1950 . . . . $350—450

Rolex. Ladies. 18K gold, 16mm. square case with raised glass. Unusual fitted bracelet with axe head links. ca 1955. . . . . $600–800

Rolex. Ladies. White dial, subsidiary seconds, 9K gold, 21mm. round case, molded lugs. ca 1951 . . . . $175–225

Rolex "Milky Way". Ladies. White dial, raised gold stars & dots for numerals. Round platinum case, 22-diamond set bezel, 4-diamond end-pieces & platinum bracelet with 24 diamonds. ca 1960. Depending on the size of stones, ... $1,400–1,800

Rolex "Orion". Ladies. White dial, raised gold chapters. Square platinum case, 20 diamonds set in bezel, 10-diamond endpieces, platinum band with 58 diamonds. ca 1960 . $900–1,100

Rolex "Platinum & Diamond Bracelet". Ladies. White dial, raised gold chapters. Round platinum case set with 20 diamonds & platinum bracelet set with 68 diamonds. ca 1960. $850–1,000

Rolex "White Gold & Diamond Bracelet". Ladies. Square white dial, raised gold chapters. 14K white gold square case set with 34 diamonds & 14K white gold bracelet. ca 1960. . . . . $500–600

Rolex "Ladies Platinum & Diamond Cord". White dial, raised gold dots for numerals. Square platinum case covered with 26 round diamonds, black cord band. ca 1960 .$475–550

Rolex "Ladies Platinum & Diamond Cord". White dial, raised gold dots for numerals. Square platinum case set with 26 diamonds, two of which are tapered baguettes covering lugs, black cord band. ca 1960 . . . $475–550

Rolex "Ladies Platinum & Diamond Cord". White dial, raised gold dots for numerals. Round platinum case covered with 24 round diamonds, platinum band set with 36 round diamonds. ca 1960 . . . . $900–1,100

Rolex "Ladies Platinum & Diamond Cord". White dial, raised gold dots for numbers. Round platinum case with molded lugs, set with 2 diamonds, and bezel set with 18 diamonds. ca 1960. . . . . $385–450

Rolex "Ladies Diamond & Gold Cord". White dial, raised gold dots for numerals. 14K white gold square case with 4 diamonds, molded lugs, black cord band. ca 1960 . . . $225–275

Rolex "Ladies Diamond Bracelet". White dial, raised gold dots for numerals. 17J movement. 14K white gold case with 6 diamonds, molded lugs. 14K white gold bracelet. ca 1960.
. . . . $425–500

Rolex "Ladies Diamond Cord". White dial, raised gold dots for numerals. 17J movement. 14K white gold square case, set with 8 diamonds. Single extended lugs, black cord band. ca 1960. . . . . $235–275

Rolex "Ladies Diamond Cord". White dial, raised gold dots for numerals. 17J movement. 14K white gold square case, single molded lugs set with 2 diamonds. ca 1960 . . . . $235–275

Rolex "Ladies Diamond & Gold Cord". White dial, raised gold dots for numerals. 14K white gold round case. Fancy molded lugs set with 8 diamonds and 2 diamonds set on cord runners. Faceted sapphire crystal, black cord band. ca 1960 . . . . $375–425

Rolex "Ladies Diamond & Gold Cord". White dial, raised gold dots for numerals. 14K white gold square case with 4 diamonds. Molded lugs and black cord. ca 1960. . . . . $225–275

Rolex "Ladies Diamond & Gold Cord". White dial, raised gold dots for numerals. 17J movement. 18K white gold round case, molded lugs set with 6 diamonds. Faceted sapphire crystal, matching 14K white gold grooved band. ca 1960 . . . . $450–550

Rolex "Ladies Diamond & Gold Cord". White dial, raised gold dots for numerals. 14K white gold square case with 8 diamonds. Molded lugs, black cord band. ca 1960 . . . $225–275

Rolex "Ladies Platinum & Diamond Cord". White dial, raised gold dots for numerals. Round platinum case, 18 diamonds set in bezel and molded lugs set with 14 diamonds. Black cord band. ca 1960 . . . . . $425–500

Rolex "Ladies Diamond Crown Bracelet". White dial, raised gold dots for numerals. 17J movement. 14K white gold square case with 12 diamonds. Molded lugs and 14K white gold mesh bracelet. ca 1960 . . . . $325–400

Rolex "Ladies Diamond & Gold Cord". White dial, raised gold dots for numerals. 14K white gold round case, molded lugs set with 8 diamonds, faceted sapphire crystal, black cord band. ca 1960 . . . . $225–300

Rolex "Ladies White Gold & Diamond Cord".
White dial, raised gold dots for numerals. 14K
white gold round case, bezel set with 18 diamonds. Molded lugs set with 14 diamonds,
black cord band. ca 1960 . . . . . $435—495

Rolex "Swan Neck". White dial, raised gold
dots for numerals. 17J movement. 14K yellow
gold square case with swan neck lugs. ca 1960.
. . . . $335—400

Rolex "Ladies Diamond & Gold Cord". White
dial, raised gold dots for numerals. 14K white
gold round case, 2 large diamonds on lugs,
faceted sapphire crystal. 14K white gold band
or black cord band. ca 1960. . . . . $165—200

Rolex "Swan Neck". White dial, raised gold
dots for numerals. 17J movement. 14K yellow
gold square case with swan neck lugs. ca 1960.
. . . . $285—350

Rolex "Ladies Diamond & Gold Bracelet".
White dial, raised gold dots for numerals. 17J
movement. 14K white gold round case, square
molded lugs set with 8 diamonds. Faceted sapphire crystal, 14K gold band. ca 1960.
. . . . $375—450

Rolex "Diamond Swan Neck". White dial,
raised gold dots for numerals. 17J movement.
14K yellow gold square case, raised crystal,
swan neck lugs set with 6 diamonds. ca 1960.
. . . . $385—450

Rolex "Ladies Diamond & Gold Cord". White
dial, raised gold dots for numerals. 14K white
gold round case. Molded lugs set with 14 diamonds. Faceted sapphire crystal, black cord
band. ca 1960 . . . . $245—300

Rolex "Swan Neck". White dial, raised gold
dots for numerals. 17J movement. 14K white
or yellow gold round case with swan neck lugs.
ca 1960. . . . . $285—350

Rolex "Ladies Diamond & Gold Cord". White
dial, raised gold dots for numerals. 17J movement. 14K white gold round case. Molded
lugs paved with 14 diamonds. Faceted sapphire
crystal, black cord band. ca 1960 . . $235—300

Rolex "Diamond Chameleon". White dial,
raised gold stars for numerals. 17J movement.
18K yellow or white gold round case, scrolls
set with 6 diamonds, slot in back for quick
change of straps. ca 1960 . . . . . . $285—350

Rolex "Diamond Chameleon". White dial, raised gold dots for numbers. 17J movement. 18K white gold round case set with 2 diamonds, slot on back for quick change of straps. ca 1960 . . . . $275—325

Rolex "Ladies Gold Strap". White dial, raised gold bars for numerals. 17J movement. Geometric form, 18K yellow gold case, extended lugs & black suede strap. ca 1960 . . $215—250

Rolex "Orchid Gold Strap". Waterproof, white dial, raised gold bars for numerals, subsidiary seconds. 17J movement. 14K yellow gold round case, molded lugs, gold kid band or black suede band. ca 1960 . . . . $155—210

Rolex "No Dial". Ladies gold strap, yellow gold dial. Imported, 18K gold square case with engraved bezel, black suede strap. ca 1960. . . . . $235—300

Rolex "Orchid Gold Strap". Waterproof, white dial, raised gold dots for numerals. 17J movement. 18K yellow gold round case, extended lugs & suede strap. ca 1960 . . . . . $245—305

Rolex "Ladies Gold Strap". White dial, raised gold numerals, center seconds. 17J movement. 14K gold round case, molded extended lugs & black suede band. ca 1960 . . . . . $135—170

Rolex "Orchid Gold Strap". Waterproof, white dial, raised gold dots for numerals. 17J movement. 18K yellow gold round case, wide bezel & extended lugs, suede strap. ca 1960.
. . . . $235—285

Rolex "Ladies Gold Strap". White or black dial, raised gold bars for numerals, subsidiary seconds. 17J movement. 14K yellow gold case with engraved bezel & extended lugs, black suede strap. ca 1960 . . . . $200—250

Rolex "Orchid Gold Strap". Waterproof, white dial, raised gold bars for numerals. 17J movement. 18K gold round case with extended lugs & 14K gold flushfit mesh band or suede strap. ca 1960. . . . . $650—800

Rolex "Ladies Gold Strap". White dial, raised gold dots for numerals. 17J movement. 14K yellow gold square case, molded lugs & black suede strap. ca 1960 . . . . $215—250

Rolex "Gold Cord". White dial, raised gold dots for numerals. 17J movement. 14K yellow or white gold molded square case, single molded lugs, black cord. ca 1960 . . $175—225

Rolex "Lady Date-Just' Oyster Perpetual". Silvered dial with Cyclops date window. Sweep second, 26J rotor self-winding movement. 18K yellow gold case with diamond-cut fluted bezel. ca 1960. . . . . $1,200—1,500

Rolex "Gold Bracelet". White dial, raised gold bars for numbers. 17J movement. 14K yellow gold round case, 14K gold mesh bracelet. ca 1960 . . . . $435—495

Rolex "Lady Date Oyster Perpetual". Silvered dial with Cyclops date window. Sweep second, 26J rotor self-winding movement. Tonneau oyster case. ca 1960. 14K solid gold case with smooth bezel . . . . $600—750
Stainless steel, w/14K smooth bezel 250—350
Stainless steel . . . . 100—120

Rolex "Gold Bracelet". White dial, raised gold dots for numerals. 14K yellow gold round case. 14K gold bracelet. ca 1960 . . . . . $500—575

Rolex "Ladies Oyster Perpetual". Radium dial & hands. Sweep second, 26J rotor self-wind movement. Stainless steel, tonneau case. ca 1960 . . . .$60—80

Rolex "Gold Bracelet". White dial, raised gold dots for numerals. 17J movement. 14K white gold square case with simple 14K gold mesh bracelet. ca 1960 . . . . $425—500

Rolex "Ladies Oyster Perpetual". Steel grey finish dial with dot markers. Sweep second, 27J rotor self-winding movement. Stainless steel. tonneau case with 14K yellow gold, engine-turned bezel. ca 1960. . . . . $150—200

Rolex "Gold Bracelet". White dial, raised gold dots for numerals. 17J movement. 14K gold round case with 14K gold mesh bracelet. ca 1960 . . . . $425—500

Rolex "Zephyr Ladies Oyster Perpetual". Steel grey dial with luminous dots. Sweep second, 26J rotor self-winding movement. Tonneau stainless steel case with 14K yellow gold engine-turned bezel. ca 1960. . $150—200

Rolex "Ladies Oyster Perpetual". Luminous hands & markers on steel grey dial. Sweep second, 26J rotor self-winding movement. Tonneau case. ca 1960. 14K yellow gold case with diamond-cut fluted bezel. . . . $500—600 Stainless steel case with 14K diamond-cut fluted bezel . . . . $200—300

Rolex "Ladies Oyster Perpetual". Steel grey dial, subsidiary seconds. 27J rotor self-winding movement. Tonneau oyster case. 14K YG with diamond-cut fluted bezel. . . . $450—550 Stainless steel with 14K WG diamond-cut fluted bezel . ca 1960 . . . . . . $200—250

Rolex "Ladies Oyster Perpetual". Steel grey dial with subsidiary seconds. 17J self-winding movement. Tonneau oyster case. ca 1960. Stainless steel case with: 14K yellow gold faceted bezel. . . . $200—250 Engine-turned bezel. . . . . 60— 90 Smooth bezel . . . . 50— 80

Rolex "Lady Oyster Perpetual". Various color dials & bezels. Calendar models have 2½ magnification Cyclops eye in crystal. Sweep second, 26J rotor self-wind movement. Tonneau Oyster case. All of the later Oysters, and many of the early ones, were available with matching bracelets. The values given here are for heads only. Bracelets are not included in the values. ca 1969.

NOTE: The above illustration has the modern stick hands, numerals & markers now being used, which raises the value of the stainless steel cased watches by $35 to $50, and the gold cased watches $50 to $100.

Rolex "Gold Bracelet". White dial, raised gold dots for numerals. 17J movement. 14K yellow gold round case, 14K yellow gold snake bracelet. ca 1960 . . . . $435—500

Rolex. Ladies. Subsidiary seconds. 18K gold, 20mm. square case, with a heavy fitted, molded link bracelet. ca 1965. . . . . $600—800

Rolex. Ladies. Champagne dial. 14K gold, 15mm. square case with diamond-set bezel and gold flexible Rolex band . . . $900—1,000

Rolex "Cellini". Ladies. Reflective skyblue face. 18K white gold oval case. Sapphire crystal & bezel set with 26 full-cut diamonds & matching Florentine mesh bracelet. ca 1970.
. . . . $2,500—3,200

Rolex   Chronograph. Tachometer base 1,000m. Silvered dial, subsidiary seconds, 30 minute recorder (chronograph hand missing). ca 1920. . . . . $1,000—1,200

Rolex "Oyster". Round dial, subsidiary seconds. 14K gold, 32mm. cushion case with milled bezel. ca 1930 . . . . $400—450

Rolex. Extra prima movement. 18K gold, 25x35mm. tonneau case. ca 1924. . $400—475

Rolex "Prince". Tu-tone silvered duo-dial. Extra prima movement. 9K or 18K white & yellow gold striped, 25x43mm. flared rectangular case. ca 1933. 18K . . . . . $2,500—2,900
9K . . . . 2,200—2,600

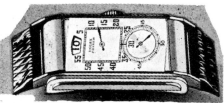

Rolex "Prince Railway H.S. (Jump Hour)". Silvered duo-dial (upper window for jump hours, middle dial for minutes, lower dial for subsidiary seconds). Rolex prima extra, 15J nickel movement timed to 6 positions. Curved, 20x45mm. rectangular case with stepped sides. ca 1933. Platinum. . . . . $3,500—4,000
18K gold . . . . 2,800—3,000
14K gold . . . . 2,500—2,700
9K gold. . . . . 2,300—2,500
Gold-filled . . . . 600— 700

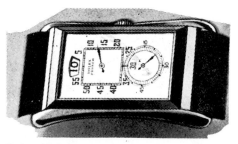

Rolex "Prince Brancard H.S. (Jump Hour)". Silvered duo-dial (upper window for jump hours, middle dial for minutes, lower dial for subsidiary seconds). Rolex prima extra, 15J nickel movement timed to 6 positions. Curved, 26x42mm. rectangular case with tapered (hourglass) sides. ca 1933.
Platinum . . . . $3,500—4,000
18K gold . . . . 2,800—3,000
14K gold . . . . 2,500—2,700
9K gold. . . . . 2,300—2,500

Gold-filled . . . . 800—1000

Rolex "Prince Railway". (Doctor's watch). Silvered duo-dial. Rolex prima extra, 15J rectangular, nickel lever movement timed to 6 positions. Curved, 20x48mm. rectangular case with stepped sides. ca 1933.

Platinum $2,500–2,800
18K gold 2,200–2,500
14K gold 1,600–1,800
9K gold 1,500–1,700
Gold-filled 450– 650

Rolex "Dauphin Biseaux". Silvered dial. 17J movement. Rectangular strap case with polished beveled ends. ca 1933.

18K gold $500–650
14K gold 450–550
Gold-filled 125–185

Rolex "Dauphin Railway". Black or silvered dial. 17J movement. Curved rectangular case, stepped sides. ca 1933. 18K gold . . $550–700
14K gold 500–650
Gold-filled 150–200

Rolex "Elegant". Tu-tone gold and silver finish dial. 17J movement. Rectangular, beveled edge, strap case. ca 1935.

9K yellow gold $200–250
Stainless steel 100–125

Rolex "Prince Dauphin". Tu-tone gold finished dial. 17J movement. Rectangular case with tapered (hourglass) sides. ca 1936.

18K gold $550–700
14K gold 500–650
Gold-filled 150–200

NOTE: Read Page 6 before using this book to value your wrist watch.

Rolex "Prince Railway". (Doctor's watch). Silvered duo-dial (upper dial for hours and minutes, lower for subsidiary seconds). Rolex prima extra, 15J rectangular, nickel lever movement timed to 6 positions. Curved, 20x48mm. rectangular case with stepped sides. ca 1936.

Platinum $2,500–2,800
18K gold 2,200–2,500
14K gold 1,600–1,800
9K gold 1,500–1,700
3-color gold-filled 550– 750
Gold-filled 450– 600

NOTE: All values are given for the head only unless the bracelet is included in the description.

Rolex "Prince Branchard". (Doctor' watch). Silvered duo-dial. Rolex prima extra, 15J rectangular, nickel lever movement timed to 6 positions. Slightly curved, 26x42mm. rectangular case. ca 1939. Platinum. . . . $2,500–2,800
18K gold 2,200–2,500
14K gold 1,600–1,800
9K gold 1,500–1,700

Gold-filled 450– 600

Rolex "Oyster Royale (Manual Wind)". Various dials with plain or luminous numerals, subsidiary or sweep seconds, manual wind movement. 33mm. tonneau oyster case, with square ends. ca 1935 (Were made for many years).

18K yellow gold.	$600—700
14K yellow gold.	550—650
9K or 10K yellow gold	400—500
Yellow gold top	300—400
Stainless & gold	175—250
Gold-filled top, steel back	125—150
Stainless Steel	75—125

Rolex "Oyster Perpetual Bubble Back". Various colored dials with plain or luminous numerals. Subsidiary or sweep second, self-winding rotor movement. 33mm. tonneau oyster case with square ends. ca 1935 (Were made for many years).

18K yellow gold.	$800—900
14K yellow gold.	700—800
9K or 10K yellow gold	500—600
Yellow gold top	500—600
Stainless & gold	250—350
Gold-filled top, steel back	150—200
Stainless steel	100—150

Rolex Chronograph. Gold matte dial, subsidiary seconds, precision gold train, round movement, 30 minute register, tachometer base 1 mile spiral. 18K gold, 29mm., heavy gold square case with molded lugs. ca 1940.
.... $1,400—1,800

Rolex "Oyster Perpetual". Moonphase calendar, white dial, center seconds, day & month windows with outer date ring. 14K gold, 34mm. round case with milled bezel.
.... $4,000—4,500

Rolex "Oyster Manual Wind, Round End". Radium dial, sweep seconds. ca 1944.

18K yellow gold.	$500—550
14K yellow gold.	450—500
9K yellow gold	425—475
Gold top, stainless back	200—250
Stainless & gold	150—200
Stainless steel	50— 85

Rolex "Precision" Oyster. Moonphase calendar. Silvered dial, subsidiary seconds, day & month windows with outer date ring. 38mm. round stainless steel case. . . . . $1,400—1,600

Rolex "Oyster Perpetual Chronometer". Sweep second, self-winding. Referred to as bubble back. ca 1942.

18K yellow gold	$800–1,000
14K yellow gold	700– 900
9K or 10K yellow gold	600– 700
Stainless & gold	200– 275
Stainless steel	125– 175
Gold watch with steel back	375– 450

Rolex "Oyster Perpetual". Radium dial, self-winding rotor movement. Tonneau, 29x38mm. case. ca 1943. Stainless steel $150–175
14K gold 700–900

Rolex Chronometer. 12 hour chapter ring on bezel, 17J, 14K gold. ca 1942 . . . . $500–600

Rolex. Automatic, signed "Perpetual Autoroter Chronometre". Silvered dial, subsidiary seconds. 18K gold molded square case . . . . . .
. . . . $1,200–1,400

Rolex Precision. White matte dial, raised gold numerals, subsidiary seconds. 17J movement. 14K gold, 28mm. square case. Signed case, dial & movement $500–600

Rolex Perpetual Chronometer. Silvered dial, raised gold stars & triangles for numbers, subsidiary seconds. 18K gold, 34mm. molded square case. ca 1945 . . . . $950–1,050

Rolex "Chronometer". Silvered dial with raised black numerals. Subsidiary seconds chronometer movement. Tonneau case. ca 1943. Stainless steel . . . . $ 75–100
14K. 250–275
18K. 300–325

Rolex "Army". Radium silvered dial, center seconds. 17J manual wind movement. Stainless steel cushion oyster case with screw-down crown. ca 1945 . . . . $125–165

ROLEX
OFFICIALLY CERTIFIED CHRONOMETERS

Prior to November 15th, 1951, the Swiss Federation of Watch Manufacturers ruled that the term "chronometer" was descriptive of: "A precision watch regulated in different positions and various temperatures, capable of obtaining an Official Timing Certificate."

On November 16th, 1951, the Federation modified this ruling. It now reads as follows: "A precision watch regulated in different positions, HAVING OBTAINED an Official Timing Certificate."

In accordance with this new Swiss regulation, no watch may be termed "CHRONOMETER" unless its precision has been proved by a Swiss Government Testing Station or by an Observatory.

Every Rolex chronometer offered for sale has previously obtained an OFFICIAL Timing Certificate and bears the words **OFFICIALLY CERTIFIED CHRONOMETER** on the dial. A "Rolex Red Seal" was attached to every Rolex Chronometer for easy identification.

This new definition, therefore, vindicates a policy which Rolex had applied strictly for a great many years.

We have not mentioned in our descriptions of Rolex watches the words **CERTIFIED CHRONOMETER** because it appears on the original dials and the number of **POSITIONS OF ADJUSTMENTS** appears on the movement.

ROLEX

Rolex "Day Date Oyster", (with the proper band becomes known as the **"President"**). Combines all of the features invented and perfected by Rolex. Oyster case, sweep second perpetual rotor self-winding, superlative chronometer movement and the date and the day spelled out in full with a choice of over 25 languages. Available only in 18K white or yellow gold and platinum, with matching "President" bracelet. A wide choice of dial colors and bezels, including partial & full diamond. This head and band (and other Rolex products) have been extensively copied and reproduced in recent years. New Rolex watches are as they should be—Expensive—and be careful when offered a new or slightly used one at a seemingly bargain price. Rolex "Day Date" have been made over 27 years and condition, age, and custom features affect the final value of these fine watches.

Rolex has held its value as well or better than most other wrist watches and can be compared perhaps with a Mercedes automobile in this respect.

NOTE: All Rolex values are given for the head only unless it has a fitted bracelet. You must add the bracelet value for the total value of your watch.

Rolex "Day Date Oyster". ca 1960. President head, 18K yellow . . . . $1,400—1,800
18K white . . . . 1,200—1,600

Rolex "Oyster Chronograph". Silvered dial with applied triangular bar markers. Subsidiary seconds, 30 minute & 12 hour register. The outer chronograph rings with various markings. 17J movement. Various case metals. ca 1960.
18K gold . . . . $1,250—1,500
14K gold . . . . 900—1,000
Stainless steel . . . . 325— 400

Rolex "Oyster Perpetual Date". Various colored dials with polished gold markers, date window & cyclops lens. Sweep second, 25J rotor self-wind chronometer movement. ca 1960.
Stainless steel . . . . $200—275
14K gold . . . . 375—550

Rolex "Oyster Date". Silvered or smoked gold dial with date window and cyclops lens. Sweep second, 17J movement, stainless steel case. ca 1960 . . . . $175—250

Rolex "Date-Just". Silvered or gold dial with polished gold markers, date window & Cyclops lens. Sweep second, 25J rotor self-winding chronometer movement in oyster cases with fluted bezel. ca 1960. 18K gold . . . $750—950
14K gold & steel . . . . 650—800
Stainless steel . . . . 200—260

Rolex "Oyster Perpetual". Silver or gold finish dial. Sweep second, 25J rotor self-wind chronometer movement. 14K gold case with polished end pieces and fluted diamond-cut bezel. ca 1960. . . . . $475—550

Rolex "Oyster Perpetual". Silvered dial & polished markers. Sweep second, 25J rotor self-winding chronometer movement. Case has a flat engine-turned bezel. ca 1960. Stainless steel. . . . . $175—240
14K gold . . . . 375—450

Rolex "Oyster Perpetual". Steel grey dial with polished white markers. Sweep second, 25J rotor self-wind chronometer movement. Stainless steel case. ca 1960 . . . . $100—125

Rolex "Tru Beat Jump-Seconds". Silvered dial with distinct seconds marks. Sweep jump-seconds hand. 25J rotor self-wind chronometer movement. Stainless steel oyster case. ca 1960. (Not pictured) . . . . . . $150—175

Rolex "Oyster Perpetual". Silvered dial with polished markers. Sweep second, 25J rotor self-winding chronometer movement, in a case with engine-turned bezel. ca 1960. Stainless steel . . . . $180—250
Steel & 14K gold . . . . 240—285
14K gold . . . . 400—475

Rolex "Oyster Perpetual". Silvered dial with polished markers. Sweep second, 25J rotor self-wind chronometer movement. Stainless steel case with a 14K gold fluted bezel. ca 1960. . . . . $185—240

Rolex "Oyster Perpetual". Steel grey dial with lapped white markers, sweep second, 25J rotor self-winding chronometer movement. Gold filled case. ca 1960 . . . . $190—230

NOTE: Read Page 6 before using this book to value your wrist watch.

Rolex "Zephyr Oyster Perpetual". Silvered dial with dot markers. Sweep second, 25J rotor self-wind chronometer movement. Stainless steel case with a 14K gold, diamond-cut bezel. ca 1960. . . . . $185—250

Rolex "Oyster Perpetual". Applied gold markers on silvered or gold florentine dial. Sweep second, 25J, self-wind chronometer movement. Large size, 18K gold case with diamond cut, fluted bezel. ca 1960 . $500—575

NOTE: All values are given for the head only unless the bracelet is included in the description.

Rolex "Oyster Perpetual". Black dial and polished gold markers. Sweep second, 25J rotor self-wind chronometer movement. Stainless steel case with a 14K gold, fancy engraved bezel. ca 1960 . . . . $200—240

Rolex "Oyster Perpetual". Applied gold markers on silver finish. Sweep second, 25J, rotor self-winding chronometer movement. Large size, 18K solid gold case. ca 1960 . . $425—500

Rolex "Oyster Perpetual". Applied lapped finish markers on grey or gold finish dial. 26J rotor self-winding chronometer, in a thin model, 14K gold case. ca 1960 . . . $400—475

NOTE: All values are given for the head only unless the bracelet is included in the description.

Rolex "Oyster". Silvered dial, sweep second, 17J movement. Stainless steel oyster case. ca 1960 . . . . $75—100

Rolex "Oyster". Silvered dial, sweep second, 18J chronometer movement. 14K gold oyster case. ca 1960 . . . . $300—350

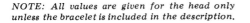

Rolex "Oyster Perpetual". Silvered dial with black markers. 25J rotor self-winding chronometer movement. 14K gold case with polished bezel and end pieces. ca 1960 . . . . $375—450

NOTE: Read Page 6 before using this book to value your wrist watch.

Rolex "Super-Thin Oyster Dress". Silvered dial, subsidiary seconds. 18J chronometer movement. 18K gold, thin-style case. ca 1960. . . . . $300—350

Rolex "Oyster Perpetual". Applied lapped finish markers on grey finish dial. 25J rotor self-winding chronometer movement. ca 1960.
Stainless steel . . . . $125—175
Steel & gold . . . .   225—275
14K gold . . . .   375—450

Rolex "Gold Dress". Gold finish dial. Sweep second, 18J chronometer movement. 18K gold case. ca 1960. . . . . $315—365

Rolex "Gold Dress". Silvered dial with subsidiary seconds. 18J chronometer movement. 18K gold case. ca 1960 . . . . $315—365

Rolex "Gold Dress". Silvered, applied gold, polished marker dial. Sweep second, 17J movement. 14K gold case. ca 1960 . $290—340

Rolex "Gold Dress". Silvered dial. Sweep second, 18J chronometer movement. 14K gold, 35mm. case with engine-turned bezel. ca 1960. . . . . $275—325

Rolex "Gold Dress". Silvered dial, subsidiary seconds. 17J chronometer movement. 14K gold, 35mm. case with engine-turned bezel. ca 1960. . . . . $260—310

Rolex. Chronograph. Silvered dial, subsidiary seconds, 30 minute & 12 hour recorder with outer telemeter & tachometer rings. 17J movement. 39mm., 18K gold round case. ca 1950. . . . . $1,200—1,400

Rolex Chronograph. Gold matte dial, subsidiary seconds, 30 minute register, tachometer ring & outer telemeter. 18K gold, 31mm. tonneau case. ca 1945 . . . . . . $1,200—1,400
Gold top & steel back . . . . . . 400— 650
Stainless steel . . . . 200— 300

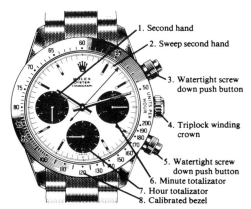

1. Second hand
2. Sweep second hand
3. Watertight screw down push button
4. Triplock winding crown
5. Watertight screw down push button
6. Minute totalizator
7. Hour totalizator
8. Calibrated bezel

Rolex "Cosmograph Oyster". Dials & bezels in 4 color combinations. Subsidiary seconds, 30 minute and 12 hour recorder. Black or steel bezels calibrated in units per hour, for calculating speeds, production rates, etc. Manual wind, 17J, superlative chronometer in steel or gold case, tested to 165 feet. ca 1971.
18K gold . . . . $1,350—1,750
14K gold . . . . 1,050—1,400
Stainless steel . . . . 400— 500

Rolex "Submariner Oyster". Black dial with heavy radium dots & markers. 60 minute time elapse rotating bezel. Sweep second, 25J rotor self-winding movement. Stainless steel case originally tested to 660 feet under water. ca 1960 . . . . $225—300

Rolex "Explorer Oyster". Black dial with heavy duty radium figures & markers. 25J rotor self-winding, sweep second chronometer movement. Stainless steel, 35x42mm. case, originally tested to 330 feet underwater. ca 1960. . . . . $200—225

Rolex "Submariner Oyster". Black dial with heavy radium dots & markers, 60 minute time elapse rotating bezel. 17J rotor self-winding, sweep second, movement originally tested to 330 feet under water. Stainless steel case. ca 1960 . . . . $275—325

Rolex "Explorer Oyster". Black dial with heavy radium figures & markers. 25J rotor self-winding, sweep second chronometer movement. Stainless steel, 35x42mm. case, originally tested to 330 feet under water. ca 1969 . . . . $200—250

Rolex "Submariner Oyster". Black or blue dial with heavy radium dots and markers with a matching 60 minute time elapse rotating bezel. Date window with cyclops lens. 25J rotor self-winding, sweep second chronometer movement. Stainless steel, crown guard case, originally tested to 660 feet under water. ca 1960. $325—475

Rolex "Explorer II Oyster". Black dial with heavy luminous radium figures and markers, with a window date & cyclops lens and a red triangle hand indicating 24 hour time on a fixed bezel. 25J rotor self-winding, sweep second chronometer movement. Stainless steel crown guard case. ca 1973 . . . . . . $275—350

Rolex "Milgauss Oyster". Silver dial with polished or luminous markers. Sweep second, 25J rotor self-winding chronometer movement that will maintain accuracy in magnetic fields up to 1000 Gauss. Stainless steel case. ca 1969.
. . . . $200—250

Rolex "GMT-Master Oyster". Black dial with heavy luminous dots & markers, date window with Cyclop lens. Red triangle 24 hour hand reads rotating bezel setting in second time zone. Sweep second, 25J rotor chronometer movement in stainless steel case. ca 1960.
. . . . $275—375
Same with 17J movement . . . . . . 225—300

Rolex "Date-Just". Various colored dials with polished gold markers, date window & Cyclops lens. Sweep second, 25J rotor self-winding chronometer movement. Oyster cases with fluted bezels. ca 1969. 18K gold $800—950
14K gold & steel . . . . 550—750
Stainless steel . . . . 275—400

Rolex "Thunderbird Date-Just". Same as above except has Turnograph Bezel carved in 18K gold, with minute markers. ca 1969. (Not pictured). 18K gold. . . . . $1,450—1,850
14K gold & steel . . . . 650— 850

Rolex "GMT-Master Oyster". Five colors used in combinations for matching bezel and dial, with optional radium hands & markers. Date window with Cyclops lens. Red triangle 24 hour hand reads rotating bezel setting in second time zone. Sweep second, 30J rotor chronometer movement in crown-guard case. ca 1969. 18K gold . . . . $1,800—2,200
14K gold & steel . . . . 550— 750
Stainless steel . . . . 350— 400

Rolex "Day Date Oyster". ca 1970. President head, 18K yellow . . . . $2,000—2,200
18K white . . . . 2,000—2,200
44 Diamond Bezel . . . . 800—1,000
10 Diamond dial . . . . 350— 500

Rolex "Sea Dweller Oyster". Black dial with heavy radium dots and markers. 60 minutes on a time elapse rotating bezel. Date window with cyclops lens. Sweep seond, 25J rotor self-winding movement. Originally tested to 2,000 feet under water. Stainless steel, crown guard case. ca 1971 . . . . $375—550

Rolls. Self-winding, subsidiary seconds, 24x41mm. rectangular case with moulded sides enclosing the winder. ca 1931. $600—800

Rolex. Plain dial, bar numerals. 14K gold, 30mm. round case, 14K gold braid strap. ca 1965 . . . . $800—1,200

Rolex, Geneve. Silvered dial. 18K white gold, 28mm. square case with 14K gold mesh bracelet. . . . . $800—1,200

Rozanes. Lighter, watch & lipstick case. Oval silvered dial. Square 14K gold engine-turned case with stripes, 1-5/8 inches . . . . $450—600

Rolex. Silvered dial signed "Officially Certified Chronometer". Subsidiary seconds. Yellow gold square, 25mm. case with a faceted bezel. . . . . $650—800

Rolex "Cellini". Men's. Reflective skyblue dial. 18K gold geometric, ridged case, sapphire crystal . ca 1970 . . . . $600—700

Rulon "Chrono King". Calendar chronograph base 60 with subsidiary seconds, 30 minute & 12 hour recorders, window day & month, with outer date ring. 17J movement. Round case with heavy lugs. ca 1946.
14K yellow gold. . . . . $250—325
Stainless steel . . . . 100—125

SANTA FE WATCH COMPANY
821 Kansas Avenue
Topeka, Kansas

Santa Fe Watch Company was a non-manufacturing mail order watch company who contracted with the Illinois Watch Company and Swiss companies (some Bulova) to make watches for them. A 1933 Santa Fe catalog (in the library of Luther and Vivian Grinder, Owensboro, Kentucky) offered pocket and wrist watches by Illinois (the advertising cuts show "Illinois" on the dial) and were said to be complete with box and certificate. A fold-out, 11x17 brochure also offered 18 styles of Bulova wrist watches. Swiss wrist watches have been seen with "Santa Fe" or "Santa Fe Special" on the dial and because of the dial marking, will probably bring a premium of $5 or $10 over the same watch with "Illinois" or Swiss markings. A box and certificate would add $15 to $25 to the total value.

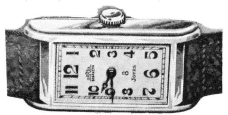

Sarda "8 Day". 18J movement. Molded rectangular case. ca 1931. 14K yellow gold.$325—400

Silver	125—150
Gold-filled	100—125
Chrome	65— 95

NOTE: Sarda (French) offered 600 case styles and variations in their 1931 catalog.

Sarda "Besancon Chronograph". Subsidiary seconds, 30 minute recorder, outer telemeter & tachometer rings. 18J movement. 37mm. round case. ca 1931.

14K yellow gold	$400—500
14K gold-filled	150—200
Silver Niello	150—225
Chrome	75—100

Sarda "Besancon Chronograph". Round dial, subsidiary seconds, 30 minute recorder and outer tachometer ring. ca 1933. 14K yellow gold, cushion case . . . . $325—400

Sarda "Besancon Chronograph". Subsidiary seconds, 30 minute recorder, outer telemeter & tachometer rings. 18J movement. 14K yellow gold, round case & lugs. ca 1935 . . $325—400

Sarda "Besancon". Tu-tone gold dial, subsidiary seconds. 18J movement. Gold-filled, curved rectangular case. ca 1938 . . . .$30—45

Sarda. Round case, large link lugs. ca 1938.

14K yellow gold	$100—115
Gold-filled	15— 20
Chrome	10— 15

Sarda. Subsidiary seconds. Molded tonneau case. ca 1938. 14K yellow gold . . . $100—125
14K gold-filled . . . .   15— 25
Chrome. . . . .   10— 15

JAMES SCHULZ
36 W. 47th Street, New York City
; 30 Rue Du Stand, Geneva, Switzerland

Manufacturer and Importer

Schulz, James "Ladies Platinum & Diamond". 16 baguette diamonds set in a rectangular case. ca 1931. Value varies according to size, quality and color of diamonds . . . . . . $800—1,000

Schulz, James. Solid tonneau case with hour & minute windows. ca 1931.
Gold-filled . . . . $50—70
Chrome. . . . . 40—60

Schulz "Split Second Chronograph". 1/5 second split timer is rare on wrist watches. Silvered dial with subsidiary seconds & 30 minute recorder. 18K heavy gold tonneau case. ca 1940. . . . . $1,000—1,400

Schulz "Minute Repeater". Moonphase perpetual calendar with chronograph base 60. Subsidiary seconds, 60 minute recorder, day, date & month indicator. 18K heavy gold tonneau case. ca 1940 . . . .$20,000—25,000

Schwob "Man's Plated". Subsidiary seconds. 7J or 15J movement. 8¾x12mm., molded tonneau case. ca 1935. White or yellow rolled gold plate . . . .$8—16

Schwob "Duo-Dial". Top for hours, bottom for seconds. 7J movement. 8¾x12mm. rectangular case with graduated sides. ca 1935.
10K yellow rolled gold plate. . . . . $100—125
Stainless steel . . . .   80—110

Schwob "Man's Stainless". Subsidiary seconds. 7J movement. 8¾x12mm. faceted rectangular case. ca 1935. 10K yellow rolled gold plate . . . .$8—15
Stainless steel . . . . 5—10

Seeland "Skipper". Subsidiary seconds. 7J or 17J movement. 10K rolled gold plate, steel back, molded and engraved tonneau case. ca 1940 . . . .$8—18

Seeland "George". Subsidiary seconds. 7J or 17J movement. 10K rolled gold plate, molded tonneau case. ca 1940 . . . .$8—18

Seeland "Paul". Subsidiary seconds. 7J or 17J movement. 10K rolled gold plate, stainless steel back, molded tonneau case. ca 1940. . . . .$8—18

Seeland "Contour". Subsidiary seconds. 17J movement. 10K rolled gold plate, curved tonneau case. ca 1940 . . . .$7—15

Seeland "Charles". Subsidiary seconds. 7J or 17J movement. 10K rolled gold plate, steel back, molded tonneau case. ca 1940 . . .$7—15

Seeland "Vincent". Subsidiary seconds. 17J movement. 10K rolled gold plate, curved rectangular case. ca 1940 . . . .$10—15

Seeland "Chrome Chronograph". Telemeter-tachymeter chronograph with subsidiary seconds and 30 minute recorder. 7J or 17J, stop-start-flyback movement. Round chrome case. ca 1940. . . . .$40—60

Seeland "Clifton". Subsidiary seconds. 7J or 17J movement. 10K rolled gold plate, tonneau case. ca 1940 . . . .$10—15

Seiko "World Time". Waterproof. Center seconds, date window. 17J, Automatic movement. Round stainless steel case. ca 1965.
. . . .$40—65

Seneca "Platinum & Diamond". Ladies, 17J adjusted movement. Platinum rectangular case, set with 60 diamonds. ca 1930 . . . $775—950

Seneca "Platinum & Diamond". Ladies, 17J adjusted movement. Platinum rectangular case, set with 48 round diamonds and 2 half-moon shape diamonds. ca 1930. . . . . . . $550—700

Seneca "Platinum & Diamond". Ladies, 17J adjusted movement. Platinum rectangular case set with 2 Navette-cut and 36 round diamonds. ca 1930. . . . . $550—700

Seneca "Platinum & Diamond". Ladies, 17J adjusted movement. Platinum rectangular case set with 10 baguette-cut and 38 round diamonds. ca 1930 . . . . $600—775

Seneca "Diamond & Platinum Bracelet". 17J adjusted movement. Rectangular platinum case and lugs, set with 2 baguette-cut and 185 round diamonds. ca 1930 . . . . $2,250—2,750

Semca. Ladies. 14K gold rectangular case with molded single lugs. ca 1946 . . . .$40—60

Semca. Ladies. 14K gold & diamond round case with diamond lugs. ca 1946 . . . . . $175—250

Semca. Subsidiary seconds. 14K gold square case. ca 1946 . . . . $100—125

SETH THOMAS CLOCK CO.

Discontinued the manufacture of wrist and pocket watches in the United States about 1915. The wrist watches of U.S. production are represented by the few shown at the beginning, made about 1912. Seth Thomas again in 1953 began to offer a line of Swiss made watches marked with the famous old Seth Thomas name.

Seth Thomas. Ladies, 8''', 17J movement. 10K rolled gold plate, molded square case & lugs, stainless steel back. ca 1953 . . . .$15—25

Seth Thomas. Ladies, 8''', 17J movement. 10K rolled gold plated square case, molded lugs, stainless steel back. ca 1953 . . . . .$7—15

Seth Thomas. Ladies, 5''', 17J movement. 10K gold-filled round, beveled case. ca 1953. . . . .$15—25

Seth Thomas. Ladies, 5''', 17J movement. 14K gold square case with leaf-shaped lugs. ca 1953. . . . .$35—55

Seth Thomas. Ladies. Luminous hands & numbers, center seconds, waterproof, 8¾''', 17J movement. Chrome top, stainless steel back, round case. ca 1953. . . . .$5—10

Seth Thomas. Ladies, 8''', 17J movement. 10K white or yellow rolled gold plate case, molded lugs, stainless steel back, with 1/10 10K gold-filled bracelet. ca 1953 . . . . $20—30

Seth Thomas. Ladies, silvered dial, 8''', 17J movement. 10K rolled gold plate tonneau case, engraved bezel & lugs. ca 1953 . . . . . $15–25

Seth Thomas. Ladies, silvered dial, 8''', 17J movement. 10K rolled gold plate, molded octagonal case & lugs. ca 1953 . . . . . $15–25

Seth Thomas. Ladies, 8''', 17J movement. 10K gold-filled tonneau case, molded lugs. ca 1953. . . . . $20–30

Seth Thomas. Ladies, 8''', 17J movement. 14K gold tonneau case, molded lugs. ca 1953. . . . . $35–55

Seth Thomas. Ladies, 8''', 17J movement. 10K gold-filled tonneau case, molded lugs. ca 1953. . . . . $20–30

Seth Thomas. Glass enamel dial on a 7J, 0 size, Grade 1 movement. 36mm. round, nickel, 4 size pocket watch style case with wire lugs. ca 1912. . . . . $35–50

Seth Thomas. Glass enamel dial with red 5/60 outer track on an 0 size, Grade 1 movement. 32mm. round, nickel, pocket-style case with wire lugs. ca 1912. . . . . $35–50

Seth Thomas. Subsidiary seconds. 10K rolled gold plate, scalloped square case, molded lugs & stainless steel back. ca 1955. . . . . . $10–20

Seth Thomas. Raised gold figure dial, subsidiary seconds. 8¾''' movement. 10K rolled gold plate, fancy molded rectangular case, stainless steel back. ca 1955 . . . . . . $10–20

Seth Thomas "Favorite Rotor". Automatic, waterproof, center seconds, 17J movement. 10K gold-filled round case, ca 1955 . .$10—25

Seth Thomas "Thinner Automatic Rotor". Raised gold-filled numbers, waterproof, center seconds, 17J movement. Round stainless steel case. ca 1955 . . . .$10—20

Seth Thomas "Aristocrat Rotor". Automatic, waterproof, center seconds, 17J movement. 14K gold round case. ca 1955 . . . . .$65—95

Seth Thomas "Dress Rotor". Automatic, waterproof, subsidiary seconds, 17J, 9¼''' movement. 10K gold-filled & stainless steel back, unusually thin molded round case. ca 1955 . . . .$10—25

Seth Thomas "Calendar Rotor". Automatic, waterproof. Silvered dial, luminous figures, center seconds, date window, 17J movement. Round stainless steel case. ca 1955 . . .$10—25

Seth Thomas "Ultra-Thin". Raised gold figure dial, subsidiary seconds, 11½''' movement. 10K rolled gold plate round case, stainless steel back. ca 1955 . . . .$15—25

Seth Thomas "Sports Rotor". Automatic, waterproof, raised gold numerals & center seconds, 17J movement. Round stainless steel case. ca 1955 . . . .$10—20

Seth Thomas "Sportman's Rotor". Automatic & waterproof. Luminous dial, center seconds, 17J movement. 10K gold-filled top, stainless steel back, round case, molded lugs. ca 1955. . . . .$15—25

Seth Thomas "Nimrod". Waterproof, raised gold figures, center seconds. Round stainless steel case. ca 1955 . . . . $15—25

Seth Thomas "The Graduate". Waterproof. Raised gold figures, center seconds. 10K rolled gold plate case, molded lugs, stainless steel back. ca 1955 . . . .$7—18

Seth Thomas. Raised gold figure dial, subsidiary seconds, 10½''' movement. 10K rolled gold plate square case, molded lugs, stainless steel back. ca 1955 . . . . $20—30

Seth Thomas "Square Rotor". Automatic, subsidiary seconds, 17J movement. 10K gold-filled square case, stainless steel back, molded lugs. ca 1955. . . . . $20—35

Seth Thomas. Subsidiary seconds. 10K rolled gold plate, molded tonneau case & lugs, stainless steel back. ca 1955 . . . . $20—30

Seth Thomas "Original Rotor". Automatic, waterproof, luminous dial, center seconds, 17J movement. 10K gold-filled round case, stainless steel back. ca 1955 . . . . $10—20

Seth Thomas "Companion". Waterproof. Luminous dial, center seconds. Round case, chrome bezel, stainless steel back. ca 1955 . . . $5—10

Seth Thomas. Raised gold figures, subsidiary seconds, 10½''' movement. 10K gold-filled, molded square case & lugs. ca 1955. . .$15—25

JOSEPH M. SHANHOLTZ
723 Sanson Street
Philadelphia, Pa.

Advertised in 1947 as being a manufacturer of platinum and palladium jewelry, and selling to leading jobbers in all parts of the country.

Shanholtz "Palladium & Diamond". Ladies. Rectangular case and large linked bracelet. ca 1947 . . . . $400—600

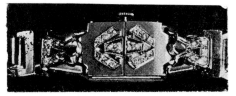

Shanholtz "Palladium & Diamond Hunting". Ladies. Rectangular case, double door lid and large linked bracelet. ca 1947 . . . . $600—800

Smith & Son, S. "Allies Watch". White glass enamel, subsidiary seconds dial. 13''', pin set movement. Round, wire lug case. ca 1918.
Silver screw back & bezel . . . . $25—50
Silver hinged case . . . . 25—50

Solrex. Ladies. Gold finished or silvered dial. 10½''', 7J or 15J movement. 14K gold, hand engraved, round case. ca 1918. . . . . . $40—60

Sheffield "Calendar". Chronograph base 60. Luminous numerals & hands, white, pink or black dial, center seconds & date window. Round chrome case. ca 1950 . . . . . . $10—20

Solrex. Ladies. Gold finished or silvered dial. 10½''', 7J or 15J movement. Round, hand engraved, green gold-filled case. ca 1918.
. . . . $10—20
Gold-filled bracelet . . . . 3— 5

Solrex. Ladies. 9¾''', 15J movement. Hand engraved, green gold-filled, octagonal case. ca 1918. . . . .$10—20
Gold-filled bracelet . . . .   3— 5

Solrex. Ladies, 8¾''', 15J movement. Hand engraved, 14K green gold, tonneau case set with 4 diamonds. ca 1918 . . . .$40—60

Solrex. Ladies. Gold finished or silvered round dial. 9¾''', 15J movement. Green gold-filled, cushion case. ca 1918. . . . .$10—20

Solrex. Ladies, 8¾''', 15J movement. 14K green gold, hand engraved, octagonal case. ca 1918. . . . .$40—60

Solrex. Ladies. Silvered dial, black enameled numerals. 15J movement. 14K white gold, rectangular case. ca 1932. . . . .$40—60

Solrex. Ladies. Silvered dial, black enameled figures. 17J baguette movement. 18K white gold, molded baguette case. ca 1932 . . .$45—65

Solrex. Ladies. Silvered dial, black enamel figures. 17J baguette movement. 18K white gold, molded baguette case. ca. 1932. .$45—60

Solrex. Ladies. Silvered dial, black enameled numerals. 15J movement. 14K white gold-filled, engraved rectangular case with black enamel. ca 1932. . . . .$50—75

Solrex. Ladies. Oval silvered dial, black enameled figures. 15J movement. 14K white gold, hand engraved, tonneau case, with black enameling. ca 1932 . . . .$40—60

Solrex. Ladies. Silvered dial, black enameled figures. 15J movement. 14K white gold, hand engraved, tonneau case. ca 1932 . . . .$45—65

Solrex. Ladies. 17J baguette movement. 18K white gold, molded baguette case. ca 1932.
. . . .$40—60

Solrex. Ladies. Silvered dial, black enamel figures. 15J movement. 14K white gold, hand engraved, tonneau case, with black enameling. ca 1932. . . . .$50—75

Solrex. Plain or luminous dial, subsidiary seconds. 3/0 size, 15J movement. 14K gold, cushion case. ca 1918. . . . .$15—25

Solrex. Ladies. Square silvered dial, black enameled numerals. 15J movement. 14K white gold-filled, engraved tonneau case. ca 1932. . . . .$10—20

Solrex. Plain or luminous dial, subsidiary seconds. 3/0 size, 15J movement. Sterling silver, cushion case. ca 1918 . . . .$15—25

Solrex. Plain or luminous dial, subsidiary seconds. 3/0 size, 15J movement. Round, sterling silver case. ca 1918 . . . .$15—25

Solrex. Plain or luminous dial, subsidiary seconds. 3/0 size, 15J movement. Cushion, nickel case. ca 1918. . . . .$15—25

Solrex. Plain or luminous dial, subsidiary seconds. 3/0 size, 15J movement. Round, sterling silver case with cutout cover for dial. ca 1918. . . . .$25—35

Solrex. Plain or luminous dial, subsidiary seconds. 3/0 size, 15J movement. Gold-filled, cushion case. ca 1918. . . . .$15—25

Solrex. Plain or luminous dial, subsidiary seconds. 3/0 size, 15J movement. Round, sterling silver case. ca 1918 . . . . $15—25

Solrex. Plain or luminous dial, subsidiary seconds. 3/0 size, 15J movement. Round, nickel case. ca 1918 . . . . $15—25

SOLREX
Trademark of
Marshall Field & Co.,
Chicago, Ill.

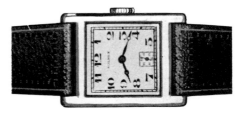

Solrex "Tank". Silvered dial, black enameled numerals, subsidiary seconds. 17J movement. 14K white gold, rectangular case. ca 1932. . . . . $125—150

Solrex. Luminous dial, subsidiary seconds. 3/0 size, 15J movement. Gold-filled, cushion case. ca 1918. . . . . $15—25

Solrex. Silvered dial, subsidiary seconds. 15J movement. 14K white gold-filled, hand engraved, molded rectangular case. ca 1932. . . . . $20—35

Solrex. Plain or luminous dial, subsidiary seconds. 3/0 size, 15J movement. Sterling silver, cushion case. ca 1918. . . . . $15—25

Solrex. Luminous hands and numerals, subsidiary seconds. 15J movement. 14K white gold-filled, cushion case. ca 1932 . . . . $25—45

Solrex. Silvered dial, luminous hands and numerals, subsidiary seconds. 15J movement. 14K white gold-filled, octagonal case. ca 1932 . . . .$30—50

Solrex. Silvered dial, radium hands and numerals, subsidiary seconds. 17J movement. 14K white gold-filled, curved rectangular case with faceted corners. ca 1932 . . . .$30—50

Solrex. 15J tonneau movement. Molded rectangular, 14K white gold-filled case. ca 1932. . . . .$20—35

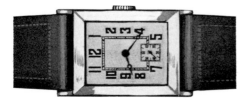

Solrex. Silvered dial, black enameled numerals, subsidiary seconds. 17J movement. 14K green gold, rectangular case. ca 1932 . . . .$90—125

SPARKES MANUFACTURING CO.
Jefferson & Clifford St.
Newark, New Jersey

Made custom cases in yellow gold or combination pink & green 14K gold. ca 1940

Sparkes "Fortuna Bracelet". Ladies 14K gold, ½ spherical case & matching link bracelet. ca 1940 . . . . 10% to 20% over gold value

Sparkes "Bona Dea Bracelet". Ladies. 14K gold square case & marquis link bracelet. ca 1940. . . . . 10% to 20% over gold value

Sparkes "Cassandra Bracelet". Ladies. 14K gold rectangular case & large round link bracelet. ca 1940 . 10% to 20% over gold value

Sparkes "Bona Dea Bracelet". Ladies. 14K gold marquis shaped case & matching link bracelet. ca 1940 . 10% to 20% over gold value

STABILIS
Trademark of
Marshall Field & Co.
Chicago, Ill.

Stabilis. Luminous dial. 11''', 17J movement. 14K yellow gold, cushion case. ca 1918.
. . . . $90—120
Sterling Silver . . . . 20— 35

Stabilis. Luminous dial. 11''', 15J movement. 14K yellow gold, cushion case. ca 1918 . . . . $90—120
Sterling silver . . . . 20— 35

Steven, David G. Raised gold markers on dial, center seconds. 14K gold round case & gold mesh band. ca 1961 10% to 20% over gold value

Sunset Watch Case Co. Ladies. Round white dial. 14K green gold butterfly case, hand engraved and enameled. Ribbon band with 14K gold clasp. ca 1925 . . . . $400—550

Swiss Skeleton Watch. 18K gold, 35mm. round case. ca 1970 . . . . $1,500—1,700

Tavannes. Ladies. Silvered dial. 9''', 15J round movement. 22x28mm. rectangular case. ca 1920. 14K gold . . . . $150—200
Silver . . . . 50— 75

Tavannes. Ladies. Silvered dial. 9''', 17J round movement. 23x33mm. platinum tonneau case set with diamonds & precious stones. ca 1920.
. . . . $250—350

Tavannes. Ladies. Silvered dial. 9''', 17J round movement. 22mm. platinum cushion case set with diamonds & precious stones. ca 1920.
. . . . $150—225

Tavannes. Ladies. Silvered dial. 9''', 17J movement. 21mm. round platinum case set with diamonds. ca 1920 . . . . $75—100

Tavannes. Ladies. Silvered dial. 9''', 17J round movement. 23mm. platinum octagonal case set with diamonds & precious stones. ca 1920. $175—225

Tavannes. Ladies. Round white dial, Roman numerals. 9''', 15J movement. 14K gold round case, octagonal engraved bezel set with diamonds. ca 1920 . . . . $125—150

Tavannes. Ladies. White dial, Roman numerals. 9''', 15J movement. 22mm., 14K gold round case set with diamonds. ca 1920. . . . $75—100

Tavannes. Ladies. Silvered dial. 10''', 15J movement. 24mm. 14K gold round case set with diamonds. ca 1920 . . . . $75—100

Tavannes. Ladies. Silvered dial. 10''', 15J movement. 24mm., 14K gold round case set with diamonds & precious stones. ca 1920. $75—100

Tavannes. Ladies. Silvered dial, 10''', 15J movement. 22mm., 14K gold round engraved case set with diamonds. ca 1920 . . . . . . $85—100

Tavannes. Ladies. Silvered dial. 10''', 15J round movement. 25mm., 14K gold, faceted octagonal case with alternating facets set with diamonds & precious stones. ca 1920 . . $85—100

Tavannes. Ladies. Roman numeral dial, subsidiary seconds. 11''', 15J movement. 30mm., grooved round case. ca 1920.
Gold-filled . . . . $35—50
Nickel . . . . 30—45

Tavannes. Ladies. Small, plain white dial. 11''', 15J movement. 29mm. round case, numerals enameled on bezel. ca 1920.
Silver . . . . $30—35
Gold-filled . . . . 25—30
Nickel . . . . 15—20

Tavannes, Ladies Strap. Subsidiary seconds, 10/0 size movement. 24mm. cushion case, engraved & enameled. ca 1926.
14K gold . . . . $90—110
14K gold filled . . . . 30— 55

Tavannes, Ladies Strap. Subsidiary seconds, 10/0 size movement. 25mm. cushion case, engraved & enameled. ca 1926.
14K gold . . . . $75—90
14K gold filled . . . . 20—25

Tavannes, Ladies Strap. Subsidiary seconds, 10/0 size movement. 25mm. tonneau case, enameled & engraved. ca 1926.
14K gold . . . . $75—90
14K gold filled . . . . 20—30

Tavannes, Ladies Strap. Subsidiary seconds, 10/0 size movement. 25mm. 14K WGF tonneau case. ca 1926 . . . . $20—30

Tavannes, Ladies Strap. Subsidiary seconds, 10/0 size movement. 25mm. cushion case. ca 1926. 14K gold . . . . $75—110
14K gold filled . . . . 20— 30

Tavannes, Ladies Strap. Subsidiary seconds, 10/0 size movement. 24mm. 14K white tonneau case, engraved & enameled. ca 1926.
14K gold . . . . $90—110
14K gold filled . . . . 40— 60

Tavannes "Ladies Bracelet". 14K gold, domed rectangular case, link bracelet. ca 1940.
. . . . 10% to 20% over gold value

Tavannes "Diamond, Emerald & 14K White Gold". Square case and molded lugs. ca 1940.
. . . . $150—175

Tavannes. Ladies. 14K gold, molded rectangular case with graduated ends and single lugs. ca 1940 . . . . $30—50

Tavannes. Silvered dial. 9''', 15J round movement. 22x28mm. oval case. ca 1920. 14K gold . . . . $150—200
Silver . . . . 40— 60

Tavannes "Ladies Gold Cord". Raised gold markers on dial. 14K gold square case, large molded cord lugs. ca 1947 . . . . $40—60

Tavannes. Luminous hands & numerals, subsidiary seconds. 15½''', 17J movement. 39mm. round case. ca 1920. 14K gold . . . $200—250
Silver . . . . 100—110
Nickel . . . . 30— 40

Tavannes. Silvered dial. 11''', 15J round movement. 29mm. square case. ca 1920. 14K gold . . . . $175—225
Silver . . . . 50— 65

Tavannes. 8¾''' movement. 28mm. engraved square case. ca 1926. 14K gold . . . . $90—110
14K gold filled . . . . 20— 30

Tavannes. White dial, Roman numerals, subsidiary seconds. 15''', 6J movement. 37mm. round groved bezel case. ca 1920. Silver$75—85
Nickel . . . . 30—40

Tavannes. Subsidiary seconds, 3/0 size movement. 31mm. 14K white or green gold filled cushion case. ca 1926. . . . . $20—30

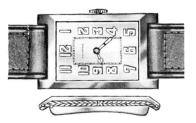

Tavannes. 8¾''' movement. 24x35mm., 14K green gold rectangular case. ca 1926 . $95—125

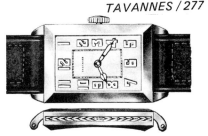

Tavannes. 6¾''' movement. 14K white gold, 24x35mm. rectangular case. ca 1926.
14K gold . . . . $150—225
14K gold filled . . . . 30— 40

NOTE: Read Page 6 before using this book to value your wrist watch.

Tavannes. Subsidiary seconds. 24x35mm., 14K green or white gold tonneau case. ca 1926.
. . . . $150—175

Tavannes. Subsidiary seconds, 6/0 size movement. 30mm. cushion case. ca 1926.
14K gold . . . . $90—110
14K gold filled . . . . 15— 20

Tavannes. 6¾''' movement. 24x35mm. engraved rectangular case. ca 1926.
14K gold . . . . $150—225
14K gold filled . . . . 30— 40

Tavannes. Subsidiary seconds, 6/0 size movement. 30x33mm. 14K white or green gold filled, engraved tonneau case. ca 1926 . $25-35

NOTE: All values are given for the head only unless the bracelet is included in the description.

Tavannes. Subsidiary seconds, 10/0 size movement. 28x32mm. 14K white or green gold filled rectangular case, engraved & enameled. ca 1926. . . . . $25—35

Tavannes. Subsidiary seconds, 6/0 size movement. 30mm. 14K white or green gold filled cushion case. ca 1926. . . . . $20—30

Tavannes. Subsidiary seconds, 6/0 size movement. 14K white or green gold filled engraved cushion case. ca 1926. . . . .$20—30

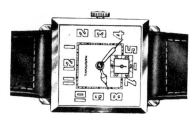

Tavannes. Subsidiary seconds, 6/0 size movement. 29mm. 14K green or white gold filled square case. ca 1926 . . . .$20—30

Tavannes. Subsidiary seconds, 10/0 size movement. 14K white or green gold filled rectangular case with faceted corners. ca 1926 . $15—25

Tavannes. Subsidiary seconds. 14K white gold, 25x28mm. tonneau case. ca 1926. . $150—200

Tavannes. Subsidiary seconds, 6/0 size movement. 30x33mm. tonneau case. ca 1926.
14K gold . . . . $125—150
14K gold filled . . . . 20— 30

Tavannes. Subsidiary seconds, 6/0 size movement. 14K green gold or sterling silver, 30mm. faceted square case. ca 1926. 14K . $100—125
Silver . . . . 25— 40

Tavannes. 8¾''' movement. 29mm. square, 14K green gold case. ca 1926 . . . . $100—125

Tavannes. 8¾''' movement, 22x30mm. faceted rectangular case. ca 1926. 18K gold $150—175
14K gold . . . . 110—125

Tavannes. 8¾''' movement. 23x38mm. elongated rectangular case. ca 1926.
14K gold . . . . $150—200
14K gold filled . . . . 25— 40

Tavannes. Subsidiary seconds. 14K gold, square case and lugs. ca 1940 . . . . $100–125

Tavannes. Platinum finished dial, raised gold or luminous figures and hands. 20x47mm. curved, elongated rectangular case. ca 1930.
14K green gold $175–225
14K white or green gold-filled. . . . 35– 55

Tavannes. Subsidiary seconds. 14K gold, molded square case with graduated ends. ca 1940 . . . . $100–125

Tavannes "Gold-Filled Strap". Platinum finished dial with luminous hands & numerals, subsidiary seconds. 15J movement. Engraved rectangular case. ca 1930.
14K white or green gold-filled. $25–45

Tavannes "Man's Gold Strap". Raised gold markers on dial, subsidiary seconds. 14K gold rectangular case with scalloped lugs. ca 1947.
. . . . $100–125

Tavannes "Gold-Filled Strap". Luminous dial & hands, subsidiary seconds. 15J movement. Curved rectangular, 14K white or green gold-filled case. ca 1930 . . . . $35–55

Thorensen "Chronograph". Radium silvered dial, subsidiary seconds, 30 minute recorder with outer tachometer ring. 17J movement. Round gold-filled case. ca 1950 . . . . $40–75
Chrome. 30–60

Tavannes. Silvered dial, subsidiary seconds, 15J movement. Gold plated, rectangular case with bowed sides. ca 1935 . . . .$10–20

Tide "Chronograph" with 12 hour recorder, center seconds. Stainless steel round case. ca 1949. This watch virtually gazes at the moon, and anyone living or working near the sea has a geodetic chart on his wrist . . . . . . $40—60

NOTE: Read Page 6 before using this book to value your wrist watch.

Tiffany "Ladies Gold, Garnet & Diamond". Square case with bracelet. ca 1940 . $325—375

NOTE: All values are given for the head only unless the bracelet is included in the description.

Tiffany & Co. Silvered dial. 14K gold, 35mm., long tonneau curvex case. ca 1914 . $350—425

Tiffany & Co. Moonphase calendar, chronograph. Gold finished dial, subsidiary seconds, 30 minute & 12 hour recorders, day & month windows & outer date ring. 18K gold, 39mm. round case . . . . $1,100—1,200

Tiffany & Co. Moonphase, calendar, chronograph. Gold matte dial, subsidiary seconds, 30 minute & 12 hour registers, day & month window with outer date ring. 18K gold round case . . . . $1,000—1,100

Times Watch Co. Ladies. Platinum and diamond tonneau case. ca 1924. Value varies according to size, quality and color of diamonds.
. . . . $250—350

Tissot. Silvered dial. 17J movement. 14K gold, 16x20mm. rectangular case with heavy lugs & gold bracelet fittings. ca 1947 . . 20% over gold

Tissot "Center Seconds". Silvered dial with ultra-flat movement. 14K round, 31mm., gold case. ca 1947 . . . . $75—100

Tissot. Tu-tone dial, subsidiary seconds. 14K, 23x25mm., rectangular gold case. ca 1947.
. . . . $115—135

Tissot "Chronograph". Tachometer base 1000m., with subsidiary seconds, 30 minute & 12 hour recorder. 14K gold, 35mm. round case. ca 1947. . . . . $250—300

Tissot "Automatic". Subsidiary seconds. 14K gold round case. ca 1959. . . . . . . $120—140

Tissot. Chronograph, metal dial, subsidiary seconds, 30 minute & 12 hour recorders with outer telemeter & tachometer ring. 17J movement. 18K gold, 35mm. round case. $200—225

Tissot "Automatic". Black dial with raised gold numerals & sporting hands. Subsidiary seconds, self-winding movement. 14K gold, 32mm. round case. ca 1947 . . . . . $100—130

Tissot "Sea Star". Chronometer. Black dial, subsidiary seconds, 30 minute recorder with outer tachomer ring. ca 1966.
14K gold . . . . $225—300
Stainless steel . . . . 40— 60

Tissot "Automatic" Model T-400 (Large Size). Raised gold markers on dial, subsidiary seconds. 14K gold square case. ca 1954. . . . $300—350

Tissot "Sea Star". Automatic calendar. Black dial, date window at 3. 14K gold or stainless steel tonneau case with revolving calibrated bezel. ca 1966. 14K gold. . . . . . . $125—150
Stainless steel . . . . 25— 40

Touchon & Co. Ladies, white matte dial. 15J Movement signed Audemars Piguet & Co. Platinum rectangular, 29mm. case. Bezel & lugs set with diamonds. . . . . $700—900

Tourneau "Admiral". Hacking sweep seconds, round case. ca 1942 .
Gold Filled. . . . .$25—40
Stainless steel . . . . 20—30

Touchon & Co., retailed by Tiffany & Co. White matte dial, subsidiary seconds. 14K gold, slightly curved, 40mm., long rectangular tank case . . . . $300—400

Tourneau. Chronograph base 1 mile & 1m. with subsidiary seconds, 30 minute and 12 hour recorders, luminous dial, in a heavy round stainless steel, non-magnetic case. ca 1942. . . . . $75—100

Tourneau "Neptune". Sweep second, waterproof, non-magnetic 17J. Round intergal lug stainless steel case. ca 1941 . . . .$35—60

Tourneau. 14K raised gold numerals & indexes. Round, 14K gold case. ca 1942 . 20% over gold

Tourneau. Chronograph base 1 mile with subsidiary seconds and 30 minute recorder. Stainless steel case. ca 1942 . . . .$35—65

Tourneau. 14K raised gold numerals & spots. Rectangular 14K gold case with tri-facet crystal. ca 1942 . . . . $175—250

Tourneau "Triton". Sweep second, luminous dial, waterproof, stainless steel, round case. ca 1943. Mens $35–60
Ladies $20–35

NOTE: Read Page 6 before using this book to value your wrist watch.

Tourneau. Raised gold chapters, subsidiary seconds, 17J movement. 14K gold rectangular case, hinged lugs & arched crystal. ca 1946. . . . . $100–125

NOTE: All values are given for the head only unless the bracelet is included in the description.

Tourneau. Telemeter, chronograph, subsidiary seconds, 30 minute & 12 hour recorders. Round case. ca 1946. 14K gold . . . $250–300
Stainless steel 75–100

Tudor "Princess Oyster Date Chrono-Time". Self-winding, waterproof up to 165 feet. Blue, silver or tu-tone dial, center seconds, date window. Round stainless steel oyster case, blue 60 minute time elapse bezel, twinlock screw-down crown. Integral bracelet included in value. ca 1970 . . . . $100–150

Tudor "Prince Oyster Date Ranger II". Self-winding & waterproof up to 165 feet. Silver, blue, brown or gold dial, center seconds, window date. Round case with blue or yellow striped bezel & twinlock screw-down crown. Integral bracelet included in value. ca 1970. Gold-filled & steel. $175–225
Stainless steel 125–175

Tudor "Prince Oyster Date". Self-winding, waterproof up to 165 feet. Blue, silver, champagne, or tu-tone dial, center seconds, date window. Round case with notched bezel to mark seconds, twinlock screw-down crown. Integral bracelet included in value. ca 1970. Gold-filled & steel. $125–175
Stainless steel 100–150

Tudor "Ranger Prince Oyster Date". Self-winding & waterproof up to 165 feet. Silver, black or champagne dial, center seconds, date window. Round case with twinlock screw-down crown. Bracelet not included. ca 1970.
Stainless & GF bezel $175–250
Stainless steel 150–200

Tudor "¾ Size Submariner Oyster Date". Man or Ladies. Self-winding & waterproof up to 330 feet. Black or blue dial, center seconds & date window. Round stainless steel case with black or blue calibrated bezel & twinlock screw-down crown. Oyster stainless steel bracelet included. ca 1970 . . . . $200–250

Turler. Calendar, center seconds, day & month windows, with outer date ring. Round, GF case.
. . . . $30–50

Udall and Ballou. 14K gold rectangular case, mounted on a money clip. ca 1936 . $125–150

Udall and Ballou "Gold Bracelet". Tu-tone 14K green & yellow gold, geometric case, with snake bracelet. ca 1936. . . . . $250–300

"Ultra Deluxe" Watch Lighter. Platinoid & gold plated. ca 1928 . . . . $50–75

Ulysse Nardin "Ladies Ribbon". 14K gold engraved rectangular case, black enamel bezel. ca 1925. . . . . $60–75

Ulysse Nardin "Ladies Ribbon". Oval dial, engine-turned center. 14K gold engraved & enameled rectangular case. ca 1925. . . $60—75

Ulysse Nardin Ribbon, Platinum, Diamond & Semi-Precious Stone". Ladies "Art Deco" design rectangular case. ca 1928. $1,000—1,500

Ulysse Nardin "Ladies Ribbon". Platinum with paved diamond Art Deco design rectangular case. ca 1927 . . . . $1,250—1,750

Ulysse Nardin "Ladies Ribbon, Platinum, Diamond & Semi-Precious Stone". Art Deco design rectangular case. ca 1928. . $900—1,200

Ulysse Nardin "Ladies Ribbon". Platinum with paved diamond Art Deco design rectangular case. ca 1927 . . . . $1,250—1,750

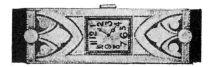

Ulysse Nardin "Ladies Ribbon". Platinum with paved diamond, Art Deco design rectangular case. ca 1927 . . . . $1,550—2,000

Ulysse Nardin "Ladies Strap". Oval dial. 14K gold, tu-tone striped rectangular case. ca 1928. $95—150

Ulysse Nardin "Ladies Cord". Plain platinum rectangular case, single lugs. ca 1928 . . $60—75

Ulysse Nardin "Ladies Ribbon". 14K gold engraved tonneau case. ca 1928 . . . . . $60—75

Ulysse Nardin "Ladies Gold Cord". Black dial. 14K gold rectangular case with graduated lugs. ca 1940. . . . . $40—60

Ulysse Nardin "Ladies Ribbon". 14K gold, plain rectangular case. ca 1928 . . . . . $60—75

Ulysse Nardin "Ladies Gold Strap". Black dial. 14K yellow gold rectangular case. ca 1940. . . . . $50—75

Ulysse Nardin "Ladies Gold Hunter Diamond Bracelet". Round black dial. Rectangular case and matching mesh band. ca 1940.
. . . . .10% to 20% over gold & diamond value

Ulysse Nardin. Black dial. Subsidiary seconds. 18K gold rectangular shaped 20mm. tank case. Flexible lugs. ca 1925 . . . . . $325—375

Ulysse Nardin "Gold Strap". Silver dial with luminous numerals & hands. 17J adjusted movement. 18K white gold with plain brushed finish, rectangular case. ca 1930. . . $200—250

Ulysse Nardin. Luminous hands & numerals, subsidiary seconds. 18K gold rectangular case. ca 1927. . . . . $140—165

Ulysse Nardin. Pink silvered dial, luminous hands & numerals, subsidiary seconds. 17J movement. 18K white gold, 24x39mm. rectangular case. ca 1930 . . . . $135—165

Ulysse Nardin. Luminous hands & numerals, subsidiary seconds. 14K gold square case. ca 1928 . . . . $125—150

Ulysse Nardin. Luminous hands & numerals, subsidiary seconds. 14K gold tonneau case. ca 1925. . . . . $175—200

Ulysse Nardin. Subsidiary seconds. 14K gold rectangular case. ca 1928. . . . . . . $125—150

Ulysse Nardin. Luminous hands & numerals, subsidiary seconds. Tu-tone, 14K gold tonneau case with engraved hinges for lugs. ca 1928. . . . . $400—500

Ulysse Nardin "Gold Strap". Subsidiary seconds. 18K yellow gold rectangular, curvex case. ca 1940 . . . . $300—350

NOTE: Read Page 6 before using this book to value your wrist watch.

Ulysse Nardin, Locle, Geneve. Chronograph. White enamel dial, subsidiary seconds & 30 minute recorder. 19J movement. 18K gold, 38.5mm. round case. . . . . $450—550

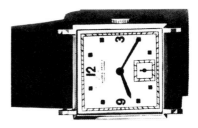

Ulysse Nardin "Gold Strap". Subsidiary seconds. 14K yellow gold square case. ca 1940. $175—225

Ulysse Nardin. Pulsimeter Chronograph, white enamel dial. Subsidiary seconds & 30 minute recorder. 18K gold 34mm. round case. . . . . $500—550

Ulysse Nardin, Chronometer Co. Moonphase, calendar, chronograph. Subsidiary seconds, 30 minute & 12 hour recorder, day & month windows with outer date ring. 18K gold, 39 mm. round case . . . . $1,000—1,200

Ulysse Nardin "Chronograph". Black dial, subsidiary seconds and 30 minute recorder, with outer tachometer ring. ca 1940 .$375—425

Ulysse Nardin. Silver dial, subsidiary seconds. 18K gold curvex case. 31mm . . . . $300—350

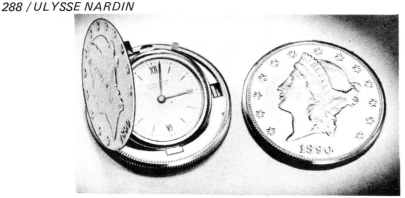

Ulysse Nardin. $20 gold coin watch. 17J movement. Watch hidden in gold coin. ca 1957.
. . . . $1,300—1,800

Ulysse Nardin "Reporter". 14K gold applied dial. 17J, sweep second movement. Ultra thin, stainless steel, water resistant round case. ca 1963 . . . .$25—40

Ulysse Nardin "Sea Captain Automatic Calendar". 14K gold applied dial. 17J or 21J, sweep second, date at 3, movement. Round case. ca 1963. 14K gold top, stainless steel back . . . . $60—85
Stainless steel . . . . 40—60

Ulysse Nardin "Sovereign". 14K gold applied dial. 17J movement. 18K gold square, flat case. ca 1963 . . . . $175—210

Ulysse Nardin "Atlas Automatic Calendar Chronometer". 14K gold applied dial. 21J, self-winding, sweep second, date at 3, movement. 18K solid yellow gold round case. ca 1963 . . . . $200—225

Ulysse Nardin "Diplomat". 14K gold applied dial. 17J, sweep second movement. 14K solid yellow gold, round case. ca 1963 . . $110—135

Ulysse Nardin "His Excellency". 14K gold applied dial. 17J movement. 18K yellow gold case. ca 1963 . . . . $150—185

Ulysse Nardin "President". 14K gold applied dial, subsidiary seconds. 17J movement. 18K yellow gold round case. ca 1963 . . $130—165

Ulysse Nardin "Royal". 14K gold applied dial, subsidiary seconds. 17J movement. 18K yellow gold round case. ca 1963 . . $135—175

Ulysse Nardin "Statesman". 14K gold applied dial, subsidiary seconds. 17J movement. 14K yellow gold round case. ca 1963 . . $110—135

Ulysse Nardin "Skipper". 14K gold applied dial. 17J, sweep second movement. Round case. ca 1963. 14K yellow gold . . . . . . $110—135
Gold-filled . . . . 35— 45

Ulysse Nardin "Governor". 14K gold applied dial, subsidiary seconds. 17J movement. 14K gold round case. ca 1963. . . . . . . $110—135

Ulysse Nardin "Supreme Automatic Chronometer". 14K gold applied dial. 21J, self-winding sweep second movement. 18K yellow gold round case. ca 1963. . . . . $160—200

Ulysse Nardin "Nautilus Automatic". 14K gold applied dial. 21J, self-winding, sweep second movement. 14K yellow gold round case. ca 1963 . . . . $120—145

Ulysse Nardin "Polaris Automatic". 14K gold applied dial. 21J, sweep second movement. 14K yellow gold round case. ca 1963 $125—150

Ulysse Nardin "Explorer Automatic". 14K gold applied dial. 17J, sweep second movement. Round case, gold-filled top, stainless steel back. ca 1963 . . . . $45—65

Ulysse Nardin "Continental". 14K gold applied dial. 17J, sweep second movement. 14K yellow gold, square, flat thin case. ca 1963. $140—175

Ulysse Nardin "Commodore Automatic". 14K gold applied dial. 21J, self-winding, sweep second movement. 14K yellow gold round case. ca 1963. . . . . $125—150

Ulysse Nardin "Sea Gull Automatic". 14K gold applied dial. 17J, sweep second movement. Round case, gold-filled top, stainless steel back. ca 1963 . . . . $45—65

Universal Geneve. Ladies, 18K gold rectangular case with scalloped edges. ca 1943 . . . $60—85

Universal Geneve "Ladies Duo-Compax". Tachometer chronograph, base 60 seconds, subsidiary seconds, 30 minute recorder. 23mm. square case. ca 1945. 14K gold . . . $500—600
Stainless steel . . . . 250—300

Universal Geneve. Ladies. Silvered dial. 17J movement. 14K white gold bracelet with rectangular, palladium case set with 26 diamonds. ca 1946 . . . . $200—250

Universal Geneve. Ladies. Silvered dial on a 17J movement. 18K gold square cord case with molded lugs. ca 1946 . . .10% to 20% over gold

Universal Geneve. Ladies. Silvered dial on 17J movement. 14K gold bracelet set with diamonds & rubies. Round case with stone-set lugs for cord or fitted bracelet. ca 1946. Head only . . . . $200—275

Universal Geneve. Ladies. Round 14K case with heavy lugs. ca 1946 . . . . $50—75

Universal Geneve "Ladies Gold Cord". Silvered dial, raised gold markers. 17J movement. 14K gold round case with 4 round cylinders. ca 1949 . . . . $100—125

Universal Geneve. Ladies. Square 14K case with intergal 14K gold mesh bracelet. ca 1964. . . . . $200—275

Universal, Geneve. Ladies, tiger eye oval dial & surrounded by tiger eye-set gold petals. 35mm. oval case . . . . $350—375

Universal, Geneve. Self-winding, blue metal dial, 25J movement. 18K gold, 30mm. oval case . . . . $350—400

Universal "Cabriolet". Silvered dial, subsidiary seconds, 15J, 7¾''' movement. Polished steel, 43x24mm. rectangular reversible case. ca 1930.
. . . . $350—375

Universal, Geneve, "Uni-Compax". Chronograph, silvered dial, subsidiary seconds, 30 minute recorder with outer tachometer ring. 18K gold, 27mm. square case . . . . $550—650

Universal Geneve. Silvered dial, raised gold numerals, subsidiary seconds. 17J movement. 14K gold round case. ca 1949 . . . . $110—135

Universal Geneve. Subsidiary seconds, 18K gold round case with moulded lugs. ca 1943.
. . . . $175—225

Universal Geneve. Subsidiary seconds. 17J movement, 14K gold round case. ca 1943.
. . . . $125—150

Universal Geneve. Tu-tone dial, center seconds, 24 hour inner chapter ring. 17J movement. Waterproof round case in stainless steel, 14K or 18K gold. ca 1944 . . 18K gold . . $125—150
14K gold . . . .   90—125
Stainless steel . . . .   25— 40

Universal Geneve "Duo-Compax". Tachometer chronograph, base 1,000m., subsidiary seconds, 45 minute recorder. Round 39mm. case. ca 1945. 14K gold . . . . $150—200
Stainless steel . . . . 50— 75

Universal Geneve "Aero Compax". Tachometer chronograph base 1,000m., with subsidiary seconds, 30 minute, 60 minute and 12 hour recorders. Also a memento dial set from crown at 9. Round 39mm. stainless steel case ca 1946. . . . . $200—250
14K yellow gold. . . . . 700—800
18K yellow gold. . . . . 800—900

Universal Geneve "Tri-Compax". Moonphase calendar in color, tachometer chronograph base 1,000m., subsidiary seconds, 30 minute, 60 minute and 12 hour recorders, window day & month. round 39mm. case. ca 1946.
18K gold . . . . $1,100—1,300
14K gold . . . . 1,000—1,200
Stainless steel . . . . 250— 350

Universal, Geneve, "Tri-Compax". Moonphase calendar, chronograph. Waterproof, gold finished dial, subsidiary seconds, 30 minute, 12 hour & date recorders, day & month windows with outer tachometer ring, base 400m. 18K gold, 34mm. round case . . . . . $1,100—1,300

Universal Geneve. Moonphase calendar, subsidiary seconds, automatic date recorder. A combined moonphase-month indicator in color and day window. Radium dial & hands. Round 34mm. case. ca 1947. 14K gold . . . $550—650
Stainless steel . . . . 150—200

Universal Geneve "Gold Diamond Dial". 12-diamond dial with engine-turned center. 18K yellow gold round case with integral gold band. ca 1954. . . . . $350—425
18K white gold . . . . 300—350

Universal Geneve "Tri-Compax". Moonphase calendar chronograph. Subsidiary seconds, 30 minute and 12 hour recorders, incorporated moonphase and date recorder, day & month window. Round case, heavy lugs, black bezel calibrated for tachometer. ca 1970.
14K yellow gold head . . . . . $1,000—1,200
Steel, white or black dial with stainless bracelet . . . . $300—350
Steel, white or black dial . . . . . . 275—325

Universal Geneve "Space Compax". Waterproof chronograph. Black dial, luminous figures, subsidiary seconds, 30 minute & 12 hour recorders. Stainless steel round case, revolving black bezel with luminous division of 0 to 60 minutes, heavy lugs and armored waterproof crown and buttons. ca 1970.
. . . . $150—200
With stainless bracelet . . . . 160—210

Universal Geneve "Compax". Tachometer Chronograph. Black dial with subsidiary seconds, 30 minute and 12 hour recorders. Round case, heavy lugs, with tachometer scale on black bezel. ca 1970. Steel, black dial . . . $125—175
Steel, white dial . . . . 125—175
Steel, black dial with steel bracelet . 150—200
Gold-filled, white dial . . . . 150—200
Gold-filled, black dial . . . . 150—200

Universal Geneve "Aero-Compax". Chronograph, 24 hour dial, subsidiary seconds, 15 minute & 12 hour recorders. Round stainless steel case, heavy lugs, revolving black and white 24 hour bezel. ca 1970 . . . . $175—225

VACHERON & CONSTANTIN

Vacheron Constantin. Ladies. Platinum rectangular case, set with diamonds & sapphires. ca 1927. Value varies according to the size, quality and color of the diamonds and other precious stones . . . . $1,000—1,200

Vacheron Constantin. Ladies. Platinum rectangular case, set with diamonds & sapphires. Value varies according to the size, quality and color of the diamonds and other precious stones. ca 1927 . . . . $1,200—1,400

Vacheron Constantin. Ladies. Platinum rectangular case, set with diamonds & sapphires with matching bracelet. ca 1927. Value varies according to the size, quality and color of the diamonds and other precious stones.
. . . . $1,600—1,800

Vacheron Constantin. Ladies. Platinum rectangular case, set with diamonds. ca 1927. Value varies according to the size, quality and color of the diamonds. . . . . $1,400—1,800

Vacheron Constantin. Ladies. Platinum rectangular case, set with diamonds & sapphires. ca 1927. Value varies according to the size, quality and color of the diamonds and other precious stones. ca 1927 . . . . $1,200—1,400

Vacheron Constantin. Ladies rectangular, platinum, diamond & sapphire case with matching bracelet. ca 1927. Value varies according to the size, quality and color of the diamonds and other precious stones . . . . . . $2,000—2,500

Vacheron Constantin. Ladies. Platinum rectangular case set with diamonds & sapphires. ca 1927. Value varies according to the size, quality and color of the diamonds and other precious stones. . . . . $1,000—1,200

Vacheron Constantin. Ladies. Silvered dial, raised 18K gold markers, subsidiary seconds. 17J movement. 18K yellow or white gold, molded oval case. ca 1938 . . . . . $250—300

Vacheron & Constantin "Ladies Gold Cord". Tu-tone gold colored dial with subsidiary seconds. 17J movement. 18K yellow gold rectangular case with heavy cord lugs. ca 1939.
. . . . $300—400

Vacheron Constantin "Ladies Ruby". 18K gold square case and large molded flower lugs set with rubies. ca 1940 . . . . $200—250

Vacheron & Constantin, Geneve. Ladies, 20mm. round 14K gold case with 16 diamonds & mesh band. . . . . $2,200—2,800

Vacheron & Constantin. Gold plated dial, subsidiary seconds. 18K gold cushion case.
. . . . $550—625

Vacheron & Constantin, Geneve. Minute repeater, silvered dial, 31J movement. 18K gold cushion case, slide repeat at 9 o'clock. All original. . . . . $9,000—9,500

Vacheron & Constantin, Geneve. Five minute repeater. White enamel dial, Louis XV hands. Strikes on 2 gongs. 18K gold, 33mm. round case . . . . $4,500—5,000

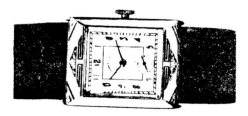

Vacheron & Constantin, Geneve. White dial, subsidiary seconds, 15J, 9¼''' movement. Tu-tone, 14K gold, 35x26mm., "art deco" designed rectangular case. ca 1925. $1,200—1,400

Vacheron & Constantin. Black dial with unusual cross numerals. Rectangular, 24x35mm 18K gold case. ca 1930. . . . . $700—750

Vacheron & Constantin, Geneve. Silvered dial, subsidiary seconds. 18K gold, 20mm., tu-tone rectangular case with rose gold lugs. ca 1930. . . . . $1,100—1,350

Vacheron & Constantin, Geneve. Gold finished dial, subsidiary seconds. 14K yellow gold, square case. ca 1935 . . . . $575-650

Vacheron & Constantin. Subsidiary seconds. 18K gold, 22x38, curved rectangular case. ca 1936. . . . . $600—750

Vacheron & Constantin. Dial signed Vacheron & Constantin, Geneve, Asprey. Subsidiary seconds. 18K gold, 32x21mm. rectangular case. ca 1937 . . . . $600—750

Vacheron Constantin. Silvered dial, subsidiary seconds. 17J movement. 18K yellow gold square case. ca 1938 . . . . $600—650

Vacheron & Constantin. Black dial with raised gold numerals, subsidiary seconds. 17J movement. Rectangular 18K yellow gold case with polished, slanted ends. ca 1939 . . . $600—750

Vacheron Constantin. Tu-tone dial, subsidiary seconds. 18K gold, round case. ca 1940.
. . . . $400—500

Vacheron & Constantin. Raised gold numerals on tu-tone silvered dial. 17J movement. Square tank, 18K yellow gold case. ca 1939 .$600—750

Vacheron Constantin. Tu-tone dial, subsidiary seconds. Square, 18K yellow gold molded case and large rectangular lugs. ca 1940 . $600—750

Vacheron Constantin. Tu-tone dial, subsidiary seconds. 18K yellow gold, round case. ca 1940 . . . . $400—500

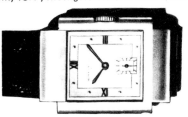

Vacheron & Constantin, Geneve. Curvex, gold matte dial. Subsidiary seconds, 18J movement. 18K gold rectangular, 39mm. case. Signed case, dial & movement. ca 1940.
. . . . $750—850

Vacheron & Constantin. 18K gold, 26mm. square case with champferred sides. ca 1940.
. . . . $600—650

Vacheron & Constantin, Geneve. Moonphase calendar, silvered dial, subsidiary seconds, day & month windows with outer date ring. 17J movement. 18K gold, 34mm. round case. Signed case, dial & movement. ca 1945.
. . . . $2,500—2,800

Vacheron & Constantin, Geneve. Silvered dial, subsidiary seconds, 17J movement. 18K gold rectangular case . . . . $650—750

Vacheron & Constantin, Geneve. White matte dial with raised gold numbers, center seconds. 18K gold, 37mm. round case . . . . $400—425

Vacheron & Constantin, Geneve. Gold finished dial, subsidiary seconds, 18J movement. 18K gold, 27mm. square case with heavy moulded bezel & lugs . . . . $650—750

Vacheron & Constantin. 18K gold, round case. ca 1946. . . . . $375—400

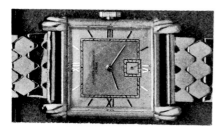

Vacheron & Constantin "Curvex". Silvered dial, subsidiary seconds, 17J octagonal movement. 18K gold, 30mm. curved rectangular case. ca 1950 . . . . $600—675

Vacheron & Constantin. Tu-tone dial, subsidiary seconds, 17J movement, 14K heavy gold square case with moulded lugs. ca 1946. $700—750

Vacheron & Constantin, Geneve. Telemeter chronograph. Gold matte dial, subsidiary seconds & 30 minute recorder. 19J movement, 18K gold, 36mm. round case. Signed case, dial & movement in original box. ca 1950. . . . . $1,700—2,200

Vacheron & Constantin, Geneve. Silvered dial, subsidiary seconds, 17J movement. 18K gold, 36mm. rectangular case with tri-faceted crystal. $650—750

Vacheron & Constantin. Subsidiary seconds, winder at 12 o'clock. 18K gold, 30mm. round case. ca 1950 . . . . $450–500

Vacheron & Constantin. Tu-tone dial, subsidiary seconds. 18K gold, 31mm. round case, with moulded strap lugs. ca 1950 . . $400–450

Vacheron & Constantin, Geneve. Calendar, raised gold numerals, gold matte dial. Subsidiary seconds, day & month windows with outer date ring. 17J movement. 18K gold, 36mm. round case. Movement, case & dial signed, original strap & leather box. ca 1950. $1,400–1,600

Vacheron & Constantin, Geneve, "Chronometro Royal". Metal dial with raised gold markers. 18K gold, 39mm. round case. $400–450

Vacheron & Constantin, Geneva. Calendar, subsidiary seconds, day & month windows with date ring in red. 18K gold, 35mm. round case with moulded lugs. ca 1950 . . . $1,350–1,550

Vacheron & Constantin, Geneve. Gold plated dial, center seconds, 18J movement. 18K gold, round case. Signed case, dial & movement. $400–425

Vacheron & Constantin. Center seconds. 18K gold, 38mm. round case with moulded strap lugs. ca 1950. . . . . $400–450

Vacheron & Constantin, Geneve. Ultra-thin, white matte dial, 17J movement. 18K gold, 34mm. round case with reeded bezel & matching mesh bracelet $800–1,000

Vacheron & Constantin "Royal Chronometer". Silvered dial, center seconds. 18J, 12½''' movement. 18K gold, 36mm. round case. ca 1951. . . . . $450—500

Vacheron & Constantin, Geneve. Self-winding, moonphase calendar, chronograph. Tu-tone silvered dial, center seconds, day, date & month recorders, with outer tachometer ring. 29J movement. 18K gold, round case with gold mesh band . . . . $6,500—7,500

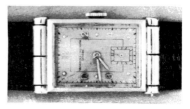

Vacheron & Constantin, Geneve. Curvex, gold matte dial. Subsidiary seconds, 17J tonneau movement. 14K gold, 37mm. slightly curved rectangular case with hinged lugs. Signed dial & movement. ca 1955 . . . . . . $700—900

Vacheron & Constantin "Man's Gold Strap". Tu-tone champaigne dial with applied gold numerals on textured background. Sweep second, self-winding movement. 18K yellow gold case with reeded design bezel and hidden lugs. ca 1954. . . . . $450—500

Vacheron & Constantin. Center seconds, round 18K gold, 35mm. case with moulded strap lugs. ca 1960. . . . . $450—500

Vacheron & Constantin. Calendar, subsidiary seconds & outer date ring, day & month windows. 18K gold, 35mm. round case. ca 1954. . . . . $1,400—1,600

Vacheron & Constantin, Geneve. 18K, tu-tone white & yellow slim square case, 25mm. 18K band. ca 1961 . . . . $1,200—1,400

Vacheron & Constantin, Geneve. Self-winding, silvered dial, center seconds. 18K gold round case . . . . $700—750

Vacheron & Constantin, Geneve. Automatic, calendar. Gold finished dial, center seconds, date window. 14K gold, 35mm. round case with large moulded lugs . . . . $800—850

Vacheron & Constantin. 18K gold, 33mm. round case. ca 1961. . . . . $400—425

Vacheron & Constantin, Geneve. Self-winding calendar, gold finished dial with date window. 14K gold, 35mm. shaped, square case. . . . . $900—1,000

Vacheron & Constantin. Champagne dial, 18K gold, 22x30mm., slim rectangular case. . . . . $650—725

Vacheron & Constantin, Geneve. Silvered dial, 18K gold, 28mm. cushion case with basket weave design. . . . . $500—550

Vacheron & Constantin, Geneve. Self-winding, white gold matte dial. 36J movement. 18K gold, bowed, 32mm. square case, with 18K gold mesh band . . . . $1,400—1,600

Vacheron & Constantin, Geneve. Silvered dial, 18K gold, 35mm. cushion-shaped, basket weave design on case, original gold band $1,200—1,400

Vallette, Paul. Ladies. Silver dial. 15J movement. 14K, engraved white gold case with 4 diamonds and 2 sapphires. ca 1927 . . . $30—50

Vallette, Paul. Ladies. Engine-turned rectangular dial with diamond center. 14K tu—tone rectangular case, extended hinged lugs. ca 1929 . . . . $150—225

Vallette, Paul "Ladies Ribbon". Engraved tonneau nickel case. ca 1929 . . . . . . $10—20

Vallette, Paul. Ladies. Engine-turned, rectangular dial with round center. 14K gold, tu-tone rectangular case, extended double lugs. ca 1929 . . . . $125—200

Vallette, Paul. Ladies. Rectangular, engine-turned dial with round center. Platinum & diamond rectangular case. ca 1929 . $175—250

Vallette, Paul. Ladies. Rectangular dial. 14K gold, molded "Art Deco" design, rectangular case, with cord lugs. ca 1930 . . . . . . $65—85

Vallette, Paul "Ladies Cord". Rectangular dial. 14K gold, plain rectangular case, cord lugs. ca 1930 . . . . $40—60

Vallette, Paul. Ladies. Platinum & diamond "Art Deco" design rectangular case, 3 emerald cut diamonds, cord lugs. ca 1930 . . $275—350

Vallette, Paul. Ladies. Rectangular dial. 14K gold, plain rectangular case with faceted corners and cord lugs. ca 1930 . . . . $40—60

Vallette, Paul. Luminous hands & numerals, subsidiary seconds. 14K gold, embossed rectangular case. ca 1929 . . . . $175—200

Jallette, Paul. Luminous hands & numerals, subsidiary seconds. Rectangular case. ca 1930. Platinum . . . . $175—210
18K gold . . . . 140—160

Vallette, Paul. Chronograph, subsidiary seconds & 30 minute recorders. Round case. ca 1931.
14K gold . . . . $300—350
Gold-filled . . . . 75—100
Nickel . . . . 35— 55

Vedette "Ladies Gold". Tu-tone dial. 14K yellow gold faceted rectangular case. ca 1936.
. . . . $80—100

Vedette "Man's Gold". Subsidiary seconds. 14K yellow gold faceted case. ca 1936.
. . . . $150—200

Vog. Ladies. Tu-tone dial. 18K gold tonneau case. ca 1929 . . . . $40—55

Vog. Ladies. Silvered dial. Plain 18K gold, strap rectangular case. ca 1929 . . . . . $45—65

Vog. Silvered dial, subsidiary seconds. Man's 18K gold square case with hinged lugs. ca 1929.
. . . . $225—275

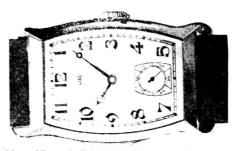

Vog. Silvered dial. Subsidiary seconds. Man's 18K gold tonneau case. ca 1929. . . . $150—175

Vulcain. Ladies, oval, silvered dial. 18K gold, 38mm, shaped oval case . . . . $125—150

Vulcain "Ladies Gold Bracelet". 14K gold rectangular case & large, marquis-shaped link bracelet. ca 1946 . 10% to 20% over gold value

Vulcain. Raised 14K gold hour & minute markers. Ladies rectangular 14K gold case with matching band. ca 1946 . . . . . 20% over gold

Vulcain "Ladies Gold". Tu-tone dial, 14K gold applied numerals & dots. 17J movement. 14K yellow gold square case with pear shaped single lugs. ca 1955. . . . . $30—50

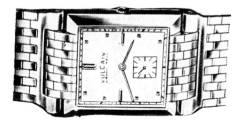

Vulcain. Raised 14K gold hour & minute markers. Square 14K gold case with matching link band. ca 1946 . . . . 20% over gold

Vulcain "Diamond & Gold". Ladies. 14K gold applied markers.17J movement. 14Kyellow gold, tonneau case and white gold lugs, set with 2 diamonds. ca 1955. . . . . . $30—50
Gold-filled expansion bracelet. . . . . . 3— 5

Vulcain "Gold Strap". Subsidiary seconds. Square, 14K yellow gold case with hinged lugs. ca 1946. . . . . $135—165

Vulcain "Ladies Gold". 14K gold applied markers. 17J movement. 14K yellow gold geometric designed case and lugs. ca 1955. . . . . $30—50
Gold-filled expansion bracelet. . . . . . 3— 5

Vulcain "Ladies Gold". 14K gold applied markers. 17J movement. 14K yellow gold, molded tonneau case, single lugs. ca 1955. . . . . $30—50
14K expansion bracelet . . 10% over gold value

Vulcain "Automatic Gold-Filled". Waterproof. Raised gold-filled numerals and luminous markers, center seconds. 17J movement. Round gold-filled case, stainless steel back and gold-filled expansion band. ca 1955 . . . . . $10—20

Vulcain "Diamond & Gold". Ladies. 14K gold applied raised numerals and markers. 17J movement. 14K yellow gold square case and single lugs, set with 4 diamonds. ca 1955 . . . $60—85
14K expansion bracelet . . 10% over gold value

Vulcain "Automatic Steel". Waterproof. Raised numerals and radium tipped markers, center seconds. 17J movement. Round stainless steel case. ca 1955 . . . . $8—18

Vulcain "Man's Gold". 14K raised gold applied numerals and markers, center seconds. 17J movement. 14K gold square case. ca 1955.
. . . . $125—150
Gold-filled expansion bracelet. . . . 3— 5

Wakmann "Calendrice". Ladies. Day window & outer date ring. 17J Universal movement. Square, 14K yellow gold case. ca 1940 . . . . $175—225
Yellow gold-filled. . . . . 70— 90

Vulcain. Raised gold dots on dial, center seconds. 17J movement. Yellow gold-filled, rectangular case. ca 1955. . . . . $20—30
Gold-filled expansion bracelet. . . . . . 3— 5

Vulcain "Cricket Alarm". Raised gold-filled numerals and radium tipped markers, center seconds and outer ring for alarm. 17J movement. 14K yellow gold round case. ca 1955.
. . . . $140—160
Yellow gold-filled top . . . . 70— 90
Stainless steel . . . . 40— 50

Wakmann "Calendrice". Ladies. Day window & outer date ring. 17J Universal movement. Round, 14K yellow gold case. ca 1949 . . . . $150—200
Yellow gold-filled. . . . . 60— 80

Wakmann. Ladies. Silvered dial. 17J movement. Square case & link bracelet. ca 1965.
Gold-filled . . . . $10—15
Rhodium plated . . . . 5—10

Wakmann "Custom Insignia Chronograph".
Subsidiary seconds, 30 minute recorder &
outer tachometer ring. 17J movement. 14K
gold round case. ca 1965 . . . . . . $150—175

Wakmann "Ladies Braille" dial. 17J movement.
Round case with spring transparent crystal
cover. ca 1965. Gold-filled top . . . . $20—30
Stainless steel . . . . 20—30

Wakmann "World Travel". Silvered dual dial,
global design, left for travel time, right for
home time. 34J movement. Round case. ca
1965. 18K gold . . . . $225—300
Gold-filled top. . . . . 40— 55
Stainless steel . . . . 25— 40

Wakmann "Hunting Braille Watch". Raised
braille dots on dial. 17J movement. Round
chrome hunting case with stainless back. ca
1949 . . . . $25—40

Wakmann "Alarm". Waterproof. Center
seconds with outer ring calibrated with ¼ hour
markings to set alarm by. 17J movement.
Round case. ca 1965. Gold-filled top . . $40—50
Stainless steel . . . . 35—45

Wakmann "Diver's Watch Calendar". Waterproof. Black dial, luminous hands & markers, date window. Automatic, 17J movement. Round stainless steel case, revolving calibrated bezel. ca 1965 . . . . $20—35

Wakmann "Braille" dial. 17J movement. Round case with spring transparent crystal cover. ca 1965. Gold-filled top . . . . $25—30
Stainless steel . . . . 25—30

Wakmann "Military". Waterproof. Black, 24 hour dial, center seconds. 17J movement. Round stainless steel case. ca 1965 . . . $50—75

Wakmann "Chronograph". Black or white dial, subsidiary seconds, 30 minute recorder with outer 1 mile base tachometer ring. Round case. ca 1965. 18K gold . . . . $160—200
Gold-filled top. . . . . 35— 50
Stainless steel . . . . 25—40

Wakmann "Global Time" . Dial marked for 7 time zones: Greenwich, Hawaii, Pacific Mountain, Central, Eastern & Daylight Savings. Automatic calendar, 17J movement. Round stainless steel case. ca 1965 . . . . $50—75

Wakmann "Chronograph". Black or white dial, subsidiary seconds, 30 minute & 12 hour recorders, with outer combination decimals & 1/5 scale ring. Round case. ca 1965.
18K gold . . . . $175—200
Gold-filled top. . . . . 30— 45
Stainless steel . . . . 25—40

Wakmann "Calendar Chronograph". Waterproof. Black or white dial, subsidiary seconds, 30 minute & 12 hour recorders, day & month windows, with outer date ring. 17J movement. Round stainless steel case. ca 1965.
. . . .$40—65

Wakmann "Chronograph". Waterproof. Tailored white dial, subsidiary seconds, 30 minute recorder, with outer 1 mile base tachometer. Round case. ca 1965.
18K gold . . . . $175—200
Gold-filled top. . . . .   35— 50
Stainless steel . . . .   25— 40

AMERICAN WALTHAM WATCH CO., WALTHAM, MASS. 1885—1923
WALTHAM WATCH CO., WALTHAM, MASS. 1923—1957

Waltham (we will use for short), first listed ladies convertible bracelet wrist watches in their 1912 Catalog. In this complete, product line catalog, was offered the Jewel Series "Ruby", 17 jewel, 6/0 size movement, in five round cases in combinations of case metals with bracelets or straps. A note explains that those combinations could also be obtained in 0 size by writing for prices.

A 1921 product catalog in the library of Roland Thomas "Rod" Minter, issued from The Waltham Watch Company Limited, Montreal, Canada (stating: Factories in Montreal and Canada), listed six styles of 3/0 size, 7 and 15 jewel, ladies convertible bracelet and ribbon watches; 12 varieties of 6/0 size, 7 and 15 jewel, ladies round convertible (disappearing eye) bracelet watches; 11 varieties of 10 ligne, 15 jewel, ladies detachable bracelet watches in round, cushion, square, decagon & octagon, plain and engraved bezel cases in both solid and gold-filled; and, last but not least, a man's "Cadet Model" tonneau case with a 7 or 15 jewel, 3/0 size round movement in a silver case with leather strap.

The 1922 product catalog continued to list most of the past models, with the addition of a man's strap watch in 6/0 size "Sapphire", 15 jewel round movement in a 14K solid green gold cushion case. All of the above listed watches were cased, timed & boxed at the factory.

Prior to 1912, Waltham sold to the trade both cased and uncased pocket watch movements, and the demand increased for wrist watch size movement, and, of course, they supplied them until the end of production to anyone who wanted to buy them without cases. (All of the American companies and most European companies did this as a regular business practice).

The 1928 product catalog offered six, 7¼ ligne rectangular ribbon wrist watches; nine, 6/0 size strap wrist watches; six, 10 ligne strap wrist watches; and six, 7¼ ligne strap wrist watches. From then on, the line continued to expand with literally hundreds of case styles until 1957, the end of U.S. production. Since then, the Waltham name has been used on imported wrist and pocket watches (usually Swiss).

Waltham "Sapphire Ladies Bracelet". Glass enamel dial with subsidiary seconds. 13J, 6/0 size round movement. Round, plain polish & engraved-bezel case. 14K gold . . . . . $50—75
20 Yr. gold-filled . . . . 10—20

Waltham "Ladies Convertible Bracelet and Strap". Glass enamel or gilded metal or silver dial. 17J, "Ruby", 6/0 size nickel round movement. Round case. By unfastening the bracelet from the convertible wrist watch (top illustration), it can be worn either as a chatelaine, a charm or a locket, or in the pocket. All Waltham wrist watches made at this time wind at 12 and the crown is protected by a patent bow. Cased, timed & boxed at the factory. They were also supplied in 0 size, with the values a little more. ca 1912.
14K solid gold . . . . $50—75
20 Yr. gold-filled . . . . 10—20

Waltham "Ladies or Man's". Radium silvered dial. 7¼''', 15J or 17J movement. Rectangular case and matching band. ca 1931.
14K yellow gold . . . . $100—125
Gold-filled . . . . 30— 40
Gold-filled bracelet . . . . 3— 5

Waltham "Ladies Gold". Etched rectangular dial. 7¼''', 15J movement. 14K gold, engraved tonneau case with black and white enamel. ca 1930 . . . . $35—55

Waltham "Minuet". 17J movement. 14K gold-filled, faceted rectangular case. ca 1937 . $4—8

Waltham "Ladies Filled". Etched dial. 7¼''', 7J or 15J movement. 14K gold-filled, engraved rectangular case. ca 1930 . . . . $15—25

Waltham "Encore". Ladies, 17J movement. 14K gold-filled round case with molded, graduated single lugs. ca 1937 . . . . . . $3—7

Waltham "Miss Sagamore". Ladies. Gold-filled teardrop case to be used as a pendant, fob or chatelaine. ca 1940 . . . . $20—35

Waltham "Military Style". Glass enamel or luminous dial. 0 size, 7 or 15J round movement. Round, plain polish, jointed front, snap back, silver or 20 Yr. GF case. ca 1917. . . . . $15—30

Waltham "Man's Strap". Silvered metal luminous dial with subsidiary seconds. 15J, "Sapphire" 6/0 size, round movement. 14K green gold cushion case with a gold buckle. ca 1922. . . . . $80—120

Waltham "Filled Strap". Radium silvered or etched dial, subsidiary seconds. 6/0 size, 15J movement. 14K white, green or yellow gold-filled, tonneau case. ca 1928. . . . . . . $25—35

Waltham "Gold Presentation". Sunken silver dial, subsidiary seconds. 15J, 10/0 size round movement. 14K solid gold rectangular case with heavy flexible lugs and hard enameled numerals on raised bezel. ca 1928. 14K yellow gold. . . . . $160—185
14K green gold . . . . 140—160
14K white gold . . . . 125—150

Waltham "Filled Strap". Radium silvered dial, subsidiary seconds. 15J or jJ movement. 14K white, green or yellow gold-filled, engraved and faceted octagonal case. ca 1928 . . $25—35

Waltham "Filled Strap". Radium silvered dial, subsidiary seconds. 15J or 7J movement. 14K gold-filled white, green or yellow, engraved rectangular case with faceted corners. ca 1928. . . . . $25—35

Waltham "Filled Strap". Radium silvered or etched dial, subsidiary seconds. 15J or 7J movement. 14K white, yellow or green gold-filled cushion case. ca 1928 . . . . . . $25—35

Waltham "Gold Strap". Radium silvered or
etched dial, subsidiary seconds. 17J or 15J
movement. 14K tonneau case. ca 1928.
14K yellow gold. . . . . $100—125
14K green gold . . . . 100—125
14K white gold . . . . 80—110

Waltham "Gold Enamel Bezel". Round silvered dial with subsidiary seconds. 15J or 17J,
6/0 size, round movement. Tonneau, 14K gold
case with hard enamel black bezel. ca 1930.
14K yellow gold. . . . . $160—185
14K green gold . . . . 150—175
14K white gold . . . . 140—165

Waltham "Gold Enamel Bezel". Round silvered
dial. 15J or 17J, 6/0 size round movement.
Tonneau case with hard enamel numerals on
bezel. ca 1928. 14K yellow gold . . $150—175
14K green gold . . . . 140—165
14K white gold . . . . 125—150

Waltham "Lugless Strap". 7J or 15J movement.
Rectangular gold-filled case with faceted
corners. ca 1930. . . . .$35—45

Waltham "Gold Strap". 18K gold applied
figure dial, subsidiary seconds. 17J movement.
14K yellow gold tonneau case. ca
1928 . . . . $140—160
14K green gold . . . . 130—150
14K white gold . . . . 120—140

Waltham "Lugless Strap". Luminous dial, subsidiary seconds. 3/0 size, 15J or 17J movement.
14K green or white gold-filled, engraved
tonneau case and Hadley Cornwall mesh band.
ca 1930. . . . .$30—40

Waltham. Plain round dial, subsidiary seconds.
10''', 15J movement. 14K gold rectangular
case, round black enamel bezel. ca 1930.
14K yellow gold. . . . . $160—185
14K green gold . . . . 140—160
14K white gold . . . . 125—150

Waltham "Gold Strap". 18K raised gold figure
on round dial, subsidiary seconds. 10/0 size,
15J movement. 14K gold, skeleton-type
tonneau case with hinged lugs. ca 1930.
14K yellow gold. . . . . $150—175
14K green gold . . . . 140—165
14K white gold . . . . 130—155

Waltham "Window Seconds". Plain or radium dial with seconds meter at 9. 10''', 15J or 7J movement. 14K gold-filled molded rectangular case. ca 1930 . . . . $35–55

Waltham "Lugless Strap". Luminous dial, subsidiary seconds. 3/0 size, 15J or 17J movement. Engraved, curved back, diamond tonneau lugless case and Hadley Cornwall mesh band. ca 1930 . . . . $30–40

Waltham "Gold Strap". Radium silvered dial, subsidiary seconds. 10''', 15J movement. Engraved square case. ca 1930.
14K yellow gold. $90–110
14K gold-filled 25– 35

Waltham "Enamel Bezel". Subsidiary seconds. 3/0 size, 15J movement. Chrome tonneau case, numerals set in black enamel bezel. ca 1931. . . . . $50–75

Waltham "Filled Strap". Luminous dial, subsidiary seconds. 21J Riverside, 3/0 size, round adjusted movement. 14K white or green gold-filled, tonneau case. ca 1931. . . . . . . $35–55

Waltham "Chrome Strap". Gold-filled etched numerals on dial, subsidiary seconds. 3/0 size, 7J movement. Chrome cushion case. ca 1931. . . . . $5–10

Waltham "Enameled Strap". Subsidiary seconds. 3/0 size, 7J movement. Nickel chromium, cushion case, numbers set in black enamel bezel. ca 1931. . . . . $40–60

Waltham "Filled Strap". Luminous dial, subsidiary seconds. 3/0 size, 15J movement. White gold-filled, engraved tonneau case. ca 1931. . . . . $20–30

Waltham "Filled Strap". Gold-filled figures on dial, subsidiary seconds. 3/0 size, 15J movement. Gold-filled, engraved, diamond tonneau case. ca 1931 . . . . $10—15

Waltham "Gold Tank". 18K gold applied figures. 7¼''', 17J movement. 14K white or green gold, curved and engraved rectangular case. ca 1931 . . . . $125—150

Waltham "Filled Strap". Radium silvered dial, subsidiary seconds. 10''', 15J or 7J movement. 14K gold-filled rectangular case with faceted corners. ca 1931. . . . . $20—30

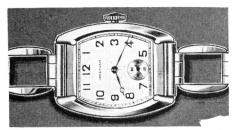

Waltham "Plated Strap". Subsidiary seconds. 6/0 size, 7J movement. 10K rolled gold plate tonneau case and large link bracelet. ca 1935.
. . . . $15—25
Bracelet . . . . 2— 4

Waltham "Plated Strap". Subsidiary seconds. 6/0 size, 7J movement. 10K rolled gold plate, tonneau case with graduated sides and matching link bracelet. ca 1935. . . . . $15—25
Bracelet . . . . 3— 5

Waltham "Plated Strap". 7¼''', 7J movement. 10K rolled gold plate, molded rectangular case. ca 1935 . . . . $15—25
Bracelet . . . . 2— 3

Waltham "Chrome Strap". 7¼''', 7J or 17J movement. Molded rectangular chrome case and large link bracelet. ca 1935.
Chrome case . . . .$5—10
Bracelet . . . . 2— 3

Waltham. Tu-tone dial. 6/0 size, 7J or 17J movement. Rolled gold plate tonneau case. ca 1935 . . . . $15—25
Chrome. . . . . 5—10

Waltham "Swagger". 3/0 size, 17J movement. 14K gold-filled, rectangular case. ca 1937.
. . . . $20—35

Waltham "Cadet". Tu-tone striped dial. 3/0 size, 21J, Riverside movement. 14K gold, striped rectangular case. ca 1937 . . $110—135

Waltham "Plated Curved". Gold figure dial, subsidiary seconds. 6/0 size, 17J movement. 10K yellow rolled gold plate, curved tonneau case. ca 1938 . . . .$20—30
Bracelet . . . . 2— 4

Waltham Watch Co. Masonic. White dial, painted Masonic symbols, 17J movement. GF, triangular case . . . . $300—375

Waltham "Filled Strap". Raised gold figure dial, subsidiary seconds. 6/0 size, 21J movement. 10K yellow gold-filled round case. ca 1938.
. . . .$25—45

Waltham "Driver's Watch". 8¾''', 17J movement. 10K rolled gold plate round case and curved rectangular frame for lugs. ca 1938.
. . . .$55—75

Waltham "Plated & Steel". Gold figure dial, subsidiary seconds. 6/0 size, 17J or 9J movement. 10K yellow rolled gold plate case, stainless steel back, link bracelet. ca 1938.
. . . .$5—15
Bracelet . . . . 2— 4

Waltham "Plated Strap". Raised gold figure dial, subsidiary seconds. 8¾''', 17J movement. 10K yellow rolled gold plate, tonneau case. ca 1938. . . . .$15—25

Waltham "Plated Strap". Tu-tone dial, subsidiary seconds. 6/0 size, 9J, 15J, or 17J movement. 10K rolled gold plate, molded tonneau case. ca 1938 . . . .$35—55

Waltham "Filled Strap". Raised gold figure dial, subsidiary seconds. 8¾''', 17J movement. 10K yellow gold-filled, molded square case. ca 1938. . . . .$35—55

Waltham "Filled Strap". Gold figure dial, subsidiary seconds. 6/0 size, 21J movement. 10K gold-filled tonneau case with graduated sides. ca 1938. . . . .$25—35

Waltham "Doctor's". Silvered dial with pulse rate scale read by a double ended sweep hand. Starting with one end on 12, doctor counts 30 beats, side markings then show pulse rate per minute. Stainless steel tonneau case. ca 1940. . . . .$35—55

Waltham. Calendar, gold-plated dial, center seconds, inner date ring. 21J movement. 14K gold, 39mm. round case. ca 1945 . . $125—175

Warwick "Diminuet". Ladies. Silvered dial. 4¾''', 17J movement. 18K white gold, hand-carved tonneau case. Platinum bezel set with 6 brilliant cut diamonds & 8 synthetic sapphires, black ribbon band & white gold clasp. ca 1924. . . . . $125—150

Warwick "Diminuet". Ladies. Silvered dial. 4¾''', 17J movement. 18K white gold, carved tonneau case set with 2 synthetic sapphires. ca 1924. . . . .$70—90

Warwick "Diminuet". Ladies. Silvered dial. 4¾''', 17J movement. 18K white gold, hand-carved tonneau case. Platinum settings with 4 brilliant cut diamonds, 6 synthetic sapphires. Black ribbon band with white gold clasp. ca 1924. . . . . $125—150

Warwick "Diminuet". Ladies. Silvered dial. 4¾''', 17J movement. 18K gold, hand-carved tonneau case set with 8 brilliant cut diamonds & 4 synthetic sapphires. ca 1924 . . $135—185

Warwick "Diminuet". Ladies. Silvered dial. 17J, 4¾''' movement. 19K white gold, hand-carved rectangular case, black ribbon band & white gold clasp. ca 1924 . . . .$70—90

Warwick "Diminuet". Ladies. Silvered dial. 4¾''', 17J movement. 18K white gold, carved tonneau case set with 2 brilliant cut diamonds & 6 synthetic sapphires. ca 1924 . . . $85—125

Warwick "Diminuet". Ladies. Silvered dial. 4¾''', 15J or 17J movement. 14 or 18K white gold, hand-carved tonneau case, black ribbon band & white gold clasp. ca 1924.
18K gold . . . .$60—85
14K gold . . . . 50—65

Warwick "Diminuet". Ladies. Silvered dial. 4¾''', 17J movement. 18K white gold, hand-carved tonneau case. Platinum settings with 2 brilliant diamonds & 4 synthetic sapphires. Black ribbon band & white gold clasp. ca 1924 . . . . $150—175

Warwick "Gold Plated". Subsidiary seconds. 10½''', 6J movement. Engraved square case. ca 1930. . . . .$8—15

Warwick "Gold Plated". Subsidiary seconds. 10½''', 6J or 15J movement. Engraved tonneau case. ca 1930 . . . .$8—15

Warwick "Gold Plated". Subsidiary seconds. 10½''', 6J movement. Engraved tonneau case. ca 1930. . . . .$8—15

Warwick "Rolled Gold Plate". Subsidiary seconds. 10½''', 6J or 15J movement. Rolled gold plate, tonneau case. ca 1930 . . . . .$8—15

Warwick "Gold Plated". Subsidiary seconds. 10½''', 6J movement. Engraved tonneau case. ca 1930. . . . .$8—15

Warwick "Gold Plated". Subsidiary seconds. 10½''', 6J or 15J movement. Engraved rolled gold plate, tonneau case. ca 1930 . . . . .$8—15

Warwick "Hinged Case Lugs". Subsidiary seconds. 10½''', 6J movement. Square designed case with hinged lugs. ca 1930. . . . . .$15—25

Weil, Raymond, Geneve. Automatic calendar, black, 3-diamond dial, center seconds, day/date window. 14K gold & steel, 34mm., tonneau case & steel band. Modern . . . . 15% over gold

Westclox "Judge". Silvered dial, subsidiary seconds. Yellow gold plated tonneau case, stainless steel back. ca 1941 . . . . $3—5

Westclox "Military 24-Hour Dial". Luminous hands & numerals on black dial. 17J, sweep second movement. Chrome plated tonneau case. Waterproof. ca 1968 . . . . $2—5

Westclox "Ben". Tu-tone dial, subsidiary seconds. Chrome molded rectangular case with stainless steel back and graduated sides. ca 1941 . . . . $3—5

Westclox "Ben". Tu-tone dial, subsidiary seconds. Chrome molded rectangular case, stainless steel back, graduated side and matching metal link band. ca 1941. . . . . $3—5

Westclox "All Sports". Large luminous numerals on black dial. 17J, sweep second movement. Chrome plated round case with two moveable bezels, one for elapsed time and one for world time zones. Waterproof. ca 1968. . . . .$7—15

Westclox "Rocket". Tu-tone metal dial. Chrome plated, molded, curved back tonneau case. ca 1941 . . . . $2—4

Westclox "Automatic Day-Date Calendar". Silvered dial with raised markers. 17J, self-winding, sweep second, day/date window at 3, movement. Chrome plated, tonneau case. ca 1968 . . . . $4—8

Westclox "Automatic". Raised numerals and markers on radial-brushed silver dial. 17J, self-winding, sweep second movement. Chrome plated round case. Waterproof. ca 1968 . $3—7

Westclox "Chrome". Silvered dial with raised numerals and markers. 21J, sweep second movement. Chrome plated tonneau case. ca 1968. Waterproof . . . . $2—5

White Star "Diagrafic Moonphase Calendar". Silvered dial with colorful combined moonphase and month indicator. Outside date ring, subsidiary seconds. Stainless steel round case. ca 1952 . . . . $150—175

Wheeler. Ladies. Silver dial. 15J movement. 18K white gold, engraved case. ca 1927 $30—50

Wittnauer "Exposition LD Bracelet". Ladies. Marquise-shaped case and lugs set with 2 diamonds, matching band. ca 1964.
. . . . 10% to 20% over gold value

Wittnauer "1/5—Second Chronograph". Subsidiary seconds, 30 minute and 12 hour recorders. 17J non-magnetic movement. Round stainless steel, 38mm. case. ca 1940. . . . . $70—90

Wittnauer "Telemeter and Tachymeter Chronograph". Silvered dial with subsidiary seconds and 30 minute recorder. 17J movement. Round stainless steel, 27mm. case. ca 1940 . . $55—80

NOTE: Read Page 6 before using this book to value your wrist watch.

Wittnauer "1/5—Second Chronograph". Silvered dial, subsidiary seconds, 30 minute recorder. 17J movement. Round stainless steel, 32mm. case. ca 1940 . . . . $50—75

Wittnauer "1/5—Second Telemeter". (Single Button). Silvered dial, subsidiary seconds. 7J movement. Stainless steel round, 29mm. case. ca 1940. . . . . $40—60

NOTE: All values are given for the head only unless the bracelet is included in the description.

Wittnauer "Telemeter 1/5—Second Chronograph". Subsidiary seconds and 30 minute recorder. 17J movement. Round stainless steel 32mm. case. ca 1940 . . . . $50—75

Wittnauer "Calendar Chronograph". Subsidiary seconds, 30 minute & 12 hour recorders, day & month windows, with outer date ring. Stainless steel round case. ca 1947. . . . . $50—75

Wyler "Incaflex Lifeguard". Dynawind heavy duty 660. Silvered dial, center seconds, day-date window. 17J, self-winding movement. Stainless steel round, one piece case. ca 1949.
. . . .$35—50

Wittnauer "Exposition MH". Waterproof. Center seconds. Self-winding movement. Cushion case and large molded lugs. ca 1964.
14K yellow gold. . . . . $100—125
RGP top, steel back. . . . . 40— 50
Stainless steel . . . . 20— 30

Wyler "Diver's Watch". Waterproof. Black dial, luminous markers, center seconds. Self-winding movement. Round stainless steel case, black bezel with elapsed time indicator. ca 1961 . . . .$10—15

Wittnauer "Exposition MI Calendar". Waterproof, self-winding. Center seconds, date window at 3. ca 1964. Round 14K gold $125—150
Stainless steel . . . . 20— 30

Wyler "Incaflex". Tu-tone luminous dial, center seconds, veri-thin stainless steel, round waterproof case. ca 1943 . . . .$10—20

Wyler "Dynawind". Silvered dial. 17J, sweep second, self-winding movement. Round stainless steel case. ca 1961 . . . .$8—16

Zenith. Ladies. 14x24mm., engraved rectangular case. ca 1926. Gold-filled. $10–15
14K & 18K gold. . . . . .10% to 20% over gold
Platinum . . . . 10% to 20% over platinum

Zenith. Ladies. 14x24mm., engraved rectangular case with faceted corners. ca 1926.
Gold-filled $10–15
18K & 14K gold . . . 10% to 20% over gold value
Platinum . . . .10% to 20% over platinum value

Zenith. Ladies. Silvered dial with stick thread hands, subsidiary seconds. Round, 20mm. 14K gold case. ca 1947. . . . . . 20% over gold value

Zenith. Ladies. Black dial with raised gold numerals & gold hands. 14K gold, 12x22mm. case. ca 1947 . . . . 20% over gold value

Zenith. Luminous hands & numerals, subsidiary seconds. 24x40mm. tonneau case. ca 1926.
Platinum $185–250
18K gold 150–200
14K gold 125–135
Gold-filled 20– 30

Zenith. Raised gold numerals on sterling silver dial. 17J movement. 18K white gold, elongated curved rectangular, 24x49mm. case. $175–250

Zenith. Luminous hands & numerals, subsidiary seconds. 42x25mm. rectangular case. ca 1926.
Platinum $185–235
18K gold 150–185
14K gold 125–135

Zenith. Luminous hands & numerals, subsidiary seconds. 10''', 15J movement. 25x40mm., 14K gold-filled tonneau case. ca 1930.
14K green gold-filled $30–45
14K white gold-filled 25–40

Zenith. Raised gold numerals, subsidiary seconds. 10''', 17J movement. 14K white gold, 24x42mm. tonneau case, leather band & white gold buckle. ca 1930 . . . . $125–150

Zenith "Gold Strap". White luminous, or 18K raised gold numerals. 10''', 17J adjusted movement. 18K white gold rectangular case, with dull finish center and bright finished faceted bezel. Drop lugs to conform to the wrist. Solid gold buckle. ca 1930 . . . . . $175—225

Zenith. Black dial with raised gold numerals & hands, subsidiary seconds. 14K gold, 32mm. round case. ca 1947 . . . . $90—115

Zenith. Raised white gold numerals, subsidiary seconds. 10''', 17J movement. 18K gold rectangular, 23x36mm. case with bright faceted bezel & drop lugs. ca 1930 . . . . $150—175

Zenith. Chronograph, silvered dial, subsidiary seconds, 45 minute recorder & outer tachometer ring. 18K gold, 36mm. round case.
. . . . $150—200

Zenith. Tu-tone gold & silvered dial, subsidiary seconds. Round, 33mm., 14K gold case. ca 1947 . . . . $75—100

Zenith "Automatic Star". White dial, center seconds. White round case. ca 1949.
14K gold . . . . $100—125
Stainless steel . . . . 15— 35

Zenith. Breguet numerals & hands on silvered dial. Center second movement. Round, 32mm. 14K gold case. ca 1947 . . . . $75—100

Zenith "Gold Automatic". Silvered dial with black numerals. Sweep second, self-winding movement. 14K yellow gold, square case, faceted bezel. ca 1954 . . . . $125—150

Zenith "Man's Gold Automatic". Silvered dial with 18K gold applied markers. 17J, sweep second, self-winding movement. Round heavy lug, 14K gold case. ca 1961 . . . . . $100—125

Zodiac "Trend". Ladies, 17J movement. 14K gold, shield-shaped case. ca 1961.
. . . . 10% to 20% over gold value

Zenith Espada. Self-winding, moonphase calendar chronograph. Polished steel dial, subsidiary seconds, 30 minute & 12 hour recorders. Day, date & month windows with outer tachometer ring, base 1000m. Stainless steel, 36mm. tonneau case. . . . . $350—425

Zodiac "Huntley Gold". 14K gold hands & numerals, subsidiary seconds dial. 17J movement. Rectangular, 14K yellow gold case. ca 1957 . . . . $125—150

Zodiac "Ladies Olympos". Champagne dial. Geometric case. ca 1961. Gold-filled top . . . .$20—25
Stainless steel . . . . 10—15

Zodiac "Chronometer". Silvered dial with gold markers & hands, subsidiary seconds. 17J movement. Round case. ca 1957.
18K gold head only . . . . $125—150
14K yellow gold bracelet. . 10% over gold value

Zodiac "Encore". Ladies. 17J movement. 14K gold, fan-shaped case. ca 1961.
. . . . 10% to 20% over gold value

Zodiac "James — Hack". Waterproof. Three-dimensional black center, white border dial, raised gold numerals, center seconds. Hacking, 17J movement. 10K, round gold-filled top with steel back case. ca 1957 . . . . $25—30

Zodiac "Stetson Gold". 14K gold markers & hands, black or white dial, subsidiary seconds. 17J movement. Round, 14K yellow gold case. ca 1957. . . . . $100—125

Zodiac "Sparton Gold". 14K gold hands & markers, subsidiary seconds dial. 17J movement. Faceted, square, 14K yellow gold case. ca 1957. . . . . $150—175

Zodiac "Regal". 14K gold markers & hands, subsidiary seconds dial. 17J movement. Square, 14K yellow gold case. ca 1957 . . . $100—125

Zodiac "Chronometer". Silvered dial, gold markers & hands, center seconds. 21J, self-winding movement. 18K gold round case. ca 1957 . . . . $135—165

Zodiac "Emblematic Masonic". Radium silvered dial, sweep seconds. 17J self-winding movement. Round, 10K yellow gold-filled top, steel back case. ca 1957 . . . . $35—55

Zodiac "Solodate Automatic". Waterproof. Center seconds, date window. 17J movement. 10K, round, gold-filled top with steel back. ca 1957. . . . . $25—30

Zodiac "Emblematic Masonic". 14K applied gold Masonic working tools dial, subsidiary seconds. 17J movement. Round, 14K yellow gold case. ca 1957. . . . . $150—175

Zodiac "Tempest Automatic". Silvered dial with sweep seconds. 17J, self-winding movement. Round stainless steel case. ca 1957. . . . . $25—35

Zodiac "Gordon Automatic". Tu-tone black center, white border dial, sweep seconds. 17J self-winding movement. Round stainless steel case. ca 1957 . . . . $25–35

Zodiac "Richard — Hack". Waterproof. Center seconds. Hacking, 17J movement. Stainless steel round case. ca 1957 . . . . $20–25

Zodiac "Ira Autographic". Center seconds with center reserve power indicator. 17J, self-winding movement. Round stainless steel case. ca 1957 . . . . $40–60

Zodiac "Solodate". Center seconds, date window at 3. Automatic, waterproof, 17J, self-winding movement. Stainless steel round case. ca 1957 . . . . $20–25

Zodiac "Concord Autographic". Center seconds with center reserve power indicator. 17J, self-winding movement. Round stainless steel case. ca 1957 . . . . $40–60

Zodiac "Leonard Moonphase Calendar". Black dial, center seconds, day & month windows with outer date ring. Waterproof, automatic, 17J movement. Round case. ca 1957.
14K gold $775–850
Gold-filled top. 150–175
Stainless steel 125–150

Zodiac "Dexter Autographic". Silvered sweep second dial with center reserve power indicator. 17J, self-winding movement. Round stainless steel case. ca 1957 . . . . $40–60

Zodiac "Ricky Powergraphic". Silvered dial, center seconds with center power reserve indicator. 17J movement. Round yellow top or stainless steel case. ca 1957 . . . . . . $40–60

Zodiac "Olympos". Waterproof, self-winding. Revolving dial, center seconds. Geometric, gold-filled top case. ca 1961 . . . . $20—35
Stainless steel . . . . 15—25

Zodiac "Olympos Calendar". Waterproof. Center seconds, date window. Self-winding. 10K gold-filled, geometric case with stainless steel case. ca 1961 . . . . $25—40
Stainless steel . . . . 20—30

Zodiac "Sea Wolf Datographic". Waterproof. Center seconds, date window at 3. 17J, self-winding movement. Round stainless steel case with movable bezel. ca 1962. . . . . . $60—80

Zodiac "Astrographic". Round black dial, date window at 3. Stainless steel cushion case. ca 1974. . . . . $50—75

Zodiac "Aerospace GMT". Black dial, center seconds, extra hour hand & date window. Stainless steel round case, with calibrated revolving bezel. ca 1965 . . . . $50—80

Zodiac Calendar "Chronograph". Tu-tone dial, subsidiary seconds, 30 minute & 12 hour recorders, day & month windows & outer seconds and date ring. 17J movement. 36mm. round case. ca 1972. 18K . . . . . . $350—400
Gold-filled . . . . 125—150
Stainless steel . . . . 75—100

Zodiac. Moonphase calendar, black dial, center seconds, day & month windows with inner date circle. 14K gold, round case . . . . . $800—900
Yellow gold-filled . . . . 200—250
Yellow gold-filled top . . . . 150—200
Stainless steel . . . . 125—175

1984 DATES TO REMEMBER

* Feb. 16—19 . .Florida Mid-Winter Regional. Sheraton-Twin Towers, Orlando, FL. Kathryn Mosley (904) 782-3989.

* Feb. 23—26 . .Pacific-Northwest Regional. Red Lion Motor Inn, Portland, OR. Betty Chisum (503) 761-6469.

* March 1—3. . .Lone Star Regional. North Park Inn, Dallas, TX. Robert Wingate (214) 620-9520.

* March 8—10 . .Southern Regional. Coliseum Ramada Inn, Jackson, MS. Fred Ingram (601) 981-6692.

* March 10—11 .Strongsville, Ohio Annual Meeting & Auction. Holiday Inn, Strongsville, OH (Rt. 82 & I-71). Don Bass (419) 625-1405.

† March 17—18 .Wichita Antique Watch & Clock Club, Public School, Wichita, KS. E. W. Ferguson (316) 683-7629.

* April 13—14 .Southern Ohio Regional. Drawbridge Motor Inn, Ft. Mitchell, KY. L. Harold Wehling (513) 871-3896.

* April 26—29 .Greater New York Regional. Travelodge International Hotel, JFK International Airport, NY. Henry Richman.

* May 10—13 . .Southwest California Regional. Hanalei Hotel, San Diego, CA. Loren L. Schmitz (714) 469-7324.

* May 18—19 . .Great Plains Regional. Holiday Inn, Omaha, NE. Richard Svehla (402) 391-3453.

* May 25—27 . .St. Louis Regional. Concourse Hotel, St. Louis, MO. Robert E. Webb (314) 723-2037.

† June 1—2 . . .Kansas City Antique Watch & Clock Club. Ramada Inn, 87th & I-435 S., Kansas City, MO. Roy Ehrhardt (816) 761-0080.

* June 6—10. . .NAWCC National Convention. Indiana Convention Center/Hyatt Regency, Indianapolis, IN.

* July 13—14 . .Midwest Regional. Ramada O'Hare, Des Plains, IL. Steve Berger (312) 394-8877.

* Aug. 3—5 . . .Missouri Regional. Ramada Inn, Columbia, MO. Jere A. DeVilbiss (314) 442-8993.

* Aug. 10—11 . .Rocky Mountain Regional. Sheraton-Denver Tech Center, Denver, CO. Roger Dankert (303) 755-0871.

* Aug. 24—26 . .Eastern States Regional. Sheraton Inn, Liverpool, NY. G. Russell Oechsle (315) 662-7912.

*Aug. 31—Sept. 1 Great Lakes Regional. Hyatt Regency, Dearborn, MI. George Hedges (313) 626-3494.

* Sept. 14—15 . .Kentucky Blue-Grass Regional. Holiday Inn Louisville South, Louisville, KY. John R. Buschermohle (502) 267-5070.

* Sept. 20—23 . .Western Regional. San Jose Convention Center/Holiday Inn, San Jose, CA. Dorothea M. Sanderson (415) 937-6272.

* Oct. 18—21 . .Mid-South Regional. Sheraton/Nashville Hotel, Nashville, TN. Dr. Cullen R. Merritt (615) 327-0404.

* Oct. 26—27 . .NAWCC Seminar No. 5. Sheraton Civic Center Plaza, Hartford, CT. (717) 684-8261.

* Nov. 2—3 . . .Mid-Eastern Regional. Raddison Hotel, Charlotte, NC. Jarvis Warren (704) 366-1530.

† Nov. 23—24 . .Kansas City Antique Watch & Clock Club. Ramada Inn Southeast, 87th Street & I-435 S., Kansas City, MO. Roy Ehrhardt (816) 761-0080.

MONTHLY SHOWS

† Tampa Time Traders. 2nd Monday evening of each month. American Legion Seminole Post 3111, 6918 N. Florida Ave., Tampa, FL. Stanley Henry (816) 839-1193.

† Kansas City Antique Watch & Clock Club. 1st Tuesday evening of each month. Ramada Inn Southeast, 87th St. & I-435 S., Kansas City, MO. Roy Ehrhardt (816) 761-0080.

† Fox Valley Watch & Clock Club. 2nd Wednesday evening of each month. Community Center, Aurora, IL. Scott Williams (815) 768-8729.

* NAWCC members only. See page 330 for membership information. Detailed information regarding these shows may be obtained from the bi-monthly publication, The Mart, or by calling the above telephone numbers. Educational programs are available at meetings.

† Open to the public. No membership required. Educational programs are available at some meetings. If interested in attending, get in touch with above mart chairman.

MAJOR WORLD AUCTION HOUSES

Auction houses play an important role in the wrist watch market. Prices realized at these auctions have a definite effect on values worldwide. Wrist watches have become an important auction item during the past three years.

The auction houses listed here have numerous auctions (2 to 8) per year. They are attended by many dealers and collectors all over the world, and the results are anxiously awaited by many others.

All of the auction houses issue beautiful catalogs (sometimes in color), on a subscription or an individual auction basis. For subscription information and auction dates, write to the addresses listed below.

SOTHEBY PARKE BERNET & CO.
980 Madison Avenue
New York, NY 10021
Telephone (212) 472-3400

Sotheby's Subscription Department
P.O. Box 4020
Woburn, MA 01801
Telephone (617) 229-2282

CHRISTIE, MANSON & WOOD LTD.
502 Park Avenue
New York, NY 10022
Telephone (212) 546-1000

Christie's Subscription Department
21-24 44th Avenue
Long Island City, NY 11101

PHILLIPS, SON AND NEALE
406 E. 79th Street
New York, NY 10021
Telephone (212) 570-4830

Me HERVE' CHAYETTE
12, rue Rossini
75009 Paris, FRANCE
Telephone 770-38-89

ANTIQUORIUM
29-31 Grand Rue
CH-1204 Geneve, SWITZERLAND
Telephone (022) 215-174

DR. HELMUT CROTT & K. SCHMELZER
Pontstrasse 21 — Postfach 164
D5100 Aachen, WEST GERMANY
Telephone (0241) 36900

KLAUS NIEDHEIDT
Niederdonker Strasse 34
4000 Dusseldorf 11, WEST GERMANY
Telephone (0211) 594401

UTO AUKTIONEN
Falkenstrasse 12 Beim Opern Haus
CH-8008 Zurich, SWITZERLAND
Telephone (01) 25-25-888

INEICHEN, PETER
C.F.Meyer-Strasse 14
CH-8002 Zurich, SWITZERLAND

BIBLIOGRAPHY AND REFERENCE MATERIAL

All of the following books are helpful in learning wrist watches. Some are in print and available from horological booksellers; some can be found in libraries; and others at flea markets and in the remains of old watchmakers' shops. This is only a partial list because of lack of space.

Kahlert, Helmut; Muhe, Richard; and Brunner, Gisbert L. *Armbanduhren, 100 Jahre Entwicklungsgeschichte.* Georg D.W. Callwey, Munchen, 1983.

Chapuis, Alfred, and Jacquet, Eugene. *The History of the Self-winding Watch, 1770-1931.* Editions du Griffon, Neuchatel, Switzerland, 1952.

De Carle, Donald. *Complicated Watches and Their Repair.* N.A.G. Press, Ltd., London, 1956.

Fried, Henry B. *The Watch Repairer's Manual, 3rd ed.* Chilton Book Co., Radnor, Pa. 1973.

Fried, Henry B. *Universal Watch Parts Catalog,* 1957.

Huber, Martin, and Banbery, Alan. *Patek Philippe.* Peter Ineichen, Zurich, 1983.

Humbert, B. *Swiss Self-winding Watches.* Journal Suisse D'Horlogerie et de Bijouterie, Scriptar S.A., Lausanne, Switzerland, 1956.

Jaquet, Eugene, and Chapuis, Alfred. *Technique and History of the Swiss Watch.* Urs Graf, Olten, Switzerland, 1953.

Lavest, R. *The Elements of Watchcraft.* Charles Rohr, Editions Horlogeres, Bienne, Switzerland, 1949.

OTHER REFERENCES

Jeweler's Circular-Keystone. *Trademarks of the Jewelry and Kindred Trades, 5th ed.* Chilton Company, Philadelphia, Pa., 1943.

A.F. Tobin. *Classification of the Swiss Watch Movements and Watchmaterials.* Andres & Cie, Beinne, Switzerland, 1936.

Any of the many material house or factory material catalogs and service bulletins will be of assistance in helping you understand Vintage wrist watches.

INFORMATION WANTED by EDITOR ROY EHRHARDT

For the preparation of future issues of this book and other clock and watch books, we need additional new and different information. Here are some samples of what we need.

Wrist Watch Point of Sale Booklets and Factory Product Catalogs, and other advertising that illustrates and describes wrist watches. We especially need information on Patek Philippe, Rolex, Audemars Piguet, Vacheron & Constantin, Cartier, Tiffany, Universal Geneve, Concord, Corum, and other lesser known Foreign and American companies.

Clocks, Wrist or Pocket Watch Periodicals, both Horological and Jewelry Trades (all languages and dates, 1850 to 1980).

Clock and Watch Auction Catalogs. Any auction house, both old and new issues.

Let me know what you have. Roy Ehrhardt, 10101 Blue Ridge, P.O. Box 9808, Kansas City, MO 64134, or phone 816-761-0080.

AN INVITATION FROM ROY EHRHARDT

TEMPUS VITAM REGIT

THE NATIONAL ASSOCIATION OF
WATCH AND CLOCK COLLECTORS, INC.
BOX 33, 514 POPLAR STREET, COLUMBIA, PA 17512

This non-profit, scientific and educational corporation was founded in 1943 to bring together people who are interested in timekeeping in any form or phase. More than 33,000 members now enjoy its benefits. The Headquarters, Museum and Library are located in the Borough of Columbia on the eastern bank of the Susquehanna River within historic Lancaster County, Pennsylvania, where a continuing heritage of clock and watchmaking spans two and one-quarter centuries.

Some of the tangible benefits of membership are the Association's publications. The bi-monthly **Bulletin** is the world's leading publication devoted to timekeeping. It contains papers written by members on technical and historic aspects of horology. Through its "Answer Box" column it also provides the member with an opportunity to direct his "knotty" horological problems to a panel of fifty volunteer authorities from around the world, many of whom are authors of definitive works in their respective areas of interest. Reviews help the collector keep abreast with the ever growing number of horological publications. Activities of the more than 100 Chapters located around the world are also included as are listings of stolen items. The **Mart**, also bi-monthly, is an informal medium in which members may list items that they wish to buy, trade, or sell. Like the **Bulletin,** its circulation exceeds 33,000. Other publications include the **Roster of Members,** a listing of books available through the Association's Lending Library, and occasional papers meriting separate publication.

Another benefit of membership is the use of the Nation's largest collection of books devoted to timekeeping. A number of the titles are duplicated in the Lending Library and may be borrowed through the mail for merely the cost of postage and, on occasion, insurance. The Library is under the supervision of a professional librarian who will also help a member in his research. A visitor can study the various horological periodicals of many sister horological associations around the world. The serious researcher may also examine rare and early works concerning horology. The Nation's only computerized Horological Data Bank is at the member's disposal as are thousands of American patents dealing with timekeeping.

Free admission to the NAWCC Museum in Columbia for both the member and his immediate family is yet another benefit. The Museum offers a rare opportunity to examine a collection of watches, clocks, tools, and other related items which range from the primitive to the modern. The "how and why" of timekeeping is emphasized throughout whether the display be of early non-mechanical timepieces or of the highly sophisticated "Atomic Clock." Movements of wood, iron, and brass are displayed for study. Many of the items exhibited are becoming increasingly rare and beyond the reach of many private collectors. Two special exhibitions are mounted each year: a three-month winter exhibition and a six-month summer exhibition. Items included in the special exhibitions are drawn from the collections of members, friends, and other museums.

Membership in the National Association also makes one eligible for membership in one or more of the more than 100 Chapters located in the United States, Australia, Canada, England, and Japan. It also makes one eligible to register for the regularly scheduled regional and national meetings each year. Chapter, regional, and national meetings usually consist of seminars, exhibits, and an opportunity to improve the member's own collection through trading, buying, or selling to other members. Finally, membership can enable a person to form lasting friendships with some of the finest people in the world: timekeeper enthusiasts!

For a brochure and membership application write to the Administrator, N.A.W.C.C., Box 033, Columbia, PA 17512.

It is easy to become a member of the NAWCC, Inc. Send the following information with your check or money order to the above address.

Name_____

(please print clearly)

$20.00
Dues (1984)

Street_____

City_____ State_____ZIP_____

Occupation_____Telephone( )_____

Have you ever been a member? YES_____NO_____ If "Yes," please give number _____

Sponsor ___*Roy Ehrhardt*___ **NAWCC No.** ___*23096*___

Street ___*P.O. Box 9808*___ City___*K. C.*___State___*MO*___ZIP *64134*

BOOKS FROM HEART OF AMERICA PRESS

WRIST WATCH BOOKS

VINTAGE AMERICAN & EUROPEAN WRIST WATCH PRICE GUIDE BOOK 1
Ehrhardt and Planes, 1984, 336, 6x9" pages, 2 lbs.............$15.00
VINTAGE AMERICAN & EUROPEAN WRIST WATCH PRICE GUIDE 1987 UPDATE
Ehrhardt and Planes, 1987, 60, 6x9" pages, 6 oz.............$10.00
VINTAGE AMERICAN & EUROPEAN WRIST WATCH PRICE GUIDE BOOK 2
Ehrhardt and DeMesy, 1988, 448, 6x9" pages, 2 lbs.............$25.00
VINTAGE AMERICAN & EUROPEAN WRIST WATCH PRICE GUIDE BOOK 3
Ehrhardt and Mycko, 1989, 224, 6x9" pages, 1 lbs.............$25.00
VINTAGE AMERICAN & EUROPEAN WRIST WATCH PRICE GUIDE BOOK 4
Ehrhardt and DeMesy, 1989, 624, 6x9" pages, 2 lbs.............$25.00
VINTAGE AMERICAN & EUROPEAN WRIST WATCH PRICE GUIDE BOOK 5
Ehrhardt and DeMesy, 1990, 656, 6x9" pages, 2 lbs.............**NEW**....$25.00
PRICE GUIDE BOOKS 1, 2, 3, 4 & 1987 UPDATE
(Special Offer No. 1) Regular $100.00.............$80.00
PRICE GUIDE BOOKS 1, 2, 3, 4, 5 & 1987 UPDATE
(Special Offer No. 2) Regular $125.00.............$100.00

POCKET WATCH BOOKS

AMERICAN WATCHES-BEGINNING TO END, ID AND PRICE GUIDE
Meggers and Ehrhardt, 1987, Revolutionizes American Watch Collecting
Identification & prices for 2 million American Pocket Watches, 464, 6x9" pages, 2 lbs.............$15.00
AMERICAN POCKET WATCH ENCYCLOPEDIA & PRICE GUIDE, Volume 1
Ehrhardt, June 1982, 216, 8 1/2x11" pages, 1 lbs. 10 oz.............$25.00
ILLINOIS, Volume 2, Ehrhardt and Meggers, 1985, 432, 8 1/2x11" pages, 2 1/2 lbs.............$50.00
AMERICAN POCKET WATCH IDENTIFICATION & PRICE GUIDE, BOOK 2
Ehrhardt, 1974 **(Prices revised in 1980)**, 192, 8 1/2x11" pages, 1 lb. 10 oz.............$15.00
FOREIGN & AMERICAN POCKET WATCH IDENTIFICATION & PRICE GUIDE, BOOK 3
Ehrhardt, 1976, 172, 8 1/2x11" pages, 1 lb. 8 oz.............CALL/WRITE
1976 POCKET WATCH PRICE INDICATOR
Ehrhardt, 1975, 64, 8 1/2x11" pages, 14 oz.............$5.00
1977 POCKET WATCH PRICE INDICATOR
Ehrhardt, 1976, 110, 8 1/2x11" pages, 14 oz.............$7.00
1978 POCKET WATCH PRICE INDICATOR
Ehrhardt, 1978, 110, 8 1/2x11" pages, 14 oz.............$10.00
1979 POCKET WATCH PRICE INDICATOR
Ehrhardt, 1979, 110, 8 1/2x11" pages, 14 oz.............$10.00
1980 POCKET WATCH PRICE INDICATOR
Ehrhardt, 1980, 110, 8 1/2x11" pages, 14 oz.............$12.00
AMERICAN POCKET WATCH COMPANIES (Pocket book with 50 inventory pages)
Ehrhardt, 1979, 96, 3 1/2x5 1/2" pages, 2 oz.............$3.00
ELGIN POCKET WATCH IDENTIFICATION & PRICE GUIDE
Ehrhardt, 1976, 120, 8 1/2x11" pages, 1 lb. 2 oz.............$10.00
WALTHAM POCKET WATCH IDENTIFICATION & PRICE GUIDE
Ehrhardt, 1976, 172, 8 1/2x11" pages, 1 lb. 4 oz.............$10.00
HAMILTON POCKET WATCH IDENTIFICATION & PRICE GUIDE
Ehrhardt, 1976, **(Revised 1981)**, 53, 8 1/2x11" pages, 1 lb. 4 oz.............$10.00
ROCKFORD GRADE & SERIAL NUMBERS WITH PRODUCTION FIGURES
Ehrhardt, 1976, 44, 8 1/2x11" pages, 12 oz.............$10.00
TRADEMARKS, Ehrhardt, 1976, 128, 8 1/2x11" pages, 1 lb. 2 oz.............CALL/WRITE
EVERYTHING YOU WANTED TO KNOW ABOUT AMERICAN WATCHES &
DIDN'T KNOW WHO TO ASK, Col. George E. Townsend, 1971
(With 1983 Price Guide by Roy Ehrhardt) 88, 6x9" pages, 8 oz.............CALL/WRITE
AMERIAN RAILROAD WATCHES, Col. George E. Townsend, 1977
(With 1983 Price Guide by Roy Ehrhardt), 44, 6x9" pages, 8 oz.............$8.00
THE WATCH THAT MADE THE DOLLAR FAMOUS, Col. George E. Townsend, 1974
(With 1983 Price Guide by Ralph Whitmer) 45, 6x9" pages, 8 oz.............$8.00
SET OF 3 PRICE GUIDES TO TOWNSEND BOOKS
(For books bought before 1983) $9.00

E. HOWARD & CO. WATCHES 1858-1903
Col. George E. Townsend, 1983 **(With 1983 Price Guide by Roy Ehrhardt)**
The last word on Howard watches: Identification-Production-Price Guide,
This manuscript was ready for publication when Col. Townsend died. The Price
Guide was written by Roy Ehrhardt, 48, 8 1/2x11" pages, Paperback, 6 oz................................$8.00

CLOCK BOOKS
CLOCK IDENTIFICATION & PRICE GUIDE, BOOK 1
Ehrhardt and Rabeneck, 1977, **(Prices revised in 1979)**
198, 8 1/2x11" pages, bound, 1 lb. 8 oz...CALL/WRITE
CLOCK IDENTIFICATION & PRICE GUIDE, BOOK 2
Ehrhardt and Rabeneck, 1979, 192, 8 1/2x11" pages, Bound, 1 lb. 8 oz..................$15.00
CLOCK IDENTIFICATION & PRICE GUIDE, BOOK 3
Ehrhardt and Rabeneck, 1983, 203, 8 1/2x11" pages, Bound, 1 lb. 8 oz..................$15.00
(All three clock books contain different clocks. You need all three to have a complete library)

F. KROEBER CLOCK CO. IDENTIFICATION & PRICE GUIDE
Ehrhardt and Rabeneck, 1983, 36, 8 1/2x11" pages, 8 oz................................CALL/WRITE

VIOLIN BOOKS
VIOLIN IDENTIFICATION & PRICE GUIDE, BOOK 1
Ehrhardt and Atchley, 1977, 192, 8 1/2x11" pages, 1 lb. 10 oz........................CALL/WRITE
VIOLIN IDENTIFICATION & PRICE GUIDE, BOOK 2
Ehrhardt and Atchley, 1978, 206, 8 1/2x11" pages, 1 lb. 10 oz.................................$25.00

MISCELLANEOUS BOOKS
AMERICAN COLLECTOR DOLLS PRICE GUIDE, BOOK 1
S. Ehrhardt and D. Westbrook, 1975, 128, 8 1/2x11" pages, 1 lb. 2 oz........................$9.00
AMERICAN CUT GLASS PRICE GUIDE
Alpha Ehrhardt **(Revised 1977)**, 120, 8 1/2x11" pages, 1 lb. 2 oz..............................$7.00
POCKET KNIFE BOOK 1 & 2 PRICE GUIDE
J. Farrell & R. Ehrhardt **(Revised 1977)**, 128, 8 1/2x11" pages, 1 lb. 2 oz..................$7.00

The books listed on these two pages are sold on a satisfaction guarantee. If you are not sure about the books you want, send a self-addressed, stamped envelope and we will send you detailed brochures on all of the publications. For orders in the U.S., send the price of the book plus $3.00 UPS for the first book and $1.00 for each asdditional book. For foreign orders, check with your post office for Book Rate, either Sea or Air, your choice. Book and carton weights are listed.

Foreign Postage Sea Mail (2 lbs. $5.00 US)
Foreign Postage Air Mail (2 lbs. $18.00 US)
Canada & Mexico (2 lbs. Land $4.00)
United States of North America (2 lb. $3.00)
Missouri Residents Add For Sales Tax 6.4225%
C.O.D. UPS $4.00 Extra
Send Your Check or Money Order (US Funds)

Send orders to:

We Sell Reliable Information

HEART OF AMERICA PRESS
10101 Blue Ridge Blvd.
Kansas City, MO 64134
(816) 761-0080
Visa & Mastercard Orders
(800) 458-8525

APPRAISAL SERVICE
on
VINTAGE CLOCKS — POCKET WATCHES — WRIST WATCHES

TELEPHONE — MAIL — APPOINTMENT

GET AN EXPERT OPINION BEFORE YOU BUY OR SELL.

I have been active in the clock and watch world as a collector, dealer, and author of price guides for the past 16 years. I have kept current with values by attending most of the regional shows of the National Association of Watch and Clock Collectors, Inc., and many of the horological auctions, antique shows, flea markets, etc., in the United States. As a result of my daily activities in the horological field, I am constantly in touch with the foremost collectors and investors.

Over the past 20 years, I have also accumulated (and have at my fingertips) a vast library of horological books, and world-wide watch and clock auction catalogs (with the auction results) from the houses listed on page 328. Also, I am a member of the International Society of Appraisers.

When the appraisal is by telephone or mail, my opinion as to value will be limited by the amount and accuracy of the information that you can supply. You will need to furnish me with as much vital information as you can, such as size, all names, trademarks and numbers, condition, originality, case material, movement quality, and if illustrated, what book and the page number. If by mail, pictures are very helpful.

DON'T GIVE AWAY — OR MISS A CHANCE TO BUY — A VALUABLE BECAUSE YOU DON'T HAVE IT PROPERLY IDENTIFIED!

APPRAISAL FEES

Telephone Call (5-minute) — $10.00 each item. This will be enough time for most items. (Appraisal Certificate $5 extra.) If additional research and return telephone calls are necessary, Minimum $20.00. Dial 816-761-0080 and ask for the ISA line. Have Visa or Master Card number ready.

By Mail or by Appointment — Minimum $15.00 each item. (Includes Appraisal Certificate)

The minimum fees will cover most appraisals. If you have items that require extensive research or phone calls and the fee exceeds the minimum, I will notify you for your approval.

I will be attending most of the NAWCC shows (such as those listed on page 327). I usually travel to and from the shows by car. Maybe I could help you with something, either enroute or at the shows, without the cost being prohibitive. Write or call me with your appraisal problems.

WILL TRAVEL FOR LARGE COLLECTIONS,
INSURANCE or ESTATE APPRAISALS.

NEED INFORMATION IN A HURRY? CALL ME!

ROY EHRHARDT, HOROLOGIST
10101 Blue Ridge, Kansas City, MO 64134, or phone 816-761-0080